A BRIEF HISTORY OF NAKEDNESS

Also by Philip Carr-Gomm

Journeys of the Soul: The Life and Legacy of a Druid Chief

The Book of English Magic (with Richard Heygate)

Sacred Places: Sites of Spiritual Pilgrimage from Stonehenge to Santiago de Compostela

What do Druids Believe?

Druid Mysteries

The Druid Way

Druidcraft – The Magic of Wicca and Druidry

In the Grove of the Druids

La Force des Celtes (with Paco Rabanne)

A Brief History
of Nakedness

Philip Carr-Gomm

REAKTION BOOKS

For my father

Published by
REAKTION BOOKS LTD
33 Great Sutton Street
London EC1V ODX, UK

www.reaktionbooks.co.uk

First published 2010

Copyright © Philip Carr-Gomm 2010

Printed and bound in Singapore
by Craft Print International Ltd

British Library Cataloguing in Publication Data
Carr-Gomm, Philip.
A brief history of nakedness.
1. Nudity – Social aspects.
2. Nudity – Religious aspects.
3. Nudity – Political aspects.
4. Nudity in literature.
5. Nudity in the performing arts.
I. Title
306.4-dc22

ISBN 978 1 86189 647 6

Contents

A young Dutchman risks punishment by the ss as he walks naked except for a fedora, socks and shoes, down a city street in the Netherlands in 1941, to protest against clothes rationing by the occupying Germans.

Introduction:
Bharat's Mirror

For me, the naked and the nude
(By lexicographers construed
As synonyms that should express
The same deficiency of dress
Or shelter) stand as wide apart
As love from lies, or truth from art.
— Robert Graves, *The Naked And the Nude*

H ere's a suggestion: stop reading and start taking off your clothes. If you were about to read this book in the bath this would, of course, present no problem, but if you happen to be standing in a bookshop, or reading this as you wait for a bus or train, your life is about to change. This book explores why this is so, and why just being naked can be so provocative that you could end up in prison before reaching chapter One. The first thing to establish, though, as you kick off your shoes, is whether you are about to end up naked or nude.

Behind every English-speaking person stands a Norman and an Anglo-Saxon, feeding words, governing attitudes. The word nakedness comes from Anglo-Saxon Germanic roots, nudity from the Norman French. Having two words to describe our unclothed state gives English a sophistication denied to many other languages. As a result, it is possible to tease apart meanings, with some suggesting that if you are nude you are unclothed and knowingly observed, while nakedness refers to the 'innocent' state of simply being uncovered. Nudity happens in art, nakedness happens in your bathroom. Nakedness represents the raw, nudity the ideal. The art critic John Berger writes: 'To be naked is to be oneself. To be nude is to be seen

7

by others and yet not recognized for oneself. A naked body has to be seen as an object in order to become nude.' He carries his thesis even further by saying, 'The nude is condemned to never being naked. Nudity is a form of dress.'[1]

To differentiate between the two terms is, however, a matter of choice. As you stand in the bookshop undressed to all the world, few will pause to question whether you are naked or nude. In attempting this brief history I have decided to write as if I were French or German, thus avoiding making a distinction between the words which I have used interchangeably, partly to avoid getting caught in semantic arguments, partly out of a concern for the problems this would pose for translators of foreign editions, and partly because I knew I would have to use one or other term repeatedly throughout the text, and without a synonym this would become intolerable.[2] In addition I was keen to focus instead on the many extraordinary questions that a consideration of nakedness poses: Why does nudity upset some people so much? Why does it excite others to such a degree? Why do some religious people condemn nudity while others recommend it? Does protesting in the nude achieve anything worthwhile? How can the Penis Puppeteers get away with displaying and manipulating their genitals on stage in the same country whose government fined CBS $550,000 for broadcasting an image of Janet Jackson's breast, covered with a nipple-shield, for less than a second? If a policeman was confronted by a naked woman painted so that she appeared clothed, and a clothed woman wearing a nude suit, which would he caution or arrest? And why is the Naked Chef never naked?

These questions, and dozens like them, arise because even though nakedness simply represents our natural embodied state, in the course of human evolution it has come to act as a catalyst for a host of contradictory thoughts, feelings and activities, in a way that has created a story which is at times tragic, at times touching, and often bizarre.

A cynic might think that this colourful history offers yet one more example of humanity's narcissism. What could be more absurd than a species that is so self-obsessed that it is endlessly fascinated by exposing and gazing upon its own form? A kinder view might see our interest as the clearest example of that attribute that distinguishes us from other animals: self-consciousness.

An incident from the legendary history of one of the world's oldest religions – Jainism – illustrates this alternative view. One day, the Emperor Bharat, son of the founder of the religion, after taking his bath, began to observe his body in a mirror, and in doing so gained enlightenment.[3]

Awareness of ourselves as embodied creatures lies at the heart of our sense of self, which explains why so much money and effort is spent on trying to change and cover our bodies, since the way we perceive them and our appearance radically affects our experience of ourselves and of the world.

Nakedness in Religion

In their celebration of nudity, the Greeks distinguished themselves from all other peoples. For them, nudity was not a matter of shame, ridicule or dishonour. Rather nudity assumed a paradigmatic signifi-cance that involved clarity of vision (an aspect of Greek religious experience) with an athletic perspective . . .
—Mario Perniola, 'The Glorious Garment and the Naked Truth'[4]

This book begins with a survey of religious approaches to naked-ness since it is religion that, before the advent of psychology, articulated and built upon humanity's concern with itself and its bodily form.

It might be thought that most religions would universally dis-approve of its leaders or followers being naked in all but the most mundane and private of circumstances, and that an active religious engagement with nudity would be virtually unknown. Some of the earliest religious icons, however, such as the 'Venuses' of Willen-dorf and Malta, are representations of naked female figures, while the religions that arose later offered male figures for veneration who were sometimes also depicted in the nude – as in Greece and India. In Christianity man is said to be created in God's image, a doctrine which has provided Christian nudists with powerful ammunition, and in Judaism primordial man is known as Adam Kadmon – a giant figure who contains all of creation within his frame. In the Jainism of India the cosmos is shaped like a standing figure, while serene images of nude men, standing or sitting, represent its 24 enlightened founders.

It is said that the truth clothes itself in paradox, and in its search for truth religion has been supplied with fertile material when considering the human form. On the one hand the body is a creation of deity – in Christian terms made 'in the image of God'. On the other hand it is both the locus of our suffering and its cause, in as much as we come into being through the interaction and medium of two other bodies. The fact that the body can be cast as both temple and prison has resulted in the ambivalent attitude to it that is found in many religious approaches.

In the first two chapters of this book, while acknowledging this ambivalence, I have focused on the way nakedness has been used to further spiritual ideals in a variety of traditions and have avoided detailing the history of many religions' attempts to inculcate shame or loathing of the body, since this book offers not so much a history

The *Venus of Willendorf.*

of attitudes to the body and its nudity, as of the ways in which nakedness has been actively pursued to further religious, political and cultural goals – in other words, in order to enlighten, empower and entertain.

The way in which religious groups and individuals have promoted being nude in the service of their ideals provides a narrative that has received little attention, and which to many may seem astonishing. In particular, it is the Christian relationship to nudity, both ancient and modern, that is perhaps the most unexpected, and which can be glimpsed in the following image. In the 2003 UK television series *The Naked Pilgrim*, the art critic Brian Sewell made a pilgrimage to Santiago de Compostela. As an ex-Catholic he was astonished to find himself moved to tears by the journey, which he finished in the traditional manner by undressing at Finisterre, making a bonfire of his clothes, and plunging naked into the sea.

Nakedness in Politics

The Duke of Wellington saw Napoleon naked every day. The perfect muscular chest of his former enemy must have become, over time, as familiar to him as his own ageing flesh. Antonio Canova's nude colossus of Napoleon Bonaparte stands to this day in the spiralling stairwell of No 1 London, the house at Hyde Park Corner that belonged to the general who defeated Napoleon at Waterloo.
—Jonathan Jones, 'Hanging in There', *The Guardian*, 11 March 2006

When it comes to our feelings about nakedness, contradictions and paradoxes abound. In religion nakedness can signify shamefulness and a lust that must be conquered, or it can symbolize innocence, a lack of shame, and even a denial of the body. In the political sphere, nakedness can symbolize raw power and authority, or vulnerability and enslavement. These contradictory associations help to explain our complex and often conflicting responses to the subject and why it offers such a fertile ground for artistic and philosophical exploration.

Two great streams of influence have moulded modern Western attitudes: one deriving from the classical pagan world, the other fed by the influences of the Judaic and Middle Eastern worlds. The latter cultures most frequently associated nudity with poverty and enslavement. The rich and powerful wore clothes and ornaments to demonstrate their wealth and prestige while prostitutes, slaves and the mad went unclad. In distinction, the Greeks elevated the naked human form to the ideal, and statesmen would be sculpted naked to demonstrate their likeness to the gods. It is no wonder, then, that the Christian inheritance, drawing as it does upon both classical and Judaic inspiration, has developed such an ambiguous set of attitudes towards nudity.[5]

Nowhere is the juxtaposition of contradictory responses to nakedness more obvious than in the realm of politics, where the most powerful people on earth require the protective 'clothing' of armoured limousines and guards, and the least powerful can hold a government or corporation to ransom by simply threatening to remove their clothing.

Nakedness makes a human being particularly vulnerable but in certain circumstances strangely powerful, which is why it has become so popular as a vehicle for political protest. By exposing the human body, protesters convey a complex message: they challenge the status quo by acting provocatively, and they empower themselves and their cause by showing that they are fearless and have nothing to hide. But at the same time they reveal the vulnerability and frailty of the human being.

Chapters Three and Four focus on the way the complexity of this message has been harnessed by protest movements, and how politicians have related to nakedness, sometimes using images of themselves in the nude to gain votes. An insight into the relevance of nudity to the political dimension can be quickly grasped with a consideration of its use in statuary designed to depict status and power.

The biblical story of David defeating Goliath, with its message of the foolishness of equating military muscle with assured victory, provided the inspiration for the statue which broke the spell of Christian guilt that had opposed the depiction of nudity in art for over a millennium. The first sculpture of a male nude made in Europe since antiquity was Donatello's bronze of David, who was naked except for boots and a hat that suggest he was also meant to

Michelangelo's
sculpture of David
contemplating his
impending battle
with Goliath,
completed in 1504.

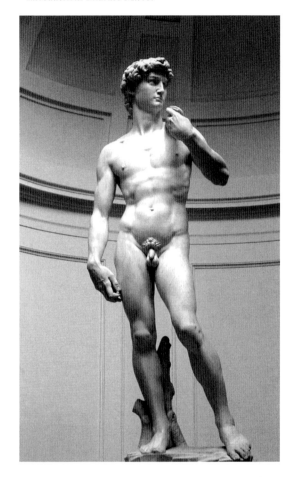

remind us of Hermes. It caused a sensation when it was unveiled in
the mid-fifteenth century and placed in the courtyard of the Medici
Palace in Florence to convey its message of victory and fearlessness.

Sixty or so years later, at the beginning of the sixteenth century,
Michelangelo created his own sculpture of David, totally nude this
time, and greater than life size, standing 5.2 metres (17 feet) tall. It was
installed in Florence's Piazza della Signoria, becoming the first male
nude sculpture to be exhibited in a public place since the demise of
the classical world. At that time Florence was threatened on every
side by more powerful states, and the statue conveyed a strong
message of innate power and its potential for effortless victory.

At the beginning of the nineteenth century the Venetian sculptor Antonio Canova was commissioned by Napoleon to create a

statue of himself in the nude. At his defeat it was given to Wellington. A naked Hitler gracing Churchill's house at the end of the war would be unthinkable, and yet it was considered perfectly acceptable for Wellington to place the statue of his defeated adversary in the nude in his London home. One hundred and fifty years later, in 1967, England's Lord Chamberlain banned the display of a nude statue of the President of the United States, Lyndon Johnson, in the play *Mrs Wilson's Diary*. Conventions, laws and attitudes are bound in a complex web determined by time, geography, class and aesthetics.

Nakedness in Popular Culture

'Despite the knowingness and even cynicism of much contemporary consumer culture, a glimpse of flesh, or indeed, even the mention of nudity, still can, in the right contexts, incite a smile, a nervous giggle or even outrage. Nudity is both big business and mundane embodiment, the staple of the porn industry and an obstacle at school gym classes. Our society's attitudes, rules and conventions around nudity are riddled with contradictions, complexities and disavowals . . .'
—Ruth Barcan, *Nudity: A Cultural Anatomy*

The contradictions referred to by Barcan make nakedness one of the most interesting lenses through which to observe human nature. Take depictions of the naked male: an image of a man 55m (180 ft) high, with an erection 9 m (30 ft) long has been tolerated, and actively maintained for hundreds of years at Cerne Abbas in Dorset, while the image of another man whose penis is flaccid and less than a millimetre long caused controversy in 2007 when a US publisher refused to include a drawing of it in a book by one of Germany's best-selling children's authors, Rotraut Susanne Berner. The drawing showed an art gallery in which a sculpture of a naked man stood in the background.

In the final two chapters of the book I have tried to paint a picture of the way in which such contradictions have played themselves out in popular Western culture, and to show how the idea of nakedness is just as significant as its actual display. Jamie Oliver

The 2004 annual nude rugby game held each winter on St Kilda beach, Carisbrook, Dunedin, New Zealand. At these matches 'reverse streaking' sometimes occurs when a clothed spectator dashes across the field to be tackled by the naked players.

has built a career on being a 'naked chef' who never gets naked; the nude scene in *Hair* that helped to create a sea change in attitudes to nudity on stage in the 1960s lasted less than 20 seconds; the film *The Full Monty*, whose main theme is nakedness, also shows less than 20 seconds of nudity, and even when a DVD version of it was released entitled *The Full Monty Fully Exposed* viewers were still denied a view of the 'Full Monty'.

Despite this, and the fact that organised nudism has declined as a social activity since the 1960s, public acceptance and enjoyment of

The wedding of Shelley Davie and Josh Hughes sponsored by a Melbourne breakfast radio show in 2008. In 2006 the British film *Confetti* featured a nudist wedding sponsored by a bridal magazine, and in 2009 a New Zealand radio station held a 'Nudie Nuptials' competition, with the winners receiving a 'dream wedding' worth $50,000. Mass nude weddings with as many as 60 couples occur every Valentine's Day at the Hedonism resort in Jamaica.

nakedness has increased to such an extent that the installation artist Spencer Tunick can now easily find thousands of volunteers who will strip naked to be filmed and photographed in public, and charitable organizations seriously consider nude fund-raising calendars. Much of the shame associated with nakedness has been discarded in favour of a recognition of its inherent comedy and its ability to demonstrate that we are all members of the same human family.

With local variations, in Europe, North America, parts of South America and in Australia and New Zealand you can now engage in a wide range of activities in the nude. You can skydive, bungee-jump, get married, perform stand-up comedy or karaoke, take yoga classes, join magical rituals, visit public swimming pools on 'nude nights', go to the cinema, bask in spas or be body-painted in the nude. You can risk a holiday in 'Naked City' at Cap d'Agde in the South of France, bathe naked in a private club or dine out in the nude in New York or Edinburgh, sunbathe in parks in the centre of Berlin or Munich, go clubbing at the 'Starkers' disco in London, work out in

A couple enjoy the thrill of nude skydiving over Australia in 1994. Despite the cold, enthusiasts regularly jump naked individually, in tandem and in formation. Some parachutists say that tradition demands a nude jump to celebrate your 100th dive.

Nude bungee-jumping for charity in British Columbia, Canada, 1997.

Nude surfing at the Rip Curl Boardmasters, Newquay, Cornwall, 2002. Surfing naked is particularly popular in Australia, where annual nude surfing events are held in Byron Bay, and on Bondi Beach in Sydney as part of the Sydney Fringe Festival.

Bouncy Boxing is apparently popular in Australia.

the nude in a Dutch gym, go on a naked cruise or hike in New Zealand or fly to your holiday in the nude on a German airline.

Despite this plethora of opportunities, and an increasingly liberal attitude towards nakedness, if you take off your clothes in the wrong place at the wrong time you can be fined, deported or thrown into jail. It is now completely acceptable to show interiors of the body but it is still not possible to grant the same freedoms to

A naked punter on the River Cam, Cambridge, in 2006. In 2009 a naked female punter appeared on a charity calendar featuring 60 Oxford undergraduates.

its surface. Gunther von Hagens' *Bodyworlds* exhibitions, which have been seen in recent years by more than 18 million people, have extended the concept of nakedness by taking real human bodies and 'stripping' them in various ways before preserving them through plastination. Now that we can see inside our bodies through this and numerous medical techniques, such as magnetic resonance imaging, images of the interior of the body are becoming more commonplace, and yet displays of the body's exterior surfaces are still subject to legal and moral restrictions. Confused? We should be. Hopefully this book, if it cannot dispel the confusion, can at least help to render it more interesting and enjoyable.

Skiers at the 'nude skiing mecca of Europe' – Obertraun in Austria, the only resort to welcome nude skiing all through the season.

The Spanish synchronized swimming team appear nude, having finished joint second in the world championships in 2003, held in Barcelona, a city renowned for its tolerance of public nudity.

The only flight of 'Naked Air' in 2003. Carrying 90 passengers and crew from Miami to a nudist resort in Mexico, in a Boeing 737 chartered by Castaways Travel of Houston, Texas, the passengers disrobed after take-off and had to dress again on landing. No hot drinks were served. In 2008 a German travel agency began selling nude air travel to a Baltic Sea resort.

On 19 August 2006, 195 contestants took part in the first World Strip Poker Championship in London, for a prize of £10,000.

Nude yoga classes for men have been held in the USA since 1998, when in New York the 'Midnight Yoga for Men' group began practising 'naked before the infinite' in the style of Indian sadhus.

Nyotaimori, or 'body sushi', a traditional Japanese practice of serving food on the naked body of a geisha, reached the West in the 1990s. Here sushi is being served at a Chinese New Year party at the Great Eastern Hotel in London in 2005.

High Priest and Priestess Stewart and Janet Farrar face each other in their Wiccan circle in Ireland *c.* 1980, in a ceremony of 'Drawing Down the Sun'.

I

Clothed with the Sky

Whenever ye have need of anything, once in the month,
and better it be when the moon is full,
then ye shall assemble
in some secret place
and adore the spirit of Me
who am Queen of all Witcheries . . .
And as the sign that ye are truly free,
Ye shall be naked in your rites, both men
And women and ye shall dance, sing, feast,
make music, and love, all in my praise.
—The Charge of the Goddess

On Lammas night, 1 August 1940, thirteen members of a witches'
coven gathered in a clearing near the Rufus Stone in the New
Forest, where some say King William II was offered as a pagan
sacrifice in the eleventh century. Although it was the summer it
was cold that night. They undressed quickly and began to rub
goose fat on their bodies to protect themselves from the elements.
One elderly man, however, refused the fat and instead offered to be
the one whose life would be given to save many lives.

As one coven member lit a small bonfire, another charged a censer
with glowing charcoal and grains of frankincense. They all then gathered in a circle around the fire to begin their rite. The High Priest cast
a circle with his athame, a small dagger. The High Priestess traced penta-
grams in the air and summoned the spirits of the four winds. And then
the entire circle of witches began to spin. Round and round the fire
they danced and ran, chanting 'Eko Eko Azarak! Eko Eko Zomelak!'

The dancing became faster and faster, the chanting became louder and louder, until suddenly two members let go of each other's hands, and moved in opposite directions so that the circle broke and turned into a line of naked bodies that repeatedly ran at the fire as they shouted: 'You cannot cross the sea! You cannot cross the sea! You cannot come! You cannot come!' Over and over they ran to the flames and shouted, until one by one they fell exhausted by the fire.

As they lay panting on the ground they visualized the force of their imprecations travelling across the Channel and straight into the mind of one man: Adolf Hitler. Several weeks earlier they had learnt of the threat that he might invade with his armies. Churchill had warned that 'all we have known and cared for' could 'sink into the abyss of a new dark age made more sinister . . . by the lights of a perverted science'. There and then the coven had decided that they would do everything in their power to stop even the thought of an invasion, and for three consecutive nights they performed that ceremony beneath the stars, in the forest beside the sea.

When the old man died a few weeks later in the local hospital from pneumonia, the rumour soon began to circulate that he had been sacrificed in a witchcraft ritual. Whether this was true, whether the whole story was true, we shall never know. Cecil Williamson, an MI6 officer, claimed that a ceremony did indeed take place to repel Hitler, but that he had helped to organize it as part of the 'secret war' being conducted against a Nazi regime known to believe in the power of the occult. Forty Canadian soldiers, wearing army blankets embroidered with magical symbols, had been instructed to perform a fake ceremony in a clearing in the Ashdown Forest in Sussex that centred on the ritual destruction of a dummy of Adolf Hitler. An account of this was then deliberately 'leaked' to Germany.

Williamson claimed his story had been taken and distorted by his erstwhile friend and colleague Gerald Gardner, a retired customs officer who had spent most of his life in the Far East, but had returned to Britain in 1938 and had begun popularizing a religion that he believed was practised long before Christianity reached its shores: witchcraft.

Ever since the witch trials of the fifteenth and sixteenth centuries and the popularization of images of nude witches during that era by Dürer and other, mainly German, artists, witchcraft has been associated with nudity. The majority of people, if asked about the relationship of nakedness to religion and magic, might well cite witchcraft as the only example of a practice in which worship and nudity have been combined. After all, religions are concerned with achieving moral purity, and encourage modesty and even a rejection of the pleasures of the body, or at least too much attachment to them. In the Judaic and Christian traditions nudity has always been shunned, since the Old Testament states that when Adam and Eve became aware of their nakedness they were filled with shame. It was surely only the witches, in their perverted 'black magic' rites, who dared shamelessly to expose their bodies while worshipping?

Contrary to these popular misconceptions, it is not only witches who worship in the nude: certain Christians, Hindus, Jains and modern pagans and druids also follow this practice. Judaism and Christianity in particular have a complex and ambivalent relationship to the naked body. The story of the relationship between nudity and religion is ancient and fascinating, and touches upon the very deepest philosophical and spiritual issues that concern what it means to be embodied and alive.

> My Lord . . .
> Here I be stripped of all finery
> No clothes, lover or home have I
> Excepting by thy Grace
> Master, I have descended the Paths towards
> Thy gates . . .
> Leaving all but my truthful spirit behind me.
> Here am I naked as the sea, as the sky,
> As grave winter itself.
> I pray Thee take pity on me and listen unto my prayer.
> —Robert Cochrane (1931–1966), who inspired several modern
> versions of Witchcraft[1]

Today, witchcraft, and its most popular variety Wicca, is considered one of the fastest-growing religions in the West. In the USA it probably claims over 400,000 followers, in the UK 100,000.[2] While many carry out their ceremonies in robes, many worship naked, and they carry out rites which were in all likelihood created in the mid-twentieth century from a variety of sources which reach far back into the past. The master-mind behind the phenomenal success of Witchcraft as an alternative religion in the modern era was Gerald Gardner who, along with Cecil Williamson, helped to run a Witchcraft Museum on the Isle of Man in the 1950s.

The fact that one man was so successful in promoting a religion that could be practised in the nude is in itself remarkable, and some have made the mistake of thinking that it was Gardner who introduced nudism into 'the craft', as it is known, since he was a committed naturist. A lifelong asthmatic, when Gardner retired to England his doctor recommended naturism to strengthen his health and alleviate his symptoms. Gardner took to naturism like a duck to water, and by 1946 he had bought a half share in a nudist resort in Hertfordshire.[3]

Although having a naturist as a promoter of a religion that advocates worship in the nude was clearly fortunate, Gardner did not simply invent the idea. Witches had been depicted in the

Three Witches by Hans Baldung Grien, Dürer's most talented pupil, who was fascinated by witchcraft, the supernatural and the erotic.

Albrecht Dürer's
The Four Witches, 1497,
although suggestive of
the common Classical
motif of the Three
Graces, shows a devil's
face to the left and a
skull and bone at the
witches' feet.

nude from the sixteenth century, but in doing this, the artists had
almost certainly fallen under the spell of the Witch Craze which
spread through Europe in those years, and which has now been
found to have its origin in the depravity, not of any so-called
witches, but in the minds and hearts of those inquisitors and
witch-hunters who tortured and killed so many innocent women
and men. As Ronald Hutton in 'A Modest Look at Ritual Nudity'
writes: 'The question of whether early modern witches actually
worked naked is rendered a non sequitur by the total absence of
evidence for any actual witch religion in the period; the satanic
cult of the demonologists does seem to have been a complete fantasy.'[4] The pictures of naked witches were undoubtedly based on
that fantasy, and in addition happened to be one of the few ways
in which German artists of that age were permitted to depict the
female nude.[5]

Although it now seems that there was no such thing as a witch religion in Europe as an organized form of worship that had survived the onslaught of Christianity, by the nineteenth century folklorists and anthropologists had begun to uncover customs and practices that were undeniably magical in intent, many of which probably represented archaic remnants of pre-Christian religious activity.

Apart from the writing of modern authors, such as Gardner, and the testimony of women extracted under torture during the Witch Hunts,[6] which must necessarily be discounted, the only recorded mention of witches worshipping naked comes from the work of an American folklorist, Charles Godfrey Leland. In 1899 he published *Aradia, Gospel of the Witches*, which recounted the alleged practices of witches who lived in the Elsa Valley of Tuscany, and who traced the origins of their faith to pagan antiquity. Aradia was the daughter of the goddess Diana and her brother Lucifer, who had been sent to earth to teach witchcraft and poisoning to those of the peasantry who had retreated to the mountains to live their lives as bandits rather than submit to their feudal masters. In stirring instructions, which now stand at the heart of modern Wiccan liturgy, witches are told to meet naked under the full moon: 'And ye shall be free from slavery, and as a sign that ye be really free, ye shall be naked in your rites, both men and women, and ye shall dance, sing, feast, make music, and love, all in my praise.'

Despite many attempts at embellishment and improvement, including those by the infamous magician Aleister Crowley and Gerald Gardner and his High Priestess Doreen Valiente, the instruction to worship naked has been retained in the various texts known as 'The Charge of the Goddess', recited regularly by many thousands of witches all over the world.

No-one knows if Leland's work represents a genuine tradition that existed in Italy. The material for the book was supplied to him by his 'witch-informant' Maddalena, and some believe she, or others, simply concocted it. Leland was considered an 'unusually unreliable scholar'[7] and until the large collection of his papers is thoroughly researched, we shall never know whether Italian witches did indeed meet naked under a full moon to dance, sing and make love in praise of their Goddess. What we do know, however, is that the association of nudity with witchcraft and folk magic can be found all over the world, which makes it certainly possible that naked worship did occur in Italy.

Although witches today almost universally consider themselves workers of benevolent magic, the term 'witch' and its equivalents have been used in most times and places to designate people who are believed to be practising harmful magic, usually to blight crops, animals or people. In Africa, for example, the 'evil witches' of the Vugusu and Logoli of western Kenya, known as *omulogi*, are said to travel around in the nude at night, as are the witches of the Lovedu of the northern Transvaal, and of the Amba of Uganda. In the Middle East, Arab peoples believed that witches haunted cemeteries and flew around at night, naked and riding on sticks, and in central India they rode on fierce beasts like tigers and crocodiles. In New Guinea the Trobriand islanders believed witches flew naked through the skies to bring death to their enemies. The shamans of the Chukchi people of Siberia, when they wished to practice harmful magic, shunned their usual, often heavy, ritual garb and were said to utter their curses naked under the light of the moon. In North America, the Navaho believed that those who practised evil magic sat in circles together wearing nothing but masks and ornaments.

As Ronald Hutton points out in 'A Modest Look at Ritual Nudity', amongst the 'African peoples who ascribed nudity to the witch-figure, it was only part of a package of role-reversals', which included moving about outdoors at night amongst people who traditionally feared darkness, and riding on unclean or untameable beasts. This analysis can be extended to the other cultures that portrayed evil witches in a similar way. The message conveyed by their depiction of role reversals is clear: people who work evil are not like us: they are the exact opposite of us.

Did any of these reversed figures actually exist, or were they products of superstition and fantasy, as most of the witches imagined by the European witch-hunters seemed to have been? We cannot be sure, but although we may never know whether the kinds of evil magic described were ever practised in the nude, we can be certain that other kinds of magic were, since nakedness was a feature of classical paganism, medieval kabbalistic magic and worldwide folk customs, all of which have informed the modern religion now known as Witchcraft.

Nakedness in Initiation

Those who would rise through the degrees of the holy mysteries
must cast aside their clothes and go forward naked.[8]
—Plotinus

Gerald Gardner travelled to Pompeii in 1951, and visited the famous 'House of the Mysteries' that contains a series of frescoes that seem to depict the initiation of a woman into a mystery school. It may even have suggested the idea to him of the ritual scourging that was introduced into the Wiccan initiatory rite, since the frescoes depict a tall bare-breasted angel raising a cane as if about to strike the buttocks of a semi-naked woman, whilst another, completely unclad, appears to celebrate the event by sounding cymbals.

A little north of Pompeii, in the Mithraeum at Capua, another set of frescoes depicts the initiation of a man into the cult of Mithras. In each scene the postulant is naked and blindfolded, guided by a clothed figure who appears to be his initiator.

The classic pattern for initiation, found the world over, involves an enactment of the process of separation from the habitual and everyday, followed by some kind of ordeal. The rite ends in a symbolic rebirth as the initiate, having survived the testing, is welcomed into the community of fellow initiates. Written accounts of Mithraic initiations suggest a host of fierce ordeals that the candidate was required to endure, including branding and immersion in water for extended periods. The frescoes, however, only suggest the brutality of this aspect of the initiation in the way the man is being handled, but no further details are provided.

As foreign as such rites may seem, their essential structure is utilized to this day in organizations that began to be popular in the early eighteenth century, and which by the end of the nineteenth century counted many millions of men in their ranks – up to a fifth of the total adult male population of the United States and a similar figure for those in Britain.[9] In an uncanny echo of the Mithraic rite of initiation, those who enter Freemasonry, or many of the trade and fraternal associations who have borrowed the Masonic form of initiation, are obliged to symbolically undress by baring their breast, having one foot bare, or by rolling up one trouser leg, and are led

A section of the fresco on the wall of the room known as 'The Initiation Chamber' in the Villa of the Mysteries, Pompeii.

blindfold into the ceremony. They are then faced with an ordeal, which in the traditional form of Masonic initiation involves being challenged at the point of a sword that touches the chest, and to then endure being led around the room by a cable-tow, a noose around the neck.

Once one learns that Gardner was initiated into Freemasonry, it comes as no surprise to discover that the Wiccan initiation rite also includes being led blindfold by a cable-tow and being challenged at the point of a sword. The difference is simply, but powerfully, that in Wicca it is not just one's trousers and shirt that are rearranged. They are taken off and one enters the magic circle naked. Gardner may have got the details from Freemasonry, but the Pompeii and Capua frescoes suggest that the idea of initiations that included ordeals endured naked are of ancient provenance.[10]

Gardner the naturist seems to have taken another idea from the Freemasons too, and in a stroke of genius, laced perhaps with a sense of mischief, transformed a rather clumsy act into a ritual gesture that unites the spiritual and the erotic, the reverential and the sensual, in the most profound way. In Masonry a secret word is passed from brother to brother in an embrace known as the 'Five

A candidate seeking initiation into the First Degree of Wicca in 1964 is challenged at the point of a sword before being allowed to enter the sacred circle.

Points of Fellowship' – a kind of geometrical hug in which the heels, knees and hands of the initiator and candidate are connected in imitation of the operation of a compass point and square. In Wiccan ceremonies the initiator dispenses with any attempt to be a human compass, and instead administers the 'Fivefold Kiss' to the candidate on the feet, knees, just above the genitals, and on the breasts and mouth.

The Kabbalah and Folk Magic

Freemasonry and classical paganism, however, were not the only sources of inspiration for the use of nudity in modern witchcraft. Much of Wiccan ceremony is derived from a work of medieval magic entitled the Key of Solomon, which appeared in the fifteenth century and which drew upon the inspiration of the Jewish Talmud and Kabbalah. Amidst its pious instructions can be found occult procedures that involve summoning spirits of the dead and sacrificing animals to detect thieves, find treasure, procure love and curse enemies. The following excerpt reveals the same emphasis on nudity and ritual bathing that is found in classical paganism:

Before commencing operations both the master and his disciples must abstain with great and thorough continence
during the space of nine days from sensual pleasures and
from vain and foolish conversation . . . on the seventh day, the
master being alone, let him enter into a secret place, let him
take off his clothes, and bathe himself from head to foot in
consecrated and exorcised water, saying devoutly and humbly
the prayer, 'O Lord Adonai,' . . . The prayer being finished, let
the master quit the water, and put upon his flesh raiment of
white linen clean and unsoiled; and then let him go with his
disciples unto a secret place and command them to strip
themselves naked; and they having taken off their clothes, let
him take exorcised water and pour it upon their heads so that
it flows down to their feet and bathes them completely; and
while pouring this water upon them let the master say:—
'Be ye regenerate, renewed, washed, and pure,' etc., . . . the
master in sign of penitence will kiss the disciples on the fore-
head, and each of them will kiss the other. Afterwards let the
master extend his hands over the disciples, and in sign of
absolution absolve and bless them; which being done he will
distribute to each of his disciples the instruments necessary
for magical art, which he is to carry into the circle . . . The first
disciple will bear the censer, the perfumes and the spices; the
second disciple will bear the book, papers, pens, ink, and any
stinking or impure materials; the third will carry the knife and
the penknife of magical art, the lantern, and the candles; the
fourth, the Psalms, and the rest of the instruments; the fifth,
the crucible or chafing-dish, and the charcoal or fuel; but
it is necessary for the master himself to carry in his hand
the staff, and the wand or rod. The things necessary being
thus disposed, the master will go with his disciples unto the
assigned place, where they have proposed to construct the
circle for the magical arts and experiments; repeating on the
way the prayers and orations . . .[11]

However much one bathes or prays beforehand, cursing people
or sacrificing animals is undoubtedly less appealing than the opportunity to indulge in some love or fertility magic. In Europe, Africa,

The Hanged Man and the Queen of Discs from the Cosmic Tribe Tarot by
Stevee Postman, 1998. This tarot deck is the only one that offers a choice of
three Lovers' cards for different sexual orientations, and appeals particularly
to contemporary Pagans.

South America and India nakedness has been used, and in some cases is still used, as an integral part of folk magic designed to attract love and enhance fertility that in its turn has influenced the rituals of modern Witchcraft.

Ripening Corn and Waist-high Flax

In British and European folk-magic nudity has mostly been used to encourage the fertility of the land and to assist in the arcane art of love magic, which promises to reveal the identity of a future spouse or lover, and sometimes to draw that person inexorably closer. This kind of magic was mostly performed by women. English customs included sweeping a room naked on Midwinter night to then dream of your future husband, entering a lake or river naked at midnight to discover his face revealed on the surface of the water, and undressing at a crossroads on St George's night. The brave woman who did this was then instructed to comb the hair on her head and her body backwards before pricking the little finger of her left hand to allow three drops of blood to fall to the ground. As this happened she was to say 'I give my blood to my loved one, whom I shall see shall be mine own.' At this point the image of her man would rise up from the ground.[12]

To discover the identity of their future husbands women were also advised to run naked around the Rollright Stones, a prehistoric stone circle in Oxfordshire, on Midsummer night. A sceptic might suggest that this story was put about by young men who could then hide behind the stones to pick their future wives from such a parade, but the prevalence of similar stories in other countries suggests a deeper meaning that connects these customs with fertility rites. Just as women would walk, dance, sing and sometimes urinate in the fields, naked under the moonlight, to encourage the growth of crops, so they were using their bodies in a similar way to encourage something more than just love. They were using their nakedness in another form of fertility magic to encourage the evolutionary aim of partnership: the birth of children.

The plant that has encouraged the most nakedness in Europe seems to have been flax – the very plant that until the advent of cotton in the nineteenth century was the main provider of clothing as linen. Flax is one of the oldest cultivated crops in the world, and is indigenous from India in the East to Europe in the west. A plethora of superstitions surrounded its sowing and harvesting and in Europe it was particularly associated with the Feminine principle: with the Goddess or 'Flax mothers' in the pagan era, and with the Virgin Mary in the Christian era. This was probably due to the fact that since prehistoric times flax has been spun and woven by women.

In Transylvania, to encourage the crops, women had to spin or wash the spinning wheel in the nude, or one of them had to spin three reels of thread while seated naked on a dunghill, or jump off a table in the nude on Shrove Tuesday evening. Many of the customs that involved nakedness have been recorded in Germany, possibly due to the interest of German scholars in nudism in the first half of the twentieth century, rather than to any propensity for Germans to engage in such practices more than their neighbours. In Saalfeld women would wander naked in the flax fields on St John's night, and in Mecklenburg the farmer's wife had to walk the fields with her skirts raised. A chant, popular in that region up to the eighteenth century, ran: 'As high as the woman lifts her skirt, as high the flax will grow.' And even in the following century, at least until the 1860s, in Riedlingen women would walk naked and urinate in the flax fields, urging the crop to grow as high as their breasts.

Men only seem to have engaged in this fertility magic amongst the Slavic minority of the Sorbs in the eastern part of the country. There they walked naked in the fields chanting 'Flax, flax, grow as high as the scrotum.' During the early part of the nineteenth century, children in Belgium were still following another custom designed to ensure a good harvest. In May they walked naked in a line along the furrows of the fields, singing 'Lady Holle is coming with her procession of flowers, Lady Holle makes all of us clean and good!' Flax was seen as healing as well as cleansing. Children in Bavaria who were ill were sent naked into a field to have flax seeds scattered over them, while anyone in Brandenburg who felt dizzy was told to walk naked around a flax field three times.[13]

Clearly all these kinds of magic are working with what is known as 'the doctrine of sympathy'. Sympathetic magic is based upon the belief that like attracts and stimulates like – so that healthy seeds and soil will foster healthy children, just as vigorous naked humans walking and chanting in the fields will stimulate vigorous and healthy crops.

In Belgium, love-sick girls placed mugwort between their breasts to attract a lover,[14] suggesting an idea of ancient provenance that the naked body exudes a kind of magical energy that is magnetic. It was also seen as an enlivening and even healing energy. In the first century AD Pliny the Elder wrote that certain herbs should only be picked by a naked virgin and that 'a poultice is more efficacious if laid upon him by a maiden, herself fasting and naked, who at the same time has to repeat certain special words'.[15] Later herbalists recommended that any woman wishing to gather the rejuvenating dew lying on the leaves of Lady's Mantle should collect it naked and alone, under a full moon in May.

Collecting herbs or dew, applying poultices, healing sick children or dizzy adults, stimulating the crops and divining your future husband – what more uses could nakedness provide? Crops could also be protected from blight by the judicious use of the nude body, provided those doing so were menstrual, according to Henry Cornelius Agrippa: 'If menstruous women shall walk naked about the standing corn, they make all cankars, worms, beetles, flyes, and all hurtfull things fall off from the corn: but they must take heed that they do it before Sun rising, or else they will make the corn to wither.'[16]

Nakedness could also be used to bring rain to parched fields. In Romania a rain-making spell required a group of young women led by an older one to strip beside the river bank and float a harrow in the water for an hour with a flame burning at each corner. In many parts of northern India and Nepal a traditional way to attract rain involved a group of naked women pulling a plough across a field at night as they prayed, usually to Vishnu. In August 2006 about fifty Nepali women revived this custom by ploughing naked in their drought-ridden fields in a desperate attempt to induce rainfall. 'This is our last weapon, we used it, and there was light rainfall', one of the women told the local newspaper.[17] In the eleventh century, along the Rhine and in the Hesse region of Germany, during prolonged periods of drought a naked girl was made to pull out a henbane plant with a finger of her right hand. She then had to tie the plant to the little toe of her right foot before being taken to the riverside, where she was sprinkled with water and chanted over.[18]

More examples could be cited of the magical use of nakedness in South America and Africa, as well as Europe and India, which all indicate that today's Wiccans and witches who work their magic in the nude are drawing upon an ancient and widespread practice – even if the accounts of Tuscan witches gathering naked in the moonlight, or the images of nude witches drawn by Dürer and his pupils, are based upon fantasy.

It probably needed a maverick naturist such as Gardner to introduce nudity into the modern practice of Witchcraft, which he did at a favourable time: it was in the 1950s that the Golden Age of nudism sedately gave way to the era of sexual liberation and greater gender equality that reached its peak a decade later in the Swinging Sixties. Rather than confining nakedness simply to the candidate seeking initiation, as in the classical mysteries, or to specific circumstances, such as the need to pray for rain or good crops, the style of witchcraft that Gardner introduced to the world in 1954 echoed the idea found in Leland's 'Gospel of the Witches' of all participants being naked at every meeting of their coven. Leland's witches, real or imagined, did this as a 'sign that they were free'. Gardner's witches, meeting first at the Hertfordshire naturist resort of Five Acres, must also have felt remarkably free as they cast aside inhibition and convention. They probably also experienced that peculiar pleasure that comes when, as an adult, one is deliberately transgressive. Ronald Hutton attributes much of the reason for the extraordinary success of Wicca, and its continued use of nudity, when he writes that

> It gave a particular value and emphasis to precisely those phenomena which western societies had long feared or subordinated, honouring the night above the day, the moon above the sun, the feminine above the masculine, and wild nature above civilisation, presenting itself as a form of paganism which made no compromises with Christianity, and holding up the figure of the witch for admiration and emulation. It was as a part of this package that nudity,

traditionally used in those same societies most commonly as a symbol of shame and weakness, was turned into one of confidence and power. Its blatant presence in ritual was just one example of the way in which, during the middle decades of the twentieth century, Wicca crashed the barriers of convention.[19]

If the sole value of worshipping naked in Wicca derived from a sense of having broken free of inhibitions and convention, one would expect that this effect would diminish with regular practice, but this does not seem to be the case. Hutton suggests that 'in combination with other components normally present, such as candlelight, incense and music, [nakedness] conveys a very powerful sense that something abnormal is going on; that the participants in the circle have cast off their everyday selves and limitations and entered into a space in which the extraordinary can be achieved.'[20]

The Portuguese Wiccan High Priest Gilberto de Lascariz has suggested further reasons for its power, including one that explains why exposing the genitals in particular might be important from a magical point of view:

Why should one be naked in Traditional Witchcraft rituals? Firstly, the adoption of nudity is irrefutable proof of one's devotion to the Craft, and it also signifies the acceptance of the body as the most precious tool in magic. The body is the vessel in which energies are transmuted. The traditional ritual system of nudity develops an enormous self-confidence, and at the same time it creates the rapport that is necessary for magic to flow amongst the participants, which can grow and develop into something potentially marvellous. Being naked is to leave everything related to our social clothing behind: the narcissism invested in our egos, through nice clothes and accessories, including the social and economic status implicit in them. By simply taking off our clothes and facing each other naked we abandon our personality, and expose ourselves to the following question: without a single item to define me, who am I really? Exposing a nude body in ritual may be connected to the ancient European belief that by exposing our genitalia we could cast away evil spirits and demons. This belief was carried on by medieval masons who decorated churches with scandalous representations of sexual organs. Ancient peoples considered genitalia a powerful talisman. A clear example is the St Michael's Chapel in the village of Monsanto, Idanha-a-Velha.[21]

Witches might scare away demons and god-fearing Christians with their genitalia, but not journalists or even liberal Christians. In a recent BBC documentary a Church of England vicar, Peter Owen-Jones, danced naked with Australian Wiccans,[22] and however much tabloid journalism might encourage us to think that only witches worship in the nude, the reality is that followers of other faiths have discovered the benefits of naked reverence too.

Naked Druids

The Britons (say historians) were naked, civilized men, learned, studious, abstruse in thought and contemplation; naked, simple, plain in their acts and manners; wiser than after ages . . .
—William Blake, in a review of his own lost picture

Wiccans use the poetic term 'skyclad' to denote nakedness in ritual, and this was probably suggested to Gardner by a druid admirer of the Jain religion, some of whose followers are known as Digambara: 'clothed with the quarters of the sky' or 'sky-clad'.

Gardner's druid friend was Ross Nichols, an academic and principal of a private college in London. Like Gardner, he was asthmatic and a keen naturist. During the Second World War these two men met on the lawns of Spielplatz, a naturist resort created in 1929 in Hertfordshire woodland just outside St Albans. When the air raid sirens were silent they swam and sunbathed while discussing their favourite subjects: magic and religion. Only once, perhaps, were their intense discussions disturbed. In 1943 a fire caused by burning chip fat set the resort's clubhouse ablaze and everyone was called upon to form a human chain to pass buckets of water. 'Nudists fight holocaust for hours' ran the local headlines.

SUN BATHING

The advertisement used by Spielplatz in naturist magazines from the 1930s to the 1950s.

After the war Gardner and Nichols continued to meet at Spielplatz and then at Gardner's own resort, Five Acres, which was a short walk away and formed one of the complex of nudist resorts in the area that became known as the 'Hertfordshire Nuderies'.[23] Both of them were agreed that Europe was in need of a new spiritual impulse that would connect people once again to an appreciation of the land and the seasons, and they became, during that post-war period, the founding fathers of a movement that by the end of the twentieth century would claim thousands of adherents: modern paganism. Whilst Gerald Gardner achieved this by promoting the religion of modern Witchcraft, or Wicca, Ross Nichols became the leading figure in the revival of interest in Druidism.

In many ways these two men took the pagan impulse and translated it in their own terms, in accordance with their very different characters. Nichols, a poet and intellectual, chose the path that was more cerebral and embraced the Bardic and Druidic tradition. Gardner, a self-educated maverick, chose the more flamboyant and practical path of folk magic and spell-working. Both paths were essentially pagan, although Nichols always maintained an allegiance with Christianity, and both he and Gardner were ordained as priests in obscure Christian churches.

Being a hedonist, it is unlikely that Gardner was interested in the ascetic path of Jainism, but Nichols admired the Jain philosophy of non-violence, vegetarianism and non-attachment, and wrote that 'Of the known cultural communities it is the Jains who seem most like a society from which Druidry could have originated.'[24] Almost certainly it was Nichols who introduced the term 'skyclad' to Gardner.[25] Skyclad is so much more romantic and poetic than the starker terms naked or nude, and Gardner's use of the word was so successful it has entered into common usage in pagan circles, with most people remaining unaware of its Indian origin.[26]

Wicca and Druidry represent two of the most significant influences in modern paganism. They both perform rituals in circles, revere Nature, and make use of the four cardinal directions and the classical four elements. Both celebrate eight seasonal festivals and offer three degrees of initiation. But when Nichols and Gardner first began to work with these approaches, there was a crucial difference between them that mirrored the distinction between the two sects of Jainism: the Shvetambara (white-robed) and the sky-clad Digambara. Druids were the 'white-robed' representatives of a form of spirituality that managed to maintain many of its ties to

Dorothy Macaskie, a founder of Spielplatz, announces lunch outside the club house that burnt down during the war, prompting the local headline 'Nudists Fight Holocaust for Hours'.

the establishment and Christianity, while witches became the naked proponents of a religion that was undeniably pagan and overtly magical. By suggesting that his witches gather in the nude, Gardner had taken a bold step that automatically distanced proponents of Wicca from the straitjacket of both the establishment and the church. Nichols, however, chose to work with a form of spirituality that was at the very fringe of alternative religious movements, while paradoxically remaining close to the heart of the British sense of identity. Druids were rather like the Beefeaters at the Tower of London: slightly ridiculous, but part of the national heritage.

In the eighteenth century an interest in Britain's pre-Christian past had initiated a period now known as the Druid Revival, in which romantic images of white-clad sages holding court at Stonehenge were promoted by figures such as William Stukeley, the founding father of archaeology. By the time Nichols encountered Druidism in the 1950s, it had developed a tradition of lore and practice that was several hundred years old, and that had nothing to do with nudity, although Nichols' predecessor, George Watson MacGregor Reid, who founded the Ancient Druid Order in the early twentieth century, was a proponent of a simple back-to-nature lifestyle that included naturist ideals, which he called 'simplicitarianism'. Adam Stout in his biographical study of the old Druid chief notes that Reid 'was a believer in the healthful effects of nudism, and on one occasion dreamed of buying a tract of land somewhere cheap and remote, upon which "an opportunity be given to all to go back to Nature for a given period, at as low a rate as possible." It was no longer possible to be naked by the sea-side, as it had been when he was a child: "This is a something lost that must be regained".'[27]

Reid may have sunbathed in the nude in private, or even at the health farm he briefly ran just before the war at Blackboys in Sussex (locals reported nude sunbathing, though the brochure noted that 'bathing costumes are used by those making use of the Sun-Bathing Field')[28] but he would never have countenanced performing a Druid ceremony unrobed. Nor would Nichols, who broke away from Reid's movement in 1964 to form the Order of Bards Ovates and Druids, which has become the world's largest druid group. Nichols certainly enjoyed being skyclad in the privacy of his naturist club or in a woodland sanctuary he created in Oxfordshire, but he never performed druid group ceremonies naked. In contrast, Gardner was able to combine his nudist lifestyle with his spiritual practice and ran his coven from a 'witches' cottage' which he bought from the Abbey Folklore Museum in New Barnet when it closed, and which he re-erected at Five Acres. It is still there, with the magic circle painted on its floor still visible.

Nichols and Reid dominated the world of Druidism from about 1910 until Nichols' death in 1975. They were sympathetic to nudism, but did not combine its practice with their druid rituals. But what about druids before and after their time?

From a survey of the contemporary literature on Druidism, it is clear that although the majority of druids today prefer to remain clothed, a number of them do practice skyclad. In 2001, in researching the life of Nichols, I discovered the existence of Spielplatz through examining his will, and wrote about his naturist interests and friendship with Gerald Gardner in my biography of him *In the Grove of the Druids*, and on the website of the Order of Bards Ovates and Druids.[29] A few years later, Emma Restall Orr, head of the Druid Network, wrote in *Living Druidry*:

> There is a cliché about Pagan religion defined as naked mud-splattered women in the midst of the forest, dancing uninhibited around a fire. Some of those who participate in Western Pagan practices shy away from the possibility, denying its existence as nothing more than media fantasy. Yet such wild expression is an important practice in Pagan Druidry, and for a number of reasons. In terms of deep reverence, being naked allows us to feel more acutely the relationship with the breeze, the wind, the skies, the light and dark, the ground beneath us, the warmth of the sun or flames, the touch of snowflakes or raindrops, the fullness of the natural world, and so encourages a richer, more genuinely felt interaction. Nakedness can also provoke or intensify the falling away of more than physical barriers, evoking an holistic vulnerability, a tangible soul honesty, not only in terms of how we relate to those around us – trees, rocks, moonlight, people, rain – but also with ourselves. Clothes allow us to hide truth, even from ourselves.

Eleven years earlier I had written a book about my own experience of Druidry walking the landscape of the South Downs, but I had hesitated to write about an episode of nakedness on this walk that I had found profoundly liberating. Emboldened by the changing spirit of the times, I decided to 'come clean' in its revised edition:

After a while I reached the outer ramparts of Mount Caburn. Entering the gateway of mound and ditch, I came to the centre of this high and powerful place. Despite it being in the middle of summer, there was no-one there: not a soul in this ancient and beautiful spot. And then I just followed my instincts and took off my clothes and spun and danced around in the sunshine, then lay on the grass feeling its softness on my back, and the sun and gentle breeze on the front of my body. I sat up and was filled with a simple, clear feeling of joy, as if, like Horace Walpole, I had cast off my cares as I had cast off my clothes. I wondered for a moment whether I was mad or indeed legal – could I be arrested for simply being myself here? Was I somehow only legally entitled to exist if covered? Why was it so pleasing and more than that, why did it feel so important to be naked at this moment?

I remembered the grand tradition of Naturism – born out of a love of the sun, the fresh air and of Nature herself, and born too out of a struggle with the grey repressive forces of prudery and Puritanism. Nakedness means freedom, and although dancing on a sun-kissed hillside with shorts on seems pretty similar to dancing with shorts off, there is all the difference in the world. It is as if your clothes take on the weight of your worries and concerns – they come to embody your defences against the world, and if you can feel confident enough and safe enough, then taking them off evokes a powerful sense of liberation, of joy and freedom; and more than that – of innocence and of openness to the world . . .

I realised that this was why so many writers who loved Nature waxed lyrical about the joys of being naked outdoors: Richard Jefferies, Francis Kilvert, George Bernard Shaw, Edward Carpenter, Thoreau, Walt Whitman. They had all discovered the 'secret' that you don't need any thing to be happy.[30]

Since 2002 I have encountered a number of druids who have told me that their practice now includes skyclad working as a result of reading recent books, such as *Living Druidry*, *The Druid Way*, or Kristoffer Hughes' *Natural Druidry*. But I have met others too, including druids from Brittany, who have decided to practise their Druidism free of clothes, not through the encouragement of a book or website, but as a result of following their own inner promptings. Druidry today is followed by most people to get closer to the natural world, which is perceived as Divine. It is often called an 'Earth or Nature Religion', and one of the best ways to feel closer to Nature, they have discovered, is to simply be in it in one's natural state.

We do not know whether the ancient druids, like the Jains, ever worshipped naked, but classical authors did recount that Celtic warriors sometimes charged into battle naked, and Geraldus Cambriensis recounted that in pre-Christian Ireland, when druids were advisors to kings, the future king would have to show himself naked to his people, slowly turning in a circle, so that he could be seen to have no blemishes, and perhaps symbolically demonstrating that he would be truthful, and would hide nothing from them. As Emma Restall Orr points out, clothes allow us to hide the truth, and the king was quite literally showing his people-to-be who he was, with no attempt to cover anything up.

At a Druid camp held in Shropshire woodland one February I witnessed an impromptu demonstration of just such an event, when three 'elders' were elected by the group of about fifty people present, seated in a great circle in a yurt, with a wood-burning stove keeping out the winter frost. When the first elder was chosen he stood up, undressed, and walked to the centre of the circle, before slowly turning as he explained that he would endeavour to hide nothing and to be as open and as honest as he could in his dealings. A hush fell on the meeting and the humility and honesty of the moment was made even stronger when those following him made similar statements but felt no need to undress.

Contemporary druids believe in the sacredness of the natural world and the human body, and reject the idea that we should feel ashamed about our bodies or our sexuality. Whether druids in the ancient past performed skyclad rites is debatable but essentially immaterial, since modern Druidry is essentially a creation of the last few hundred years that is inspired by the traditions and folklore of the past, but is not bound to any ancient form of spiritual practice through centuries of unbroken practice. As a living spirituality it is constantly growing and evolving, and since the ideals of naturism are in complete agreement with the ideals of modern Druidry it is likely that the practice of skyclad Druidry will grow with time.

As a matter of historical record, two connections that have been made with nudity and Druidry have turned out to be probably spurious. Although some writers have claimed that William Blake was a druid, there is no evidence for this, and his latest biographers, such as Peter Ackroyd, point out that an unsound source is responsible for the frequently cited story that Blake and his wife used to enjoy sitting naked in their garden. Another, often repeated story that connects nudity with a druid comes from accounts of the life of the eccentric Welsh druid and gifted healer of the nineteenth century, William Price, who enjoyed striding free of clothes across the Welsh hillsides on his way to treat patients. New research indicates that it was almost certainly his mentally unbalanced father who undertook these walks.[31]

Despite these false leads, there is one piece of evidence that links druids of the past with nakedness and in doing so it leads us once again to those mysterious figures, the Jain skyclad monks, and to the many wonders of Ancient India. Diogenes Laertius, writing in the third century, suggests a similarity between the druids and 'Gymnosophists', who were naked sages, found in India:

> Some say that the study of philosophy was of barbarian origin. For the Persians had their Magi, the Babylonians or the Assyrians the Chaldeans, the Indians their Gymnosophists, while the Kelts and the Galatae had seers called Druids and Semnotheoi, or so Aristotle says in the 'Magic' and Sotion in the twenty-third book of his 'Succession of Philosophers'. . . Those who think that philosophy is an invention of the barbarians explain the systems prevailing among each people. They say that the Gymnosophists and

Druids make their pronouncements by means of riddles and dark sayings, teaching that the gods must be worshipped, and no evil done, and manly behaviour maintained.[32]

However odd it may seem that a connection should be made between naked sages in India and priests of the Celts thousands of miles away, by the eighteenth century scholars had begun unearthing startling similarities between Celtic and Indian languages, mythology and culture, and a theory was proposed of a common Indo-European origin for both peoples. Diogenes Laertius, though, knew nothing of the similarities between Sanskrit and Old Irish. For him the connection was made as a result of Alexander the Great's incursion into India.

2

Beside the Jhelum and the Jordan

In some of the oldest scriptural texts of India, we find references
to naked saints and sannyasins . . . These naked Sadhus belonged to
the non-Vedic or pre-Aryan religion which flourished long before
the Vedic religion was introduced into India. The scriptures of these
people were known as Agamas and the same teachings were later
written as Tantras . . . The Agamas tell us of naked sannyasins as
revealing the highest expression of renunciation which suggests that
he who wants nothing of the world does not want its rags either.
—Shri Gurudev Mahendranath, *The Naked Saints of India*[1]

Probably the earliest people to combine nakedness with the sacred
were those sages of the Indus valley who emerged in the pre-
Vedic period, four thousand or more years ago, who decided to
deliberately shun clothing.[2]

Beside the Jhelum river, a tributary of the Indus, just over 2,300
years ago a group of these sadhus met the most powerful man in the
world, Alexander the Great, and a man who was to become the first
Skeptic philosopher – Pyrrho of Elis.

The Greeks called these naked sages gymnosophists, from *gymnos*:
naked and *sophia*: wisdom, and through their interactions with Pyrrho,
they may have influenced Greek philosophical thought. Some scholars argue that Pyrrho's doctrine of agnosticism – of the impossibility
of certain knowledge – was inspired by the ideas of the gymnosophist
Sanjaya, a contemporary of the Buddha and the great Jain *Tirthankara*
(enlightened teacher) Mahavira. Others believe that any similarities
in their doctrines are coincidental – that the language barrier between
the two men would have prevented the exchange of such ideas.[3]

Alexander the Great meeting the Gymnosophists, by a French artist, *c.* 1475.

More is known about Alexander's encounters with the Gymno-sophists, but here again we must move in the realm of uncertainty. There are a number of accounts of such meetings in the 'Alexander Romance', as the story of this larger-than-life figure has come to be known, and some of these accounts are probably apocryphal in their details though they may well be based on true encounters.

Alexander was a man obsessed with conquest. Over ten years, from the age of 21, he had subjugated a swathe of territory that included all of the Persian Empire, modern-day Greece, Turkey, Egypt and Afghanistan. He commanded the most powerful army in the world. He assassinated his opponents with a ruthlessness admired and emulated by tyrants ever since his time. But just as Russia defeated Napoleon and Hitler, so it was a country – its size and its weather – that finally defeated Alexander.

In 326 BC, heady with the megalomania of conquest after a decade of war, Alexander continued to push the eastern boundary of his empire to its limit. He traversed the Hindu Kush with his army of 35,000 or more soldiers and descended into the Punjab. It was here that he encountered the tradition of naked asceticism, out of which Jainism emerged, and that continues in India to this day. Although Alexander was a military man he was not, as the Greek Arrian of Nicomedia wrote, 'wholly a stranger to the loftier flights of philosophy'.[4] As a child he had been taught by Aristotle, and he had encouraged local traditions of religious worship wherever he had campaigned. So when he came upon a group of naked sadhus in the realm of Taxila he was undoubtedly fascinated by them. Proud men are impressed when they encounter strength in others, and these naked sages displayed a courage born from their disdain for worldly attachments.

Plutarch and PseudoCallisthenes both give accounts of Alexander's first meeting with the sages. These accounts may be apocryphal, since the questions posed by Alexander can be found in a number of unrelated contexts, including the Talmud, but they now form the corpus of myth that has grown up around these mysterious men, the gymnosophists.

Believing some to have sown unrest, Alexander took ten of the sages prisoner, and appointing the oldest among them to judge their answers, he proceeded to ask each a challenging question. Whoever answered poorly would be put to death. Plutarch recounts:

> The first being asked which he thought most numerous, the dead or the living, answered, 'The living, because those who are dead are not at all.' Of the second, he desired to know whether the earth or the sea produced the largest beast; who told him, 'The earth, for the sea is but a part of it.' His question to the third was, "Which is the most cunning of beasts?' 'That,' said he, 'which men have not yet found out.'[5]

The sophistry continued until the ninth had responded, at which point Alexander asked the tenth for his judgement. The naked sage replied with cunning in a way that avoided having to choose a victim: 'All that I can determine is that they have every one answered worse than another.'

Alexander was furious with this response, saying 'Nay, then you shall die first, for giving such a sentence.' Untroubled by this, the sadhu replied 'Not so, O king, unless you said falsely that he should die first who made the worst answer.'

The courage that allows a naked man to stand before the most powerful ruler on earth and give his skilful judgement, guided by his desire to preserve his colleagues' lives, is courage indeed.

The result? Alexander gave the philosophers gifts and released them. In fact he was so impressed by these men that he decided he would like his own personal gymnosophist. Arrian of Nicomedia wrote that Alexander 'so much admired their powers of endurance that the fancy took him to have one of them in his personal train'.[6] However apocryphal the questioning of the sages may have been, it is likely that the following account is true.

Alexander sent a deputy to summon the most distinguished of these sadhus to him, but instead of meekly obeying this command, Plutarch tells us that he refused to speak to the messenger until he stood naked before him: 'to those who were in the highest repute and lived quietly by themselves he [Alexander] sent Onesicritus, asking them to pay him a visit. Now, Onesicritus was a philosopher of the school of Diogenes the Cynic. And he tells us that Calanus very harshly and insolently bade him strip off his tunic and listen naked to what he had to say, otherwise he would not converse with him, not even if he came from Zeus.'[7]

When Alexander finally met Calanus, rather than punishing him for treating his messenger so rudely, he persuaded the sage to join his retinue. And it was Calanus whose simple lesson in the difficulties of maintaining empire reputedly persuaded the Macedonian invader that his troops were indeed right when they protested at the thought of marching east to further conquests. Calanus threw a dried animal hide on to the ground and stood on one edge of it and then another. Each time the rest of the hide rose up. He then stood in the centre, whereupon it flattened itself. The message to Alexander was clear: he must rule not from the borders of his empire, but from its heartland.[8]

With his court gymnosophist in tow, Alexander proceeded south. His army sped by water and land along the Indus, with much slaughter. At the river's delta he built a harbour and docks, and a hundred or so of his ships set sail for the Persian Gulf while Alexander and his army headed west by land on a journey that proved disastrous. A monsoon flood killed many of the women and children. Those who survived had to cross barren lands with little food and water.

On arriving in Persia Calanus fell ill and decided he would prefer to die rather than follow any regime that might cure him. Alexander tried to dissuade the philosopher, but in the end accepted his decision that he would like to die on a funeral pyre, and ordered one built. A solemn procession of horses, soldiers and mourners carrying oils and spices to throw on the flames accompanied

Calanus who was carried on a litter to the pyre, which he then mounted. Alexander gave the signal: bugles sounded as his troops roared with one voice and the fire was lit. The army's elephants shrieked too as the flames leapt around the old man, who sat in a state of complete calm amidst the conflagration.[9]

Within two years Alexander was dead and his empire dissolved almost as rapidly as his corpse decayed in its tomb.

The Jains

Following tradition, every Jain who becomes monk or nun, as token of this decision, obtains permission from family and authorities, distributes wealth, shaves his head and abandons jewels and clothing – exchanging them for the simple white garments of the Order. Those of the Digambara, 'sky-clad', dramatically signify this total renunciation by abandoning clothes entirely, taking literally the verse: 'Those are called naked, who in this world . . . (follow) my religion according to the commandment.' (Akaranga Sutra, 1, 6, 2 (3)).

—Eloise Hart, *A Lamp of the True Light*

Calanus' decision voluntarily to end his life was an act, known as *sallekhana*, that is still sanctioned today as part of the Jain spiritual tradition.[10] While questions about the morality of euthanasia continue to vex the West, for Jains it is not considered immoral to bring about one's own death if it is deemed appropriate.

Today's five million or so Jains, who live mostly in India but also can be found in the USA, England, Canada, Africa and Asia, are mostly clothed, but some of their monks continue the tradition of naked asceticism whose roots lie in the early Indus valley civilization of western India. When the Aryans arrived from the north in around 1500 BC they brought with them their own gods, and religion in India developed along two separate strands: one the Aryan Brahmana tradition, which evolved into the many manifestations of Hinduism, the other the indigenous Shramana tradition, which by 500 BC had evolved into five different groupings: Buddhist, Ajivika, Jain, Lokayata, and those whom we now only know as Gymnosophists, but who may have called themselves Agñanikas.[11]

Coconut milk being poured over the statue of 'Lord Bahubali' in Shravanabelagola, India, in 2006 during the festival of Mahamastakabhisheka (the great head-anointing ceremony), which is held every twelve years and which attracts several million pilgrims.

The Lokayata were rationalist materialist philosophers, while the Ajivikas, Jains and Gymnosophists were religious ascetics who renounced clothing. The Buddha was also originally a naked ascetic, and although some writers believe he probably continued to remain naked throughout his life,[12] it is more likely that he took up clothing for himself and his monks, partly to distinguish them from the other Shramanic groups, and for the very practical reason that the monks were less likely to offend others and would therefore receive more alms.

The Gymnosophists, Ajivikas and Lokayatas have all died out – although an attempt to revive the Ajivikas as a modern religion to suit atheists and nudists was made on a website in 1996.[13] The Jains, however, have continued to flourish up to the present-day.

Jains hold that a series of 24 enlightened beings, known as Tirthankaras,[14] brought their religion to the world, with the 24th and most recent being Mahavira, a contemporary of the Buddha. Mahavira and his predecessors are mostly depicted naked in the statues that adorn Jain temples.

The most striking Jain image is not of a Tirthankara, however, and is not within a temple, but stands at the crest of a great outcrop of rock in Karnataka, in the south-western state of India once known as Mysore. This tenth century statue is of a Jain saint, Bahubali. Eighteen metres high, it is reached by a flight of 614 steps, and can be seen from 30 km away as it towers over the landscape. Every twelve years a festival is held around the statue, which is ritually bathed in milk, curds, ghee, saffron, petals and gold coins.

While the image of Bahubali being bathed in milk or saffron seems a sensuous celebration of the human form, the nakedness of the Jain saints is designed to demonstrate their renunciation of physical attachments and pleasures rather than their celebration. Bahubali is said to have been a king who renounced his realm and withdrew into the forest to meditate in complete silence in a standing position until he reached enlightenment. The vines carved on his legs and arms suggest the supreme stillness he achieved in the forest.

According to Jain tradition, the monastic community founded by the last of the Tirthankaras, Mahavira, comprised 14,000 monks and 36,000 nuns by the time of his death. While the monks wore no clothing, nuns were asked to wear a simple white robe, since it was believed that they would attract harassment, or worse, if they were to go naked.

About a century after Mahavira's death, a schism developed mainly over the issue of whether monks should remain unclothed. According to the traditional account this schism arose in the fourth century BC as a result of the leader of a Jain community, Acharya Bhadrabahu, leading thousands of ascetics from Magadha in the north to southern India, to avoid the effects of a prolonged and severe famine. After twelve years they returned to their homeland to find that another leader, Acharya Sthulabhadra, had relaxed the clothing rule and monks were wearing a simple piece of white cloth. In addition a council had been convened to edit the scriptures. The returning monks could not agree with these changes and over the following centuries the rupture caused by this initial disagreement meant that by the first century AD Jainism had split into the two major sects which exist to this day: those who belong to the tradition of naked monks and are known as Digambara,[15] and those whose monks are clothed and are known as Shvetambara.

Back in the fourth century BC, the returning monks believed that in possessing clothing their colleagues were breaking one of the five vows of their discipline, which demanded celibacy, not lying or stealing, harmlessness and non-possessiveness. How could they attain their goal of *moksha*, liberation, they argued, if they broke that last vow and possessed clothing? Their clothed fellow-monks believed that it was the attitude of non-possessiveness that was paramount.

Digambara monks continue to reject clothing, however, not only because they wish to renounce worldly attachments, but also because they want to avoid killing any organisms through washing clothes. At the heart of Jainism, along with *Aparigraha*, the doctrine of non-attachment to possessions, stands *Ahimsa*, the doctrine of harmlessness that inspired Gandhi and Martin Luther King. Most Jains practise *ahimsa* by being pacifist and vegetarian. Monks and nuns apply the doctrine even more rigorously and will usually refuse transport, since the turning wheels of a car, train or bicycle are likely to kill insects. Some Shvetambara Jains today wear face masks to prevent the accidental inhalation of creatures and avoid antibiotics and disinfectants because of the harm these cause to minute life-forms.

Digambara Jains believe that a woman cannot gain enlightenment because she cannot totally fulfil the vows of Aparigraha and Ahimsa since she is obliged to wear clothes. To achieve moksha she must reincarnate into a man's body that can then remain naked. To circumvent this, the thirteenth-century Digambara writer Asadhara approved of administering vows of nudity to a woman on her deathbed, although it must be said he seems to have been the sole advocate of this method of assisting women to achieve liberation.[16]

An attempt at compromise between the two sects arose in the fourth or fifth century and was practised in the Karnataka region for possibly as long as six hundred to a thousand years. Followers of this movement, known as the Yapaniyas, took a position that from today's standpoint seems eminently sensible. They accepted the Shvetambara belief that women were equally capable of achieving moksha, and the Digambara position that monks should be naked, to which they added a relaxation of the skyclad rule to adapt to different social situations: within the forest or temple the monks were unclothed, but when leaving the sacred precincts they donned a loincloth.

Today, although the majority of Digambara Jains are lay members of the community and do not renounce clothing, in their meditative practice of samayika (often translated as 'the observance of equanimity') they temporarily take on the vows of an ascetic, and that can include divesting themselves of all ornaments and clothing. Padmanabh S. Jaini, Professor of Buddhist Studies at the University of California, writes: 'Even today a Digambara performing samayika in the privacy of his household takes off most or all of his clothes prior to arranging his limbs in the meditative posture. Jainas of all sects, having once assumed this posture, repudiate all goods and relations and resolve to sit, unmoving and undistracted, for up to forty-eight minutes . . .'.[17]

To regularly sit in meditation, free of clothes, owning nothing, attached to nothing, is designed to lead the aspirant towards the ultimate freedom of moksha. As a practice it is ancient, since we find references to it in early Buddhist scriptures, where the idea of assuming the vows of a monk for such a brief time is ridiculed: 'The Niganthas [an early term for Jains] call their laypeople on the fasting days, saying "Come here, sir. Abandoning all your clothes, speak thus: 'I belong to no one; I am nothing to anyone. I own nothing; nothing owns me.'" Having spoken thus, and having thus renounced all his possessions, [the layman] later returns and reclaims all that he has 'given away'. This kind of renunciation is nothing but a sham!'[18]

As Professor Jaini points out, this account ignores the true spirit of the practice, which is a symbolic releasing of all attachments to achieve a level of awareness that is termed 'naked' in the Dzogchen tradition of Tibetan Buddhism.[19] The Theosophical writer Eloise Hart has captured the deeper meaning of what it means to be naked for a Jain, when she writes:

Naked, 'space-clad', suggests the purity of ancient Jainism
when its followers were named Nirgranthas, 'the unbound' –
nir-grantha meaning 'no knot', thus one untied from personal
attachments. Nakedness also signifies the lucidity which
Mahavira restored to Jain traditions, when 'like a lamp he
put the Law in a true light,' discarding the obscuring lens
of superstition and ceremonial ritual [of Brahminical tra-
ditions]. . .

'Misery ceases on the absence of delusion, delusion ceases
on the absence of desire, desire ceases on the absence of
greed, greed ceases on the absence of property.'[20]

More technically this casting off of the 'illusion-garments' of our this-world thought and emotion and putting
on the 'wind as a girdle', the ethereal robes of the spirit, refers
to the time when the Self (Atma), temporarily or perma-
nently, sheds its three lower bodies; and in the two higher
'subtle ones', travels in consciousness to distant places, and
to the world of the gods and there 'develops into its natural
form, obtains perfection, enlightenment, deliverance, and
final beatitude'.[21]

Jain Digambara monks pay their respects at the feet of the Bahubali statue
in 2006.

A spiritual path that seeks to cast off 'illusion-garments' will always find followers, and recently a number of Digambara teachers, such as Muni Taran Sagar, have stimulated a renewed interest in the tradition. As a wandering ascetic he talks to vast crowds, and videos of his sermons can be viewed on the internet. A moving picture of this slight naked man addressing rows of uniformed Indian generals on the virtues of the doctrine of harmlessness can be seen on one website.[22]

Despite these sages' success in convincing contemporary citizens of fast-developing India that Jain values are needed now more than ever, the call to the ascetic life of a naked monk appeals only to a small minority of the Jain population – less than 200 choose to live skyclad, while white-robed monks and nuns number in their thousands.[23]

The Hindu Naga Babas

I was sent to the spring for a quick ritual dip, and then returned to the dark puja room, where I was made to remove my loincloth and stand naked before my five gurus. 'He looks like a Muslim. He's circumcised just like them!' joked the balding Mangal Bjarti, slicing one index finger with the other as if it were a scalpel. Everyone laughed. 'You look so funny!' said Hari Puri Baba. He was laughing so hard he had to hold his sides. 'Just like a big baby! You see, nothing in your hands, nothing on your body, you have nothing. See? No more luggage! By the authority vested in me by all the mad people of the world, I declare you cleansed of all sin!'
—Baba Rampuri, *Autobiography of a Blue-Eyed Yogi*

While there are less than two hundred naked Jains now living in India, there are thousands of naked Hindu sadhus in the country, although these may be diminishing in numbers. Lawrence Miles, an Englishman who arrived penniless in India in 1953 and became a naked sadhu and then guru known as Shri Gurudev Mahendranath, wrote in 'The Naked Saints of India':

The feature of naked sadhus is still fairly common, even in modern India. Overseas visitors seldom see them because they

The Englishman Lawrence Miles (1911–1991), who in 1953 travelled to India, eventually becoming a guru and in 1978 the founder of the International Nath Order. Photographed here in the 1980s in Mehmadabad.

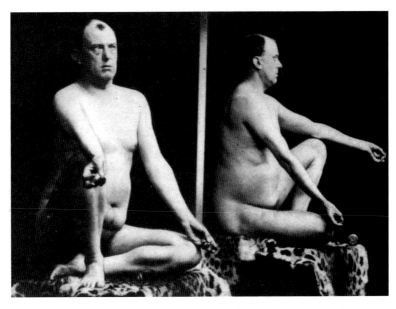

The magician Aleister Crowley demonstrating the yogic breathing technique of pranayama. Crowley met Lawrence Miles in 1934 and encouraged him to seek wisdom in India.

seldom live or visit the tourist fleshpots and city terminals. When Allen Ginsberg, the American poet, visited India some years back, he expressed in letters which were printed in City Lights his sad disappointment at not seeing even one naked sadhu. This could be surprising because in Benares, which he visited, it is doubtful if this great city of Shiva has ever been without naked sadhus and in considerable numbers.

Benares is still the one city in India where you can walk about naked and yet remain unnoticed. Even beggars display mutilated genitals to reveal a mental inclination to celibacy and a great sacrifice which would make physical delinquency impossible. In these days most naked sadhus wear a cloth in public or when travelling. They neither wish to draw needless attention to themselves or amuse the schoolboy population now sadly conditioned by modern education. Hindu Digambar sadhus have outnumbered, and still do, the naked Jains by thousands to one. Many city councils have introduced bylaws forbidding public nudity even among sadhus. A new sense of Western respectability has come to India just at a time when the West is abandoning its Puritanism.[24]

Many of the Hindu skyclad sadhus referred to by Gurudev Mahendranath are members of the Juna Akhara sect and are called 'Naga babas', naked saints. As with the Jains only the males are naked: the few women who are of equal status are called 'Naga mais' – Naga mothers – and remain clothed. It is the Naga babas of the Juna Akhara sect who decide the exact dates of the famous Kumbh Mela festivals, which are held in four different locations in twelve-year cycles.

Unlike the Jain sadhus, who from the beginning followed the doctrine of harmlessness, the Naga Babas were once mercenary warriors who, like the woad-covered Celts of old, fought naked. They were employed by Rajas and Maharajas to defend their territories against hostile neighbours and Islamic invaders. When the British came to India they were outlawed and became instead sadhus who worshipped Shiva and continued to live in their Arcuddas (gymnasia). Many Naga Babas possess sabres from these times which are hung on their walls and which they carry with them to festivals such as Kumbh Mehla or Mahashivaratri. At these great festivals thousands of Naga babas come together, some smoking chillums of

Naga Babas bathing in the Ganges at the Hindu festival of Kumbh Mela.

hashish, others engaged in various mortifications of the flesh, and many covered with ash from head to toe.

Two thousand Naga babas trekked from India to Nepal to be at the Mahashivaratri festival in Nepal in 2006,[25] and thousands attend the same festival in India. Westerners are often surprised and puzzled by the sheer numbers of these naked sages and their eccentricities, but in reality the quantity of Naga babas is small compared to the overall population of sadhus, which is believed to be in the region of 4 to 5 million in India. The tradition of mendicant ascetics has created a welfare system that cares for those people who will not, or who cannot, earn a living. Since sadhus receive alms and are revered for the blessings they bestow, and sometimes feared for the curses they can utter, some beggars pose as sadhus and some undoubtedly would be in psychiatric institutions in other countries. K. Narayan explains the colourful and chaotic diversity of the Indian sadhu tradition that now extends across the world: 'There is no overarching structure to monitor all the different kinds of ascetics . . . and even within the same sect or monastery sadhus may display a marked individuality. There are naked sadhus and ochre-colored sadhus; sadhus with matted hair, and those with shining bare scalps; poor, wandering sadhus and jet-set, Rolls-Royce-transported sadhus; sadhus who interact with a handful of Indian villagers, and sadhus who hold forth to audiences of thousands in New York or Switzerland.'[26]

Fuelled by the belief that the pathways that lead to and from the Divine are infinite, India has always had the gift and the ability to welcome and absorb the new and the different. When a non-Indian is attracted to the life of the sadhu they are usually welcomed and can become revered figures. Lawrence Miles hasn't been the only foreigner to be attracted to the life of a sadhu, naked or otherwise. The idea has proved attractive to more than one foreigner, and today there are American, Japanese and European sadhus living in India. An American Naga baba known as Baba Rampuri recently published his autobiography and runs retreats for visitors from abroad.[27]

Two points of significance seem to emerge from a study of the tradition of naked sages in India. One is the clear gender bias: it is only the males who reject clothing.[28] The other is that the motivation for being naked is not overtly the desire to exhibit the body or even celebrate its existence or form. Being naked is an act of renunciation and asceticism, not of sensuality or eroticism.

The gender bias will be found in much of the history of nakedness – on the whole it seems that men have a greater urge than women to get naked and to be seen naked.[29] Some might argue that this is culturally conditioned: that the repression of women has deprived them of the freedom to act in the way they would wish, and over the centuries they have internalized this repression and cannot now access the natural desire to be free of clothing. In addition, because men are more predatory than women, women would feel at greater risk than men in exposing themselves. Others would argue that humans often share the same patterns of behaviour as animals, and that studies of the mating behaviour of many species suggests that the male who wishes to be seen naked is simply acting out the display instinct – essentially showing off his 'wares' to attract potential mates.

While the naked sadhus may be unconsciously driven by this urge, at a conscious level they are trying to achieve a quite different aim. If they are trying to attract any mate it is Deity itself – the union they are seeking is not with a human but with the Divine – and in seeking this union they believe they are renouncing the snares of the material world.

Songs of Freedom

Dance, Lalla, with nothing on
but air. Sing, Lalla,
wearing the sky.
Look at this glowing day! What clothes
Could be so beautiful, or
More sacred?"
—Lalla[30]

Anyone who has stood naked in the sunshine or in a breeze, who has skinny-dipped or lain naked on soft grass, will know of the increased sense of connection with the world that comes from doing these things unclothed rather than clothed. However much the naked sadhus insist they are renouncing the world there must be some, at least, among them who are in reality embracing it. The very word Digambara, which is sometimes translated as 'clothed with the four directions of the sky', suggests a dynamic connection with the spatial world, with the physical reality of the breeze, and the beauty of the clear blue heavens.

Such a sensual spiritual approach, that refuses the trap of dualism, and in which the world is not rejected, nor matter disdained in favour of spirit, is certainly the aim of the 'new' naked mystics in Druidry and Wicca. But it can be found amongst the mystics of India too, and in particular in the lives and poetry of two of the few naked female sages who are recorded in history: Akka Mahadevi and Lalla.

Akka Mahadevi was born in Karnataka, southern India, in the twelfth century and although little is known of her life, 350 of her poems, sometimes called her 'Songs of Freedom', have survived. As a young girl she was brought up as a devotee of Shiva, but she was so beautiful a Jain king fell in love with her and insisted on marriage. She soon tired of the king's sexual demands, however, and left the palace and the marriage, casting aside her clothes and wandering naked into the jungle, heading for the school of two radical and democratic Shivaite devotional leaders, Allama and Basavanna.

When she arrived at the school, her hair so long it covered much of her body, Allama asked her 'Will not the lewd world react madly about your nakedness?' She replied 'Yes, it is in order not to hurt the world's eye or yet to rouse men's passions that I have covered myself with the hair cascading all around me.'[31] Soon the devotees of the school accepted her as a liberated soul, and today she is considered a saint in India. Images of her depict her as almost completely swathed in hair.

Whenever she was challenged about her nakedness she responded in song with devotional praises to Shiva, her true lover, as in this verse:

O Shiva, when shall I invoke Thee,
Ascending the sapphire hills,
Hugging the moonstones
And playing the horn?

When shall I join thee,
Lovely Lord white as Jasmine,
Shedding the shame
Of body and of mind?[32]

Akka Mahadevi died at the age of 25, and Mark Storey, in reviewing her life for a naturist magazine, concludes 'Her life, the beauty of her poems, and her willingness to challenge body-shaming cultural norms in public – in both word and deed – provide a worthy model for naturists.'[33]

Two centuries later, further north in India, Lalla, another naked female mystic, achieved fame with her lucid aphoristic verses that have made her one of Kashmir's favourite poets. Little is known of Lalla's life, and what is known is apocryphal. It is said that she was born in a village near Srinagar around 1320 and died in 1391. Her husband and his family mistreated her, but she never complained and meditated instead at holy shrines whenever she could. One day her husband believed she was wasting time, and as she returned home from fetching water he struck the pot with a stick. The pot shattered, but the water remained intact above her head and became a sacred lake.

By the age of 24 Lalla had had enough of the marriage and left home to follow the Hindu teacher Sed Bayu. Soon she was so filled with ecstasy that she began wandering and dancing naked in a state of ecstatic clarity. One of her songs clearly conveys her feelings about being skyclad:

Don't be so quick to condemn my nakedness.
A man is one who trembles in the Presence.
There are very few of those.
Why not go naked?
The ram of experience must be fed
And ripened for the sacrifice.
Then all these customs will disappear
like clothing. There's only the soul.[34]

A number of different religious impulses converged in fourteenth century Kashmir, and Lalla was influenced not only by Shaivite

Hinduism, but also by Sufism, as was the religion of Sikhism born two centuries later, in the Punjab just south of Kashmir. It is said that she studied with the Sufi master Ali Hamadani, but as with all true mystics her insights transcended the confines of religious affiliation, as she insisted 'There is no reality but God.' One of her translators, Coleman Barks, writes 'Ecstasy is only one of her moods, and not the primary one. Political disgust is another, and a Hopi-like prophetic mode: "A time is coming so deformed . . .".' He stresses the point that Lalla has essentially feminine qualities in: 'her firm location in the breath; her sense of being dissolved into the lovemaking [of Shiva and Shakti] in the jasmine garden; and her attention to a truth which is very much in motion, and which can include her doubt and her lostness.'[35]

Another translator, Jaishree Kak, writes of the way Lalla's songs are embedded in Kashmiri culture:

> Growing up in Kashmir, I have memories of spectacular Himalayan Mountains, magnificent lakes, and countless rivers snaking through the valley, and accompanying all is the echoing on festive occasions of the melodious singing of Lalla's verse-sayings, popularly known as Lalla-Vakh. Her outpourings are timeless and people of all faiths have treasured them. The oral transmission for centuries illustrates the extent to which she has been a part of folk memory. My old aunts who grew up in Kashmir have memories of women reciting Lalla's verses while they spun fine shawls at the spinning wheel. Over the centuries, Lalla became the wise woman of Kashmiri culture. She was invoked not only at moments of personal dilemma but also to celebrate moments of social togetherness. I myself remember my mother singing Lalla's verses and occasionally quoting them in her conversations.[36]

Whatever the actual facts of her life, Lal Ded or Mai Lal Diddi, Grandmother Lalla, as she is also known, has become a legendary figure, with her poetry esteemed as much as that of Rumi and Hafiz. In Sanskrit she is called Lalleshwari, the great yogini – a prophetess and practitioner of yoga.

It was said that this great yogini proved she had found a freedom that was impervious to praise or blame when one morning some children were making fun of her nakedness. A cloth merchant scolded them for their disrespect, and Lalla asked him for two strands of cloth equal in weight. She then flung these over either shoulder, and through the day, whenever someone mocked her she tied a knot in one cloth, and whenever someone praised her she tied a knot in the other. At the end of the day she asked the merchant to weigh both – surrounded no doubt by all the villagers and their children. Both naturally weighed the same, and her point was made: praise and blame have no substance.

Reading Lalla we are invited to let go of our attachments, to live from the soul, and to be free:

> The soul, like the moon,
> is now, and always new again.
>
> And I have seen the ocean
> continuously creating.
>
> Since I scoured my mind
> and my body, I too, Lalla
> am new, each moment new.
>
> My teacher told me one thing,
> live in the soul.
>
> When that was so,
> I began to go naked,
> and dance.[37]

Nakedness in Judaism and Christianity

Sincere, humble nudism is a serious way to a real union with God.
—Fr James Dodge

Discovering that nakedness could help one get closer to the Divine was not an experience confined to the East. The idea runs like a hidden seam through Judaism and Christianity too, but it is only hidden in the sense that it is unrecognized by the majority of Jews and Christians. In reality the evidence for the connection between mystical states and nakedness is clearly stated in the Bible and found in many early Christian texts, but this evidence has only been taken to heart by certain Quakers and a limited number of Catholics and Protestants.

In Judaism we see nakedness being used as a way of getting closer to God in three ways: through baptism, prophecy and ecstatic dancing. Just as Lalla danced naked in mystical ecstasy in four-teenth-century Kashmir, so did King David before the Ark of the Covenant, although he felt obliged to keep on a slip. One of his wives, however, was not amused: 'Michal the daughter of Saul coming out to meet David, said: How glorious was the king of Israel today, uncovering himself before the handmaids of his servants, and was naked, as if one of the buffoons should be naked.'[38]

David could have protested that he was not completely naked, but it is doubtful that Michal would have been interested in this nicety. The point was that a king had divested himself of his regalia and almost all of his clothing, and had made a fool of himself, in her eyes, in front of the servants.

It is ironic that it should have been Saul's daughter who reacted in this way, because her father had prophesied naked, once again reminding us of Lalla in Kashmir who engaged in prophecy as well as dance. The Book of Samuel recounts how, on arriving at Naoith, 'he too stripped off his clothes and he too prophesied before Samuel and lay naked all the day and all that night. Hence it is said, "Is Saul also among the prophets?"'[39]

A Trappist monk of the Cistercian Order of the Strict Observance, Fr James Dodge draws our attention to one word that is used twice in that quotation: 'It appears to me that the "too" is frequently overlooked, for this makes it clear that not only Saul but all the others whom he had previously sent were naked, and had been so for some time, not just a day and a night.'[40] Earlier in his essay, Dodge expresses his belief that the nakedness of the Old Testament figures such as Saul, Isaiah and David demonstrates 'humility, a sub-virtue of temperance ... Thus true, sincere, humble nudism is a serious way to a real union with God. But it can only be that, if and when our nudity is undertaken in a realization of our essential nothingness.'[41] Such an idea is reminiscent of the Buddhist concept of 'naked awareness' which is predicated on the experience of Sunyatta – the Emptiness or Nothingness that Buddhists believe underlies our experience of reality.

David may have undressed for an hour or so to dance before his God, Saul may have stripped for three days and nights to prophesy, but Isaiah had to spend three years in the nude. In the Book of Isaiah we read:

> At the same time spake the Lord by Isaiah the son of Amoz, saying, Go and loose the sackcloth from off thy loins, and put off thy shoe from thy foot. And he did so, walking naked and barefoot.
>
> And the Lord said, Like as my servant Isaiah hath walked naked and barefoot three years for a sign and wonder upon Egypt and upon Ethiopia;
>
> So shall the king of Assyria lead away the Egyptians prisoners, and the Ethiopians captives, young and old, naked and barefoot, even with their buttocks uncovered, to the shame of Egypt.[42]

Here we see Isaiah undergoing nakedness 'for a sign and wonder' – an idea that was seized upon by Quakers in the seventeenth century when some of them decided to 'go naked for a sign'. Where there is no pictorial evidence, however, we can never be sure that the word naked in any historical account indicates full nudity. David was said to have danced naked, but it transpires that he was wearing a loincloth. Isaiah, on the other hand, seems to have been completely bare, as the above passage indicates, but when the Quakers imitated the Old Testament Prophets many of them stopped short at revealing their genitals. Certainly Solomon Eccles, also known as Solomon Eagle, decided to cover his 'privities' as Pepys termed them, as he strode through Westminster Hall in the presence of the king on 29 July 1667: 'One thing extraordinary was this day, a man, a Quaker, came naked through the hall, only very civilly tied about the privities to avoid scandal, and with a chafing-dish of fire and brimstone upon his head did pass through the Hall, crying "Repent! Repent!"'[43] The poor man was living through a time in which he had good reason to be upset, as Daniel Defoe recorded in his *A Journal of the Plague Year*: 'the Quakers had at this time also a burying ground set apart to their use ... and the famous Solomon Eagle, who ... had predicted the plague as a judgment, and ran naked through the streets, telling the people that it was come upon them to punish them for their sins, had his own wife died the next day of the plague, and was carried, one of the first in the Quakers' dead-cart, to their new burying ground.'

Although the Quaker founder George Fox approved of going naked for a sign, because of its biblical precedents, there are no records of him indulging in the practice. Nevertheless the idea spread from Britain to colonial America in the late seventeenth century, with protagonists sometimes appearing in sackcloth, sometimes completely nude, and being punished with whipping or the stocks as a result. Rather than being used for prophecy, though, the practice was used as a form of pacifist protest against religious persecution, with one account describing the fate of one Sarah Goldsmith and her fellow-protesters: 'On the 3d of the 3d month, 1655, Sarah Goldsmith ... with her hair hanging down her, and without any other clothes upon her, excepting shoes on her feet ... stood about half an hour, till the tumult grew so violent, that some bystanders ... forced them into a shop, out of which the multitude call'd to have them thrown ...'.[44]

Despite the furore caused by Quakers going naked for a sign, and despite the biblical precedents, the use of nakedness to protest or prophesy was never more than a minority activity in Christianity and Judaism. But there was one religious practice which required complete nakedness, and which for at least five hundred years involved most Christians, and for perhaps as much as a thousand years most Jews.

The Baptism of Christ in the Basilica San Marco, Venice.

Naked I was born and naked shall I die. (Job 1:21)

In the time of Jesus and the Old Testament, the rite of baptism in Judaism required full immersion in the nude either into a river or a mikvah (a stone pool specially created for this purpose), and there is evidence that this had been the practice from as early as 1,000 BC.[45] For this reason, when Jesus was baptised by John the Baptist in the river Jordan he would have been naked, and was portrayed as such in paintings and mosaics.

In the Greek Orthodox church this moment is celebrated in a hymn which cries: 'O compassionate Saviour, putting on the nakedness of Adam as a garment of glory, Thou makest ready to stand naked in the flesh in the River Jordan. O marvellous wonder!'

When the Christian church created its own rite of baptism, it was based directly on the Jewish immersion rituals which required

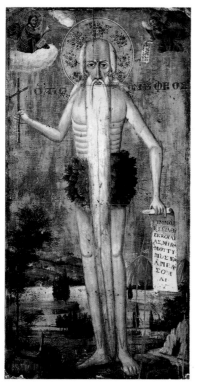

St Onuphrius lived as a hermit in the desert of Upper Egypt in the fourth or fifth centuries. Wearing nothing but a loincloth of leaves it was said that a hind instructed him in Christian rites and liturgy, and that during his 60 years in the desert his only visitor was an angel who delivered a Host every Sunday. This early depiction of Onuphrius appears on a Byzantine icon, 4th or 5th century.

nakedness, and in *c.* 200 AD St Hippolytus of Rome wrote of this, stating that total nudity was required and that women were also obliged to remove all jewellery. St Cyril of Jerusalem in *c.* 350 AD, addressing a group of naked candidates about to be immersed, declared: 'You are now stripped and naked, in this also imitating Christ despoiled of His garments on His Cross, He Who by His nakedness despoiled the principalities and powers, and fearlessly triumphed over them on the Cross.' The candidates then had to pray and receive more instruction from St Cyril, before their entire bodies (from the 'top of your head to your feet' as St Cyril says) were smeared with holy oil. Only then could they be immersed and then emerge, reborn, to be clothed in white vestments. In *c.* 400 AD Theodore of Mopsuestia explained why nakedness was necessary in baptism when he wrote: 'Adam was naked at the beginning and he was not ashamed of it. This is why your clothing must be taken off, since it is the convincing proof of this sentence which lowers mankind to need clothing.'[46]

The Mormon church in America has managed to adapt the idea of nakedness and anointing with oil in its baptismal rite by having candidates undress in private, and then don a loose tabard, enabling the priest to anoint certain parts of the body with oil whilst preserving modesty and being spared the sight of naked flesh.

In the early Christian rite of baptism we see a theme that Christianity has shared with Judaism, Classical Paganism, and modern-day Wicca – the idea that we are born into the world naked, and that a ceremony of birth into a faith should imitate this return to one's essential nature, stripped of the protection and pretensions of the everyday, symbolized by clothes. Christian supporters of nudism today talk about this as 'sacramental nakedness' – an action that helps put one 'in touch with God's grace in Christ'.

Remembering the story of Adam and Eve covering their nakedness in the Garden of Eden, most Christians today undoubtedly associate nudity with feelings of shame, and would be astonished to hear of the way in which it was a feature of the early church, and of the way it is advocated today by naturist Christians, who hold services in the nude in England and the United States. But for some early Christians, nakedness was not simply utilized at the moment of baptism. To early saints – such as St Mary of Egypt and St Onuphrius – it became a way of life and an ascetic discipline, as with certain Jains and Hindus in India. We are reminded of these Indian ascetics when we hear the story of a monastic chronicler recounting the

The Renunciation of St Francis, illustrated by Giovanni di Pauli for Dante Alighieri's *Divine Comedy*, Tuscany, c. 1450. The naked figure of St Francis receives the benediction of the Bishop of Assisi. Both Assisi and Perugia can be seen in the background.

experience of a Christian monk travelling between two monasteries in Egypt. On his way he meets three naked monks who greatly impress him with their detachment and other-worldliness.[47]

As late as the sixteenth century we read of Christian ascetics in Russia, such as St Vassily of Moscow, who renounced all clothing even in the winter, calling themselves 'Fools for Christ', and we have, of course, the most famous naked Christian of all – St Francis of Assisi.

Francis, the son of a wealthy cloth merchant, first tore off his clothing in a dispute with his father that was overseen by the local bishop. His father was attempting to strip him legally of his inheritance, but instead of defending his rights, Francis's response was to strip himself, handing his clothes to his father, saying: 'Hitherto I have called you my father on earth; henceforth I desire to say only "Our Father who art in Heaven"'.[48] At that moment, as Dante states, Francis espoused his beloved Lady Poverty, and walked naked through the snow to a nearby monastery.

We find him naked in the snow again when, some time later, he is disturbed by 'an urge of the flesh' as his biographer Celano puts it. 'But as soon as the blessed father felt it, he took off his clothes and lashed himself furiously with the chord, saying; "Come on, Brother Ass, that's the way you should stay under the whip!"' Despite 'painting welts all over his limbs black and blue', the temptation did not leave him, so he 'opened the cell, went out to the garden, and threw himself naked into the deep snow. Taking snow by the handful he packed it together into balls and made seven piles.' These seven snowmen he identified as his wife, children and servants, ordering the devil to clothe them, since they were freezing to death. 'But if complicated care of them is annoying, then take care to serve one Master!' he shouted at the devil, assuming he would find procuring clothing for a family and servants more tedious than serving his arch-enemy.[49]

We have already encountered the association of nakedness with fury and indignation in the accounts of Quakers going naked for a sign, and this motivation for the use of nakedness by Christians reached its peak in Canada between the 1930s and 1960s, when the Sons of Freedom, a sect of radical Christians inspired by Tolstoy and the Quakers, took to mass nude protests and setting fire to their homes. Since these protests were politically motivated, they are considered in more detail in chapter Three, 'Naked Rebellion'.

Given the details of any case of nakedness, rebellious or other-wise, a medieval theologian would have been able to decide to which of four categories it belonged: *Nuditus naturalis* – the natural state of humanity before the Fall, and which could be depicted in scenes of Paradise, the Last Judgement and the Resurrection; *Nuditus tempo-ralis* – the lack of earthly goods due to poverty or voluntary abnegation, as in the case of apostles, ascetics, monks and nuns; *Nuditus virtualis* – symbolizing innocence, in which the soul is laid bare before God, as in Confession; or *Nuditus criminalis* – in which vanity and lust reign supreme.[50]

Naturist Christians argue that their nakedness reflects the first three categories, with the Rev. Karen Gorham, priest of St Paul's Maidstone, and her co-author Dave Teal, lecturer in Philosophy and Moral Theology at Regent's Park College, Oxford, concluding that 'there is no essential conflict between Christianity and naturism, that there is nothing inherently sinful about the naked body, and that the realization of this is part of what it means to be at ease with oneself, to be healed, to be made whole.'[51] They finish their monograph, *Naturism and Christianity: Are They Compatible?*, with a quotation from C. S. Lewis's *The Great Divorce*, in which he imagines heaven: 'Long after that I saw people coming to meet us . . . some were naked, some robed. But the naked ones did not seem less adorned, and the robes did not disguise in those who wore them the massive grandeur of muscle and the radiant smoothness of flesh.'[52]

The Catholic writer Jim C. Cunningham argues passionately in *Nudity and Christianity* for naked worship when he writes: 'God made nothing more beautiful and dignified than the human body, which He especially designed in His Own image and likeness. God's Own Supreme Beauty is reflected in the human body as well as the soul. Whatever is beautiful in all creation, finds its perfection and fulfilment in the human nude. To love chastely and to admire the naked body is to contemplate God. "Blessed are the pure in heart, for they shall see God"'.[53]

Cunningham, eventually driven blind and losing a leg and kid-ney to diabetes, writes that after converting to Catholicism in 1973 he became 'disillusioned by conventional Christianity because it was more conventional than Christian'. He then 'seriously re-examined all of my assumed values, striving to conform them to Christ. While

The Revd Donald Sherriff giving a sermon at the Twelfth Congress of the International Naturists Federation at the North Kent Sun Club in Orpington on 10 August 1970.

studying the Fathers of the Church and their routine custom of mixed, group, nude baptism, I asked what was considered unaskable: "Why wear clothes?" I discovered that convention required always covering the body because it regarded the body as negative, if not intrinsically evil. Seeing that this was not the mind of Christ, I quit my educational professions (theology teacher, guidance counselor, headmaster) and devoted myself full-time to naturist publishing.'[54]

Although Pope Pius XI condemned naturism as 'paganly immodest' in the 1930s, by 1981 Pope John Paul II had declared that: 'Nakedness itself is not immodest . . . Immodesty is present only when nakedness plays a negative role with regard to the value of the person, when its aim is to arouse concupiscence, as a result of which the person is put in the position of an object for enjoyment.'[55] Thanks to the proselytizing work of Cunningham and others, by the 1980s naturism had become firmly established within Christianity, if not fully accepted by all, with its own websites, discussion forums, books and magazine. In the USA a number of naturist resorts have dedicated chapels and Christians can attend annual Christian Nudist Convocations, while in the UK the Christian Naturist Fellowship organizes meetings at naturist resorts, publishes a newsletter, and holds services in the nude in a small wooden chapel known as the 'campers' cabin' in Kent. Wikipedia carries a comprehensive entry entitled 'Christian Naturism' which begins by explaining that: 'Christian naturists view the story of Adam and Eve in the Garden of Eden as a model for their beliefs. When Adam and Eve were created and placed in the garden as a couple by God, they were both naked and "felt no shame".' Christian writers have also taken advantage of the more permissive times, and have started to use the term naked in its metaphorical sense to attract readers and challenge conventional approaches, publishing books such as Eric Sandras's *Buck-Naked Faith: A Brutally Honest Look at Stunted Christianity*, Craig Borlase's *The Naked Christian: Taking Off Religion To Find True Relationship* and *The Naked Christian: What God Sees When He Looks Right Through Me* by Doug Brendel.

As English naturists sit in the campers' cabin in Kent innocently listening to readings from the Bible, few perhaps realize that they are engaging in an activity that was supposedly carried out by Spanish heretics in the fourth century. The Synod of Saragossa in 380 AD condemned Priscillianism because, amongst other things, its followers read and interpreted the Bible in the nude. In that same era Church Father St Epiphanius, bishop of Salami and a staunch defender of orthodoxy, had devoted much of his energies to compiling a compendium of heretical sects, one of which was the Barbelo Gnostics, whose initiates enacted rites 'completely nude'. The bishop's colleague Hippolytus denounced another Gnostic sect, the Naasenes, for engaging in naked rituals by firelight, and a third Gnostic group was also believed to both worship and live in the nude: the Adamni.[56]

Whereas we know the Kent naturists worship in the nude, since they have been filmed for a television documentary, we cannot be so certain about these fourth-century cults, whose accusers were interested in blackening their reputations and may have had no first-hand knowledge of them.

Christ hangs naked on the Cross between the two thieves, from the Holkham
Bible Picture Book, 1320–30.

There are no more accusations of nudity in Christian worship
for about a thousand years, and then the claim was made once more,
this time against the French sect of the Turlupins, one of whom was
burnt at the stake in 1375. In the Netherlands in 1411 a group known
as the 'Men of Intelligence' were accused of practising nakedness,
as were the Adamites of Bohemia later in the century.

Ronald Hutton's incisive essay 'A Modest Look at Ritual Nudity'
points out that, as with the fourth-century accusations of heresy,
these later condemnations may well have been based upon fantasy

A 15th-century wooden crucifix by Michelangelo. Bought by the Italian State for 3.25 million euros (4.54 million US dollars) from an art dealer, experts suggest that the artist created the crucifix c. 1495, when he was 20 years old.

rather than fact, and although almost all of these sects were wiped out by military expeditions, 'none the less, for the next four centuries the Adamites were to be the classic naked worshippers in the European imagination, trotted out every time that conservative Christians wanted examples of the dreadful consequences of religious liberty.'[57] In the seventeenth century pamphleteers stirred up fears that Adamites had come to London and were seeking to cast aside not only clothes, but every vestige of discipline and order.

Were the Adamites nude or merely convenient scapegoats? We shall probably never know, but if certainty, from a Christian point of view, can be gained by turning to the Bible, then we can be sure of one thing: that in the final moments of Jesus' life he was naked as he hung on the cross. The gospel of St John recounts: 'The soldiers, therefore, when they did crucify Jesus, took his garments, and made four parts, to each soldier a part, also the coat, and the coat was seamless, from the top woven throughout, they said, therefore, to one another, "We may not rend it, but cast a lot for it, whose it shall be;" that the Writing might be fulfilled, that is saying, "They divided my garments to themselves, and upon my raiment they did cast a lot;" the soldiers, therefore, indeed, did these things.'[58]

Crucifixion was designed to inflict humiliation as well as intense physical anguish, so stripping a victim of their clothes was simply one more way to make them suffer. Most crucifixes depict Christ wearing a loincloth – for obvious reasons – but there are some notable exceptions. The crucifix from the Convent of Santo Spirito in Florence, attributed to Michelangelo and for a long time housed in the Casa Buonarotti museum devoted to the artist, was restored to the Convent by the museum in 2000. This work, which was originally a gift to the Prior of Santo Spirito Hospital, was hung behind the altar of a church, until it disappeared for some time. It was then found and placed in the museum until, under pressure from the Augustinian fathers and the Rector of the Basilica of Santo Spirito, it was restored to its original owners.

Another Renaissance artist, Benvenuto Cellini, sculpted a naked Christ on the cross – this time in marble and life-size. It is said that the model for the sculpture was his sexual partner and assistant Fernando, and Cellini originally intended the crucifix for his own tomb. Instead, though, he sold it to the Medici family who gave it to Spain, where it can now be seen in the Escorial Monastery in Madrid, draped with a loincloth and with a crown of thorns added to the head.

Spain is the location of two other naked Christs. In 1598 El Greco carved a resurrected Christ, who hardly needs a loincloth since his genitals are portrayed in a way that makes them appear to be a single testicle, faintly echoing the heresy that he was a eunuch. In choosing to portray a risen Christ as naked El Greco clearly relied on the Bible account of the resurrection, in which Joseph and Nicodemus were

El Greco's *The Resurrected Christ* sculpted for the altar of the chapel of the Hospital Tavera, Toledo, Spain, between 1595 and 1598.

allowed by Pilate to take Jesus' body from the cross. They wrapped it in linen, placed it in a sepulchre which they sealed with a 'great stone'. Later, four women including Mary Magdalene saw on passing by the sepulchre that the stone had been rolled away and that there was no body in the tomb, simply the linen that had been used to wrap the body, 'as well as the burial cloth that had been around Jesus' head. The cloth was folded up by itself, separate from the linen.'[59] Michelangelo's sculpture of the resurrected Christ in the Basilica of Santa Maria sopra Minerva in Rome was carved in accordance with this account, though now some linen has returned to cover his loins.

More recently, the Spanish photographer J.A.M. Montoya has been threatened with excommunication for his 1997 exhibition 'Sanctorum', which includes a photograph of a crucified Christ that, in complete contrast to El Greco's portrayal, depicts him with an erection.[60] Other contemporary renditions of this theme include the controversial 'Naked Christ' of childrens' illustrator Michele Coxon, which hangs in St Asaph Cathedral, North Wales and takes the concept of nakedness deeper than the skin to portray the body as a carcass using sheep bones; and the less gruesome but equally controversial life-size image of Christ in the nude made entirely of chocolate by the Canadian artist Cosimo Cavallaro. In 2007 a planned exhibition in Manhattan of the first version of the sculpture, entitled 'My Sweet Lord', was cancelled when the gallery received death threats. Rodents began to eat the sculpture while it was in storage, so the sculptor recast it and retitled it 'Sweet Jesus'. It is now displayed online with an audio-commentary by the artist.[61]

Whether in chocolate or sheep bones, carved in marble or wood, with penis erect or minimized, the image of Christ stripped of all covering is a powerful one for Christians and even non-believers. It points to the mystery of embodiment, of incarnation, provoking us into asking the existential questions 'Who are we? *What* are we?' While some religions focus their attentions almost exclusively on the soul to answer these questions, Christianity – because of its central story of God incarnating as man – sees a spiritual appreciation of the body as crucial. Pope John Paul II in his *Theology of the Body* wrote: 'The body, and it alone, is capable of making visible what is invisible: the spiritual and the divine. It was created to transfer into the visible reality of the world the mystery hidden since time immemorial in God.'[62]

With this rationale it could be argued that Christ should always be represented naked. As Michael Kowalewski writes, 'Christ's nakedness is more than a historical fact; it is of theological significance. Christ's nakedness is sacramental. It visibly communicates the poverty of spirit and purity of heart required for picking up our cross and following Christ. A Father of the Church, St Jerome, often said 'Nudus nudum Iesum Sequi' [Naked, I follow the naked Jesus].[63]

Beyond Belief – Nakedness as a Spiritual Way

Sometimes I like to run naked in the moonlight and the wind, on
a little trail behind our house, when the honeysuckle blooms. It's a
feeling of freedom, so close to God and nature.

— Dolly Parton

Although, as we have seen, nakedness has been used in some of
the major world religions as a way of pursuing spiritual goals, it
is also possible to adopt nakedness as a spiritual way in its own right
without allying oneself to any particular religion or group. Along
with the rise of Fundamentalism over the last few decades, there
has been a corresponding rise in the number of people, particularly
in the West, who identify themselves as 'spiritual' without feeling
allied to any one religious approach. The information explosion and
globalism have ensured that many people not only want to eat food
and wear clothes that come from all over the earth, but also wish to
learn about spiritual ideas and techniques from many cultures too,
so that it is not uncommon to encounter people who – for example
– practise yoga, are inspired by the writings of Christian mystics and
Sufi poets, and use a Buddhist meditation technique. They want to
nourish themselves spiritually by going beyond sectarianism, dogma,
and even belief.

Whilst some argue that this 'smørgasbord' approach to religion
is superficial, there are others – such as the philosopher Ken
Wilber, whose ideas are articulated on a website named 'Naked
Integral' – who see this as an evolutionary movement. Behind the
apparent consumerism of many New Age approaches lies the urge to
get to the essentials, to the bare bones of all religions, and to inte-
grate their wisdom in order to achieve an intense clarity of
understanding – a naked awareness.

Jain monks, Hindu sadhus and early Christian saints have all used
physical nakedness as a way of cutting back to the essentials of life,
of stripping themselves of attachments and coverings to 'stand naked
before God'. Christian and Buddhist mystics, such as St Jerome and
Nagarjuna, have used the concept of nakedness in a metaphorical
sense to urge followers to develop just such a 'naked awareness' that
clings to nothing, that hides behind nothing, and that instead

draws only upon the essential. If Ken Wilber and his colleagues at the Integral Institute are right, we will see more and more people wanting to free themselves of the restrictions of dogma while still seeking the spiritual life, and it is possible that a number of them will find that either physical or metaphorical nakedness, or both, can help them do this, as it has helped the singer Dolly Parton, and Luscious Jackson, who in *Naked Eye* sing: 'Wearing nothing is divine. Naked is a state of mind. I take things off to clear my head, to say the things I haven't said . . .'.[64]

3
Naked Rebellion

Being naked approaches being revolutionary; going barefoot is mere populism.

—John Updike

For some, undressing can be a religious act, for others it is political, and while the story of nakedness in religion is dominated by men until the arrival of Wicca in the twentieth century, the reverse situation applies in the realm of political action, where nakedness has been used most frequently by women, confirming the view that while men are easily drawn to the disembodied world of 'spirit' and the cerebral, women are more concerned with the embodied world – with the practical.

To understand how nakedness has become political we must start by exploring the way we get naked: by being stripped of clothes. Stripping can be an active or passive activity. When we are passive and someone strips us, this can be thrilling or terrifying, erotic or humiliating. Intention and context are everything. When a lover tears off our clothes because they want us naked it is exciting – flattering even. When the US soldiers at Abu Ghraib prison in Iraq stripped their prisoners it was humiliating and sadistic.

When stripping is active it can be motivated by at least six different desires. The skinny dipper strips to enjoy the sensual experience of water on skin, lovers strip to feel and excite one another as much as they can. The ascetic strips to mortify their flesh and to ignore the needs of their body, the mystic strips to commune with their deity and with Creation. In addition to the sensual, the erotic, the ascetic and the mystical motives for undressing there

Humiliation of a Japanese prisoner of war forced to bathe naked in front of the crew of the USS *New Jersey*, 1944.

Newly liberated Corsican patriots in Pisciatello punishing a woman by forcing her to strip naked and by cutting off her hair after they have accused and tried her for prostituting herself to German officers during the recent occupation in 1943.

Abuse at Abu Ghraib prison, Iraq, 2003.

is of course the simply functional, when we remove our clothes to get into bed or the bath, or to be examined by a doctor. Most naturists believe that although their nudism is sensual, perhaps even mystical, it is also essentially functional: for why wear clothes when you feel more comfortable, less hot and sticky, when wearing nothing? Not wearing clothes when sunbathing or swimming is simply sensible.[1]

The sixth motive for stripping – to gain attention – is a more complex phenomenon. For some it arises in an attempt to fulfil a deep-seated need, as in the case of an exhibitionist; in others the motivation may be more superficial and driven by the desire to enjoy the thrill of transgression, as in the case of a streaker or someone who strips for a dare. But there is a category of stripping for political reasons that transcends neurotic needs or the search for excitement, becoming instead a potent and provocative means of protesting against abuse and effecting change, or less seriously as a way of courting popularity, when politicians pose in the nude to convey the impression that they have nothing to hide.

The Legend of Lady Godiva

The first instance in British history of naked protest is probably apocryphal. In the *Flowers of History* by Roger of Wendover, written in St Albans and Westminster Abbey in the thirteenth century, the story is told of an eleventh-century couple, Lady Godiva and her husband, Leofric of Mercia. Taking pity on the local townsfolk of Coventry, Godiva asked her husband again and again to lower the crippling taxes he was imposing on them. He refused to listen, until one day, growing tired of her constant entreaties, he said that he would, provided she agreed to ride naked through the town. She accepted his challenge but issued a proclamation that all citizens should remain behind closed doors and not look out of their windows when she rode her horse with nothing but her long tresses of hair to hide her nakedness. In a later version of this story, written in the seventeenth century, an extra character was introduced: Peeping Tom, who disobeyed the order not to watch. It was this incident that provided the comedian Tony Hancock with

Lady Godiva painted in Pre-Raphaelite style by John Collier, 1898.

perfect material for a joke: 'Take the case of Doubting Thomas, who was sent to Coventry for staring through a keyhole at Lady Godiva. Can anybody prove he was looking at her? Can anybody prove it was he who shouted "Get your hair cut!"'[2]

Historians now believe the story is legendary. It is such a striking tale, they believe that if it really happened it would have been recorded in contemporary histories. In addition, there is only evidence of a tax on horses rather than people or property in that region, and since Coventry was only established as a town in the eleventh century it would hardly have been big enough for such a gesture. The evidence is stacked against it having taken place. But like all good stories, if it isn't true it ought to be, and people have found the incident inspiring from the moment it was recounted.

Mascagni's opera *Isabeau* is based on the story, and a host of singers including Eartha Kitt and Peter Gabriel have recorded songs about her, as have the Velvet Underground, Queen, Simply Red and Aerosmith. In 1974 a modern-day Lady Godiva rode a motorbike naked on to a Coventry stage, and more recently two feature films have appeared (and vanished with little trace) that translate the theme into modern-day Britain: *Lady Godiva Back in the Saddle*, released in 2007, and designed as a 'blockbuster comedy in the *Full Monty*

Female impersonator and entertainer Danny La Rue appearing as Lady Godiva in 'A Tribute to Coventry' in 1969.

To promote the DVD release of her film *Lady Godiva* in 2008, director Vicky Jewson organized a naked charity ride through London's Hyde Park. Earlier in the year the director's sister rode naked to the film's premiere.

tradition', and *Lady Godiva*, a romantic comedy released in 2008. A trawl of YouTube reveals film clips of a 1995 protest against property taxes in Phoenix, Arizona, using a naked Lady Godiva to publicize the protest, and an excerpt from an episode of the US TV series *Charmed*, in which she appears by magic to defend women's rights to breastfeed in public. British Film Institute archive footage can also be seen of a far-from-relaxed Lady Godiva, swathed in a sheet, riding in a Coventry parade in 1902.

In more recent and more permissive times, a remarkable woman has kept the name of Lady Godiva alive by riding in the Coventry carnival as if naked, though in fact wearing a flesh-coloured bikini and hair extensions. In 1982 the city of Coventry was in recession. The British Leyland factory had just closed, laying off 700 workers, and Pru Porretta took up the city's challenge to revive the practice of having a Lady Godiva ride through the streets in the annual carnival, but unlike previous processions, to at least appear to be naked this time. Ms Porretta has continued to do this for over 25 years, and has initiated a number of other projects that have raised the city's profile, including the Imagined Café to promote reading in schools, and the Godiva Sisters project, which fosters social inclusion by creating arts performances with women from diverse backgrounds. Ten years ago she also founded the annual week-long 'Coventry Women's Festival', which celebrates women's achievements and the successful struggle of women around the world against poverty and exploitation. Having raised thousands of pounds for charity, and in recognition of all her work, the city's university has awarded her an honorary MA.

Pru Porretta has understood the power of the Godiva legend, which comes from the fact that it concerns a woman – an aristocrat who sides with the poor and the exploited. Like Robin Hood she becomes a folk hero by championing the downtrodden. She takes a proposition of her husband which is part-dare, part-gamble on his part, but which also contains the threat that if she dares to defy him she will suffer the humiliation of her nakedness being on display. The power in the story lies in its alchemical nature, whereby she transforms the potential for humiliation into a moment of dignity and of pride for all the city. She asks that no-one watches, and apart from Peeping Tom, all respect and obey her.

On 15 July 2004, 40 women marched naked to the army barracks at Imphal in India to protest about a rape and killing carried out by soldiers of the Assam Rifles.

A woman with no weapon to defend herself has used her naked body to triumph over injustice.

This is a theme we encounter over and over again, particularly in modern times. In 2004 in Imphal, the capital of the northeastern Indian state of Manipur, a total of 32 women's rights organisations united to protest about a rape and killing carried out by soldiers of the Assam Rifles, and on 15 July 40 women marched naked to the barracks holding banners saying 'Indian Army Rape Us' and 'Indian Army Takes Our Flesh'. They achieved their aim of gaining publicity for their cause, although the *New Internationalist* pointed out how few Indian papers used photographs of the demonstration:

> It's an unusual thing in India to see a group of naked women walking down a public road holding banners inviting rape. Yet that's exactly what happened in the northeastern state of Manipur recently. In a fury of anger at the rape and murder of a young woman by the army, Manipuri women stripped off their saris and blouses, let loose their hair and walked through the capital city, Imphal, to the army headquarters to stage their dramatic protest. 'Our anger shed our

inhibitions that day,' said one of the activists. . . . When women protest the use of their bodies as commodities the world knows what they are talking about, though many do not sympathize with what they have to say. But when women themselves turn their bodies into commodities, people don't know how to react. In the case of the Manipuri women, this was clearly visible in media reactions to their protest. While many papers reported the incident, very few carried photos of this particular protest. Either they didn't have them – which seems unlikely – or they could not stomach the thought of showing middle-class Indian women (read 'mothers') naked! And this in a country where virtually every newspaper has a scantily dressed woman poised in a corner of the front page, disturbingly close to the masthead![3]

In the more liberal environment of New Zealand, the first country to give women the vote, women have felt empowered to use their bodies in protest even when on their own. In one instance a woman who had been raped held a public art event in which she appeared naked as she painted, in order to publicize the prevalence of sex crimes, which thrive in an atmosphere of secrecy and guilt. By turning the tables on potential offenders and showing them their objects of desire in an open way, such a protest challenges men to experience the vulnerability and imperfections of a real nude body rather than being driven by fantasies that dehumanize.

Another example of combating fantasy with reality occurred again in New Zealand in May 2008 when an Israeli tourist stripped naked in response to harassment from road-workers. The Associated Press reported:

Workmen in the small northern farming town of Kerikeri were repairing the main street when the young woman took offense at their attention. On a balmy late-autumn day, she calmly stripped bare to use an ATM – bringing an abrupt halt to both the whistles and the road work – then put her clothes back on and walked away. Sgt. Peter Masters said the woman told police she didn't take kindly to the men's wolf-whistles.[4]

Fear of the Breast

In another country, she could have been attacked, molested or arrested for this behaviour, but even in New Zealand there are some men who believe that simply the sight of a breast can be damaging. In 2005 a complaint was brought before the New Zealand Broadcasting Standards Authority for a 6 pm news item that revealed for six seconds two topless women protesting during a visit to Wellington by Prince Charles. A Mr Watts claimed that the item had breached standards of good taste and decency and was inappropriate and disturbing for children. In rebuttal the TV channel responsible for the news item wrote: 'It was as if you were telling us that you expect us to show the most awful terrorist atrocities (the attack on the Twin Towers, blood in the streets of Baghdad), the most awful crimes (school shootings, murder and rape) and introduce children to repellent concepts such as racism and intolerance – but ask us to shy away from the reality of a harmless topless protester taking part in a peaceful demonstration.' The Broadcasting Authority did not uphold the complaint.[5]

The attempt to protect others from the sight of a naked breast was taken to extremes under the Bush administration when $8,000 was allegedly spent on draping *The Spirit of Justice* – a 5.5-m (18-ft) aluminium statue of a bare-breasted woman – at the Justice Department in Washington. US Attorney General John Ashcroft claimed he was tired of photographers aiming their shots to include the breasts when he stood by the statue to deliver press conferences, but his timing was unfortunate. The United States was in crisis and his act seemed absurdly wasteful and trivial. An open letter to John Ashcroft by playwright and journalist Claire Braz-Valentine circulated the internet:

> While we live in the threat of biological warfare, nuclear destruction, annihilation, you are out buying yardage to save Americans from the appalling, alarming, abominable aluminum alloy of evil, that terrible ten foot tin tittie . . . It's not that we aren't grateful, but while we were begging the women of Afghanistan to not cover up their faces, you are begging your staff members to just cover up that nipple to

save the American people from that monstrous metal mammary. How can we ever thank you? So, in your office every morning, in your secret prayer meeting, while an American woman is sexually assaulted every 6 seconds, while anthrax floats around the post office, settling in the chests of senior citizens, you've got another chest on your mind.[6]

Fear of the breast extends to most beaches in the United States, in marked contrast to Europe and Australia, where topless bathing is considered acceptable on many beaches. In certain countries even exposing a breast in a public place in order to feed a baby has sometimes provoked condemnation. In 2007 in Andalucia in Spain a security guard ordered a mother who was breastfeeding to leave a restaurant. In retaliation, a group of 50 women staged a protest they called a 'tit-in' (*tetada*) in the shopping centre that housed the restaurant. Each began suckling their baby, and when challenged by the management, replied that breastfeeding was a natural bodily function. The management replied that so was urination but it was not done in the street.

January 2009 in Prague, Czech Republic, when 68 mothers breastfed their babies during a protest against the social networking website Facebook, which removed pictures of breastfeeding mothers from its pages.

99

Scene from an anti-war protest in 2005. One of many protests organised by 'Breasts Not Bombs'.

While women have protested for their right to sunbathe topless or to breastfeed in public, they have also made use of the power of their breasts to shock and claim attention for other causes. In 2005 a grassroots political movement emerged in Mendocino County, California, calling itself 'Breasts not Bombs'. They explain their mission as being 'dedicated to empowering women to speak out for a world that remembers what is sacred and honours the mother. Using political street theatre and the act of baring our breasts in public serves as an excellent forum to speak about the vulnerability of humanity and the earth.' Over the last four years activists in this movement have campaigned against the obscenity of war by baring their breasts and chanting 'Breasts not bombs, titties not tanks, nipples not napalm, mammaries not missiles.'7

Just as the writer of the open letter to John Ashcroft finds it impossible to believe that he could be interested in a breast at such a time, so the Breasts not Bombs campaigners use the surreality and essential absurdity of using a body-part as a protest to draw attention to the greater absurdity which sees violence as acceptable, but the display of a woman's breast, which gives life to a newborn, as unacceptable and indecent. And so, behind their chants and the photo-opportunities their protests provide the media, they are conveying the message that: 'Fixing intelligence to go to war is indecent. No bid contracts for Halliburton and Bechtel are indecent. War profiteering is indecent. Using depleted Uranium and chemical weapons in Iraq is indecent. Torturing prisoners of war is indecent. Lying to the American Public about going to war is indecent. Using 9/11 to justify every act of war and aggression is indecent. Karl Rove outing an undercover CIA operative is indecent. Letting the People of the Gulf Coast Suffer for days after Katrina is indecent.' And in their blog they repeat their message that the real obscenity is not a naked body or a bare breast: 'How many dead US soldiers are there now? When we went to the Capitol it was around 2,000, now it's over 2,100, Obscene! Now, families are fleeing from Ramadi and another American offensive is launched, Indecent! The US rejects the Montreal agreement to curb global warming! Obscene. God!! It feels like the Bush administration is trying to kill us all. Can we sue them for reckless endangering? For attempted murder? When will the American Public rise up and freak out???? Is everyone just too damn busy Christmas shopping????'[8]

It is significant that this anti-war protest was initiated by women rather than men. In most cultures women are less likely to want to be seen naked than males. They are more used to being viewed as sex objects than men. They are more subject to pressures to conform to idealized body images than men. They are more subject to sexual abuse and rape than men, and they have more to lose than men in an experience of rape, since the result can be pregnancy. For all these reasons, the act of a woman deliberately baring herself in order to make a statement is more powerful than if a man were to do the same, and indicates a deep level of commitment to a cause, on behalf of which she is willing to override her instinct to maintain the protection of clothing. It is undoubtedly for this reason that the Lady Godiva story has achieved iconic status, even though plenty of men have engaged in nude protests over the years.

Baring Witness

Fifty women in West Marin County, California, were aware of the power of baring the female body, when in November 2002, to protest against the impending war in Iraq, they spelled out the word 'Peace' with their bodies on the grass of Love Field at Point Reyes Station. The organizer, Donna Sheehan, explained that for four years she had been trying to think of a way women could 'be heard on a very deep level'. In 2002 she read an account of women in Nigeria who had threatened to strip naked to bring attention to Chevron Texaco's exploitation of the region, and who had succeeded in bringing the company to the negotiating table, when more violent protests had failed.[9] Sheehan decided to organize a photo-shoot of a group of local women who would call themselves 'Unreasonable Women Baring Witness'. Sheehan writes: 'Women from all ages and walks of life took off their clothes, not because they are exhibitionists but because they felt it was imperative to do so. They wanted to unveil the truth about the horrors of war, to commune in their nudity with the vulnerability of Iraqi innocents, and to shock a seemingly indifferent Bush Administration into paying attention.'[10]

The first Baring Witness photograph taken at Love Field, Point Reyes Station, Northern California, in November 2002. Spreading quickly via the internet and the media, this image launched a global movement, with protest groups creating messages and 'mandalas' of sometimes hundreds of naked human figures.

The power of the internet meant that soon the images of these California women were seen all over the planet, and perhaps facilitated by the rising reputation of Spencer Tunick's photography, which offered an artistic in addition to a political rationale for such a project, groups of people started posing for protest photographs – usually naked but sometimes clothed. By the end of the year the original group had dropped the 'Unreasonable women' part of their title. There was nothing, after all, unreasonable about protesting against bloodshed, and now men were joining with them in their protests. Sheehan's partner, Paul Reffell, joined her in writing the introduction to their 'Baring Witness 2004 International Peace Calendar': 'It is no accident that women would choose to go naked for the sake of peace and justice. Baring Witness used the power of the feminine, the power of beauty and nakedness to heighten the awareness of human vulnerability to inspire women and men around the world. By restoring the power of the feminine and tempering aggression, our partnership can change our relationship with each other – women with men, nations with nations – and with life on earth to peaceful sustainability. We call on the wives of our leaders, as life givers, nurturers, guardians of their families and voices of reason, to deter the men in their lives from acts of violence.'[11]

Sheehan and Reffell were invoking an idea explored in Greece in the fifth century BC. Lysistrata, in Aristophanes' play of the same name, embarks on a mission to end the Peloponnesian War by persuading the women of Greece to refuse to have sex with their husbands until they negotiate a peace treaty. Although Sheehan and Reffell did not advocate this strategy, they were aware of the potential of the sexual relationship between genders to be used consciously to promote peace, and authored a book, *Redefining Seduction: Women Initiating Sex, Courtship, Partnership and Peace*, which argues that from an evolutionary perspective it is women who should be in charge of the mate selection process.[12]

Rather than suggesting the withdrawal of sexual favours to force a peace, their approach suggested the reverse procedure, and represents a more articulated version of the doctrine 'Make Love, Not War', that was born out of the anti-war protests of the 1960s. As a logical extension of the understanding that aggression can result from frustrated sexual desire, Reffell and Sheehan and the 1960s protesters concluded that making love should be encouraged, while in more recent times the pop star Ozzy Osbourne has taken the concept one step further by launching his 'Wank for Peace' wristband and limited edition shoes. Taking the same idea, in 2008 an annual 'Wank 4 Peace day' was organized to raise funds for the charity Peace Direct. The organizer argued that 'Politicians sit around and jerk off instead of doing something about PEACE. But now we can do something about PEACE by sitting around and jerking off!'[13]

Forty years earlier, the Peace movement had been more romantic, and was content with just promoting intercourse as an alternative to annihilation. As the Swinging Sixties drew to a close, John Lennon and Yoko Ono decided to make use of the press attentions they knew they would get for their forthcoming marriage by holding a week-long 'Bed-In' at the Amsterdam Hilton in

March 1969. The year before they had released their *Two Virgins* album, which showed them both naked on the cover, and they knew that their Bed-In, designed as a protest against the continuing war in Vietnam, would suggest that they were 'making love not war'.

Although the *Two Virgins* album photograph was not part of a protest, Yoko Ono had already understood the power of nakedness as a means of gaining attention, and a few years earlier, in 1964, had sat on stage in Japan in a work of performance art entitled 'Cut Piece' that was designed as a peace protest. Members of the audience were invited to come on stage and cut off a piece of her clothing. By the end of the performance she was naked. In 2003, at the age of 70, she repeated the art-show in Paris, saying: 'Come and cut a piece of my clothing wherever you like – the size of less than a postcard – and send it to the one you love . . . When I first performed this work, in 1964, I did it with some anger and turbulence in my heart. This time, I do it with love for you, for me and for the world.'[14]

In 2009 art professor Ken Little performed the 'Yoko Ono Cut Piece' in conjunction with the University of Texas at San Antonio exhibition *Yoko Ono Imagine Peace: Featuring John and Yoko's Year of Peace.*

Nakedness in Defence of Animal Rights

We say 'nakedness is natural', but have we begun to think through all that means? It is so basic. A human being is an innocent part of nature. Our civilization has distorted this universal quality that allows us to feel at home in our skin. Other animals have coats that they accept, but the human race has yet to come to terms with being nude.
—Ruth Bernhard

When it comes to images of naked protest, Lady Godiva, Yoko Ono and the protesters of Baring Witness and Breasts not Bombs are remembered far more than any male equivalent, even though from a historical perspective the Godiva legend appeared a century later than the famous act of naked rebellion carried out by the young Francis of Assisi on his journey to sainthood. For a man passionately devoted to Lady Poverty, buildings, like clothes, could easily become enemies of the Franciscan life. Determined that the corrupting influence of wealth should never taint his brothers, he once climbed on to the roof of a building he mistakenly believed had been given to his order, and began furiously hurling off its tiles, until in a moment worthy of *Monty Python* it was explained to him that someone else owned the building. The account does not tell us whether he then arranged for the tiles to be replaced.

Despite the occasional act of overzealousness, St Francis's ministry achieved its success because it championed the exploited and extended its concern not only to the poor but also to the animal world. Francis is now patron saint of animals in the Catholic Church and is famous for addressing them as his 'brothers and sisters'.[15]

Whereas we have only skin to cover our flesh, animals and birds have fur and feathers which are now used to create objects of high fashion. To highlight the injustice that allows humans the right to remain, and be comfortable, in their own skins, while depriving animals of theirs, protesters against the fur trade and abuses of animal rights have made ample use of nakedness to draw attention to their protests.

The largest animal rights organization, with over two million supporters worldwide and an annual budget of $28 million, is PETA (People for the Ethical Treatment of Animals). With the support of many celebrities, including pop stars and fashion models, PETA has run many ad campaigns featuring nakedness with banners such as 'I'd rather go naked than wear fur', 'Be comfortable in your own skin and let animals keep theirs' and 'The Naked Truth: Burberry Butchers Bunnies'. To protest against the use of bear skins by the Coldstream Guards, for example, a nude Imogen Bailey holding a teddy bear is featured with the headline: 'Bare skin, not bear skin!'

PETA has also protested since 2002 against bullfighting, and has organized demonstrations against the annual bull run in Pamplona, Spain. Its event, known as the 'Running of the Nudes', has attracted a thousand or more participants each year from over thirty countries, who take off their clothes and don plastic bull horns or a red scarf to run through the streets of the town, creating a fiesta atmosphere designed to draw media attention and prove to the townsfolk that 'they don't need to torture animals to attract tourism'. Unfortunately the Running of the Nudes event has become so successful that it has brought more tourism to Pamplona, thus ensuring that the bull run continues.

In 2008, PETA, wise to the situation, held a round of 'Nude News Conferences' in European cities to announce a new strategy, designed to discourage tourists from visiting Spain: 'We have decided to take the Running of the Nudes outside Pamplona. First, we have no wish to bring more and more runners – and thus tourist money – to a city that continues to support an outdated and barbarically cruel form of entertainment. Second, we want to take the Running of the Nudes to capital cities across the world, in countries from which tourists embark on trips to Spain. That means that we will hold mini-Running of the Nudes in Australia, France, Germany, the UK, the United States and elsewhere'.[16]

The mastermind behind the nude protests is the senior vice-President of PETA, Dan Mathews, who has shown a remarkable flair for achieving publicity. One commentator has remarked that 'Mathews has redefined social activism. Rather than the conventional format [of protests] – placards and chants, the defiant show

Animal rights campaigners PETA (People for the Ethical Treatment of Animals) often uses nakedness to attract attention to their cause. Their 'I'd Rather Go Naked than Wear Fur' and 'The Naked Truth' campaigns have received widespread publicity.

of fist-shaking outrage – his best pranks manage to set the news agenda while making the group seem approachable. Where bloody-minded confrontation would backfire, a potent cocktail of sly wit, female beauty and celebrity often elicits public sympathy.'[17]

In addition to the naked protests, which have included seventy young women lying on the pavement near St Paul's in London wearing only teddy-bear masks to protest against the use of bearskins, PETA has lobbied fashion designers and organized catwalk invasions. At the 2004 Ferré show in Milan, Mathews leapt on to the catwalk dressed as a priest and unfurled a banner saying 'Thou Shalt Not Kill'. Mathews recounts how, as soon as security guards tried to pull him down, 'all the little old ladies in the audience started screaming "Leave the priest alone!"'[18]

PETA's protests extend to all abuses of animals' rights. In March 2009 they organized a protest outside 'Naked Chef' Jamie Oliver's London restaurant to demonstrate against his promotion of British pork. Two pregnant women, wearing only flesh-coloured underwear, crawled into cages left outside the restaurant to draw attention to the inhumane conditions on British farms that keep pregnant sows in metal stalls hardly bigger than their own bodies.

Protest movements have clearly been influenced by Spencer Tunick's installations and photographs of massed groups of naked bodies, as can be seen from this photograph of a PETA animal rights protest in Barcelona in 2007.

PETA targets the London restaurant *Fifteen* of the 'Naked Chef' Jamie Oliver in March 2009 to protest against his promotion of British pork.

Purists might object to the use of flesh-coloured pants, in the same way that some vegetarians object to 'fake meat' made out of vegetable protein, but by employing this ruse protesters achieve the publicity they seek while being able to claim to the police that they are not in fact naked.

Getting Naked for the Planet

Stripping the body in public as a way of gaining attention and making a statement is clearly suited to the defence of rights in general – not simply those of animals. One of the most creative uses of nudity to raise awareness comes from the work of the American photographer Jack Gescheidt, who started the Tree-Spirit Project in 2003. Rather than protesting against logging or destruction of the environment, Gescheidt's project seeks to enhance our appreciation of trees in the belief that the more people are able to do this, the less destructive they will be: 'I believe as more people understand the importance of trees for all they provide the ecosystem in addition to beauty and shade, all species on

Earth benefit. The fates of species are intertwined; we have the power to destroy other life forms, and without other life forms humanity will perish. We humans may only be here for a brief stay in the cosmic picture, but we have the tremendous power of free will to shape our world. Many of us in technologically advanced cultures have forgotten the ancient wisdom trees and other life forms patiently hold.'[19]

The TreeSpirit Project includes two elements: the photographs Gescheidt takes of naked people in, beside and around trees, which are then displayed on his website (www.treespiritproject.com), and the experiences of the participants when being photographed in this way. In response to the frequently asked question: 'Why are the people you photograph always naked? Isn't this really just to get attention?' Gescheidt responds:

When naked, people are: more 'present' in the meditative sense of this word, meaning in the present moment instead of thinking about the past (worry) or future (planning); therefore more vulnerable and have greater, more conscious awareness, more feeling, and therefore move and behave more freely and genuinely; more harmless to trees and other species. We humans often harm as a collective, but not when stripped of our habitual and protective layers of clothing, tools and technology; more timeless, without the many cultural and historical cues clothing provides; unified as a mass of humanity rather than seen as the individual personalities to which we are so attached; and, yes, more attention-getting. One of the goals of the TreeSpirit Project is to deliver its message of our interdependence with nature. The more people ready to take this to heart, the better.[20]

Nudity is so often utilized for titillation that it is heartening to see that it can be used with integrity not only for a political end, but at the same time to convey aesthetic and spiritual values.

While the TreeSpirit Project is very much a localized affair, based on the work of one photographer in the San Francisco Bay area, the World Naked Bike Ride is an international event that has

Tea Tree Tangle by Jack Gescheidt for the TreeSpirit Project.

been taking place every year since 2003. Originally the brain-child of Canadian political activist Conrad Schmidt, the event now occurs in over 70 locations in twenty countries. Schmidt is the founder of the Work Less Party of British Columbia – a political party whose slogan is 'Work Less, Consume Less, Live More', and whose aim is to encourage people to reduce their consumption, and be more environmentally and socially conscious. Rather than consuming, people are encouraged to spend their time on creative endeavours, spiritual exploration and sport, and to give more time to their family, friends and local community.

While the Work Less Party has failed to gain a seat in parliament, the World Naked Bike Ride took off as soon as Schmidt launched it in the same year he founded his party. In June in the northern hemisphere and March in the southern, cyclists in Sydney, Paris, New York, London, Munich and dozens of other cities, create a party atmosphere as they set off to protest against 'indecent exposure to cars' and oil dependency. A key to the enormous success of this event lies in its synergistic fusion of goals and activities. In addition to it being a protest, it is also billed as an opportunity to 'celebrate the power and individuality of our bodies and the many benefits of a car-free lifestyle',[21] so that the atmosphere created is one of fun and of a summer party rather than one of 'manning the barricades' in a spirit of defiance and rebellion. In addition the event is seen not just as a protest against the one activity of driving, but as a way of promoting and encouraging positive activities and concepts: bicycle transportation, renewable energy, recreation, walkable communities, and environmentally responsible, sustainable solutions to living in the twenty-first century.

With a decentralized organization that makes full use of the internet and allows anyone to organize and participate in a ride, the events create the opportunity for participation by a wide range of people who are interested in sustainable living, political protest, street theatre, streaking, and clothing-optional recreation. The dress code is deliberately open with the motto being 'Bare as You Dare' and many events also now feature pre-ride parties in parks with live bands, body painting, and installation art.

The use of nakedness to gain the attention of the media and politicians has come a long way from its use in Conrad Schmidt's own state of British Columbia forty and more years ago by the spirit-wrestlers from Russia.

In the thick of the World Naked Bike Ride, London, 2009.

The Sons of Freedom

CROWN EXAMINER: Now, Annie, where do you live?

A: In prison now.

CE: Oh yes, you got a term, did you, for being nude recently?

A: Yes.

CE: And before that where did you live?

A: I was hanged on the Cross.

CE: Well, all right, we will skip your hanging on the Cross for a moment. Where were you living before you went to jail?

— Proceedings of the Canadian court for 14 June 1950 in the case of Crown vs. Michael 'The Archangel' Verigin and Joe Eli Podovinikoff, accused of conspiracy involving forming a nudist sect and of instigating arson attacks [22]

In the late eighteenth century a radical sect of Christians began to emerge in the Ukraine, led by Silvan Kolesnikov, a man familiar with the writings of Western mystics such as Karl von Eckartshausen and Louis Claude de Saint-Martin. The sect at first called themselves 'God's People' but then began calling themselves *Doukhobors* (spirit-wrestlers) after a term originally used by the Orthodox Church who believed they were heretics who wrestled against the Holy Spirit. The newly named Doukhobors decided that they were indeed spirit-wrestlers, but that they fought for, rather than against, it.

The Church had good reason to believe they were heretics: they rejected its authority, were unimpressed by icons and church ritual, and accepted neither the Bible as the supreme source of divine revelation, nor the divinity of Jesus. The scene was set for a rough ride, when in addition to being in conflict with the Church, the sect's firm belief in the immorality of militarism and war brought them into conflict with the state.

By 1897, the Doukhobors had grown to be a community of thousands in various regions of Russia, and after many attempts at enforcing military conscription, and after persecution, attempts at assimilation, and various resettlement programmes, the Russian government finally decided to wash their hands of these troublesome pacifists. Having agreed to give 160 acres of land to each new male settler, the Canadian government accepted one third of the Doukhobor population in 1899, with over 7,400 migrants making the journey,

A Doukhobor woman in Canada watching a house burn, 1962.

subsidized in great part by sympathetic Quakers and Tolstoyans. Tolstoy himself donated the royalties from one of his novels to the cause, and ended up footing half the bill for this mass migration.

Once on Canadian soil, the troubled history of this group continued unabated, and after difficulties in their area of settlement, the icy Northwest Territories, many moved once more en masse to British Columbia. By 1903 an extremist minority had emerged out of this already radical movement. Calling themselves the Sons of Freedom, these Doukhobors decided to mount a sustained campaign of protest against the government, whom they believed had reneged on their promises regarding land rights and were enforcing compulsory education in government schools. On 14 May of that year, 28 men and 17 women and children walked naked in protest from their village to Yorkton, eating grass and the young leaves on trees on their way, since they took no food with them. The Commissioner ordered them to be rounded up and herded into the immigration hall, where they were told to get dressed. When they refused, the doors were nailed closed and bright lamps hung to attract mosquitoes. By morning all were dressed and all the men were charged with nudism and sentenced to three months in prison. Protests continued and intensified after one of their leaders was killed in a bomb explosion on a Canadian Pacific railway train in 1924, with the Sons of Freedom believing the government was responsible for his assassination. The police at first believed he was killed by a rival faction in the Doukhobor community, but later came to the conclusion that the crime would never be solved.

The dead leader's fanatical son, Peter Verigin (whom some accused of arranging his own father's death in the train bombing), took control of the group and in February 1931 called a meeting at the village of Bojaya Dolina, near Grand Forks, with the aim of recruiting an army of one thousand nude protesters. These were called upon the following year, when Verigin was sent to prison for committing perjury. To protest against this, 420 marched naked on 5 May. On 13 May 133 protesters marched, including 51 children, and on 4 June 69 marched. The numbers dwindled because at every protest the participants were arrested. In one of the largest mass arrests in Canadian history, a total of 725 men, women and children were imprisoned, necessitating the creation of a special penal colony on Piers Island in the Straits of Georgia.

The following year the government increased the maximum prison sentence for public nudity to three years in an attempt to deter further protests. Despite this, over the next 40 years more than 300 Doukhobor men and women were arrested for this offence.

Protests continued right up until the 1970s, with the Sons of Freedom becoming almost as much a thorn in the flesh of Canada as the IRA had become for Britain. To arson attacks and mass nude protests were added bombings, with the costs of such activities estimated at over $20 million.[23]

Although the mainstream Doukhobor community believed the violent protests of the Sons of Freedom violated the sect's pacifist principles, there were sufficient militants to maintain the pressure over decades. Finally the conflict was resolved thanks to skilful negotiation, with this successful resolution of Canada's only experience of terrorism prompting author Gregory J. Cran to analyse the process in his *Negotiating Buck Naked: Doukhobors, Public Policy, and Conflict Resolution*.

A Means of Last Resort

The Sons of Freedom seem to have been the only naked protesters who have included arson in their demonstrations, to create a spectacle that was truly shocking. In comparison, naked bike riders and Californian tree-huggers hardly seem to challenge the status quo at all. Even the four anarchist squatters who burst on to the stage at the presentation of Barcelona's 'strategic plan for culture' in 2007 must have provoked more amusement than horror as they proceeded to undress and read out their manifesto criticizing 'speculation and the censorship of popular culture'.[24]

The real anger, though, of protesters against serious abuses must have been palpable in places like Mexico and Venezuela, when the use of nakedness had become a means of last resort. In 1992 a governor of Veracruz State in Mexico appropriated 12,000 hectares of land from 14 villages and locked up over 100 farm-workers without charges. After ten years of fruitless attempts to bring attention to their cause, the protest organization formed by those affected, El Movimiento de los 400 Pueblos de Veracruz, began staging nude demonstrations in Mexico City. As Agustin Morales, a 45-year-old farmer, explained to the BBC: 'We are stripping because it is the only way to get attention. We don't have money to buy an ad in the newspapers.'[25] Another explained, 'We are only peasants, we have no other arms, all we have are our bodies.'[26]

For six years over 600 men, women and children began daily protests in Mexico City, some stripping completely, others just wearing thongs or pants. Often they would hold three demonstrations a day, waving placards and shouting their demands during the rush-hours on the widest street in Mexico City, the Paseo de la Reforma, or while dancing in front of the Monument to the Mother on the Avenida Insurgentes Centro.

For six years, farmers and their families from Veracruz State in Mexico protested against the appropriation of their land by the state governor. In 2008 the government acceded to their demands.

A city-dweller sleeps in the street while demonstrators of the '400 Pueblos' organization protest wearing masks representing former Mexican Presidents Carlos Salinas and Ernesto Zedillo, October 2003, in Mexico City.

In *The Movement of the 400 Pueblos of Veracruz: When Your Body is Your Only Weapon* Victor Allen describes how 'Where others would not even try, they refused to back down in the face of a long series of intransigent government officials. Undaunted by cold rain and the curious stares of strangers, they conducted the most extreme and relentless daily mass naked protest in history – year after year – until they achieved their goal. Showing that they had nothing more to lose and nothing to hide, they danced naked in the streets to shame the government into hearing their claim.'[27] In 2008 the government finally relented and agreed to the movement's demands.

In 2004 in Venezuela, to protest against the 13 deaths and 1,700 people injured by security forces in anti-government demonstrations, 50 opposition activists marched naked and semi-naked through the streets of Maracay, with their spokesperson saying: 'People marched naked because that is how they feel: naked and defenceless in the face of agencies who are under the control of the government . . .'.[28]

Naked protests have become increasingly popular in Central and South America over the last few years. In 2007 a group of Brazilian pensioners, all ex-workers in the oil industry, stripped in front of the headquarters of the state-owned oil company Petrobas in Rio de Janeiro to protest against the company's pension plans. In 2008 a model bared her chest in front of the Uruguay stand at a trade show in Buenos Aires to protest against the pollution from the Finnish Botnia pulp mill in Uruguay. She said she had stripped to 'defend the environment, future generations and life'.[29] In March 2009 100 women, all members of the Humanist Party, protested topless against nuclear weapons in Asuncion, Paraguay. Their breasts were painted with peace signs, radioactivity symbols and pictures of the Earth, making use of the fact that, as one spokeswoman put it: 'the public and the news media pay so much attention to breasts and bottoms'. They had discovered that each of us is a 'walking billboard' whose skin offers prime advertising space. If you want your message distributed free and worldwide, just paint it on your naked body, walk into the street, and call Associated Press.

Once again it is women who seem to have made the most use of this idea – undoubtedly because they have been used to having their bodies objectified and treated as commodities. In a single act of defiance the owner of the body takes control and decides to make use of its power to command attention, rather than subjecting itself to exploitation by commercial interests. Often such demonstrations are made by women who earn their living by showing off their bodies, but it seems that their motives are genuinely ideological rather than financial: in December 2008 the Argentinian former *Playboy* 'Playmate' Vanessa Carbone demonstrated topless against Japan's whaling activities; in March 2009 porn-star actress Laura Perego walked into the Milan stock exchange in a black coat which she took off to reveal her body painted in the colours of the Italian flag, naked apart for some tiny underwear. As traders tried to persuade her to dress, the 22-year-old Sicilian shouted 'I want to send a message to all those who mismanaged our savings . . . stripping Italians of everything but their underwear.'[30]

Such protests can easily be dismissed as publicity stunts and while they may get their message across and be perceived as witty, the real power of women protesting naked comes when there is outrage rather than wit in their demonstration. In August 2005, in an act of remarkable courage, the Syrian artist Hala Faisal became perhaps the first Arab woman to demonstrate in the nude by walking around the Washington Square Park fountain in New York, with 'Stop the War' written on her back and legs and on her buttocks in both English and Arabic. She was protesting against the US

To protest against the Iraq war and the Israeli occupation of Palestine, on a hot day in August 2005 Syrian artist Hala Faisal removed her clothes in Washington Square Park fountain in New York's Greenwich Village. Within five minutes the only recorded naked protest by an Arab woman ended with her arrest by the police, as members of the crowd shouted 'Stop the Police State.'

war in Iraq and the Israeli occupation of Palestine, and she was soon arrested. The incident provoked Ronda Kaysen, writing in Greenwich Village's *The Villager*, to ask whether one individual can have any effect on political decisions when millions marching seemed to have none: 'When I first read about Sheehan, the bereaved mother camped out at Bush's ranch, I assumed other angry mothers and wives and sisters of American soldiers would join her, that her bravery would launch a movement of its own. But so far, no one has taken up her cause. Like Faisal, alone and naked in the fountain, Sheehan will likely spend August camped out in the Crawford dust alone with only news-hungry reporters to keep her company. And if the current government will not listen to 10 million protesters, why on earth would it listen to one?' Faisal's lawyer provided her with an answer: 'Yesterday it was one woman sitting in front of the president's ranch, today it is one woman taking off her clothes in Washington Square Park, and tomorrow it will be somebody else. Ultimately, it is going to force the Bush administration to cut its losses and get the hell out.'[31]

Naked protest in the Middle East seems non-existent, unsurprisingly considering the moral strictures of Islam and Judaism.[32] In many parts of Africa, however, there is a long tradition of women using the threat of nakedness as a 'curse' and when they make their threats – or carry them out – they become a force to be reckoned with. In Gambia in 2001 30 naked women took to the streets to protest against a distasteful ritual organized by members of an opposition political party who allegedly sacrificed a dog in a ritual killing. As the women marched, they shouted, clapped, and chanted incantations and curses against those who performed the ritual. In Cape Town, South Africa, in 2006, a group of about 50 women stripped in the Mthatha prison to protest against plans to move them, and in April 2008 a group of mothers in the Yarl's Wood immigration centre in Bedford in the UK removed their clothes in desperation when a pregnant Nigerian woman who had led a clothed protest against children being detained in immigration centres was allegedly parted from her six-year-old son and taken to a solitary wing. At least 15 women then demanded to know where the woman had been taken and some of them undressed to show their disgust at the 'imprisonment' of their children. *The Independent* reported: 'A spokesperson for

Serco, the company which runs Yarl's Wood, said discussions had taken place between residents and staff, but "no significant protest" had occurred. Mercy Guobatia, 22, from Nigeria, was one of the mothers who stood naked in the centre as a symbol of the inhumane way she felt they were treated there. "I took my clothes off because they treat us like animals. We are claiming asylum, we're not animals. They treat us as if we've done something terrible."[33]

Juxtaposed against such feeling, the account of life models protesting outside the culture department in Paris on a cold December day in 2008 seems tame, and yet their cause was admirably suited to a naked demonstration. *The Guardian* reported that 'the naked and goose-pimpled models demanded a pay increase, proper contracts and, most of all, respect for their craft as they held trade union banners in the pose of Delacroix's Liberty Leading the People.' The paper quoted a model, Christophe Lemée, aged 52, who said: 'After 30 years as an actor, I began life modelling to support my own theatre projects. It's a beautiful craft and very physically demanding. You have to forget yourself and move beyond the contours of your own body. It's not my body the artists are trying to capture, but the essence of human nature, existence and all the mystery that goes with it . . . You are naked and defenceless in front of a room full of people,

Life models strip in near-freezing temperatures to demonstrate outside the city's cultural affairs bureau in Paris in December 2008.

but it's not the same brash nudity you see everywhere in modern society. It's more spiritual. I'm exposed but I know that the people looking at me are exactly the same as me under their clothes.'[34]

The Risk of Naked Protest Fatigue

With so much naked protest occurring, is there a danger in it becoming a cliché and losing its impact – of the public developing 'naked protest fatigue'? In some countries, such a way of protesting is a new phenomenon and is clearly nowhere near becoming over-used: in China nakedness has only recently been used as a means of protest, when in 2008 a schoolgirl died in mysterious circumstances. The police claimed she had committed suicide after performing several push-ups that caused injuries found on her face. A riot ensued when locals accused the police of protecting two men who could have raped and killed her, and an unlikely 'internet meme' began to circulate as a protest against government attempts to clamp down on the news, with the term 'push-up' becoming the code for the incident as thousands of bloggers and internet users communicated about the issue, and photographs of a TV personality, and others, performing push-ups in the nude circulated widely.[35]

Nakedness has been used effectively against the Chinese government in relation to its Tibet policy too. In April 2009, five days after two Tibetans were sentenced to death for their role in riots in Lhasa the year before, ten Tibetan students staged a naked protest outside the heavily guarded Chinese Embassy in New Delhi. As they chained themselves to the barbed wire protecting the building they shouted 'Human Rights in Tibet', and one of them, Dorjee Tsetan, a pupil at the Bylakuppe Tibetan Children's Village School, declared when arrested: 'We did this protest to show the Chinese leadership that their repressive policies in Tibet are naked truth [sic] no matter how hard they try to hide from the world what Tibetans in Tibet are going through.'[36] News coverage was instant and worldwide.

In other Asian countries naked protest is also a new phenomenon and in no imminent danger of losing its potential for impact and publicity. Such demonstrations are still few and far between. In 2008 Malaysian activists used the threat of nakedness to gain attention when the Malaysian People's Reform Movement announced its members were prepared to strip off outside the offices of the chief minister of Selangor state, after it more than doubled the cost of low-income housing. A party spokesperson declared: 'Protesting naked is our final act of desperation as the state government is literally stealing the clothes off our backs with this price increase.'[37] Not everyone thought this was a good idea. The spiritual leader of another opposition party, the Islamic PAS, said that only 'uncivilized' people would resort to such an act, and that 'Even [for] an animal like a cow which is stark naked, God created a tail to hide its genitals and here we are talking about human beings who have been given a mind.'[38]

A similar threat was made in 2007 in Bangkok by 300 laid-off workers from a clothing factory who threatened to protest naked in front of the Government House if they didn't receive compensation, and in 2005 fifteen students in the Philippines staged a nude protest in the streets of Manila against 'The naked truth that the government never treats education as a basic right', claiming that there was a shortage of nearly 50,000 classrooms and 3.5m desks and books.[39]

In the English-speaking world there may be a danger that naked protests are starting to lose their edge, but this is not apparent. Even when a blatantly commercial 'protest' is launched, the media responds as reliably as a dog to a bone. When the Lush chain of stores launched their worldwide protest against packaging, which involved employees in stores around the world wearing nothing but aprons sporting the headline 'Ask me why I'm naked', so much coverage was obtained, Treehugger.com remarked: 'Lush Fresh Handmade Cosmetics has made waves in innovative marketing before, but this week they set a new standard in drawing headlines without spending a single cent on advertising. OK, points given for a good message, cleverly delivered. But the campaign does leave questions open: for example, why hand out leaflets in a campaign against waste? And is naked the new marketing trend?'[40]

When, in covering the shop's campaign, the Australian *Daily Telegraph* asked its readers: 'Is it time to cover up nude protests?' only nine readers responded online, with just three agreeing – their opinion

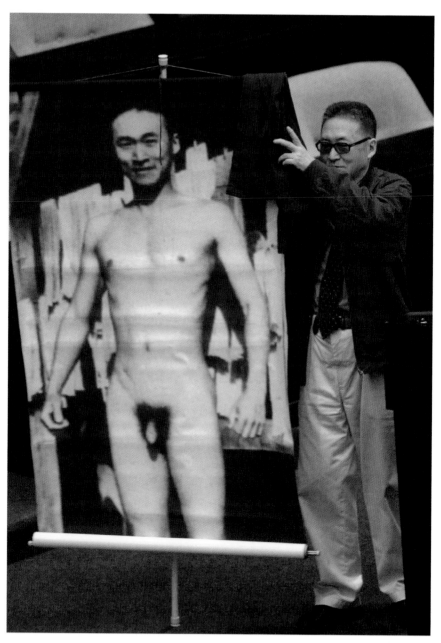

Taiwanese independent legislator Lee Ao shows a nude photo of himself taken about 50 years ago while he was still a serviceman during a protest against an arms bill at the parliament in Taipei, November 2006.

Staff in Amsterdam promote the worldwide Lush Fresh Handmade Cosmetics 'Go Naked' campaign in August 2008 to promote the concept of using less packaging – and to sell more of their unpackaged 'naked' products.

best expressed by one aptly named Cassandra: 'PUT YOUR CLOTHES BACK ON! I am sick of these protests, it's all just a stunt. Sex sells and it always has and always will, the world is just a perverted place.'[41]

The fact that nude protests still get plenty of media coverage does not necessarily mean that we are as sensitive to them as we were ten or twenty years ago. As a result, not only of the prevalence of naked protests, but also of the publicity given to Spencer Tunick's mass nude photo-shoots around the world, their ability to surprise us has undoubtedly diminished, whether or not this has affected their goal of achieving publicity.

Dalene Entenmann seems to have the measure of it. In 'Naked Trick: Bulgarian divas nude tease for breast cancer' for thecancerblog.com she writes:

> It worked for the global cosmetics company Avon in Bulgaria this week, when in a continuing effort to raise awareness for breast cancer, they launched an eye-catching public campaign using three well-known sexy celebrities

600 people pose naked on the Aletsch glacier in Switzerland in August 2007 to be photographed by Spencer Tunick for a Greenpeace Climate Change campaign.

In October 1999 the visionary doctor and social activist Patch Adams was joined by Dr Helen Caldicott, author of *If You Love this Planet* and others in an anti-nuclear protest in San Francisco.

Students run naked through the Christmas market on the Alexanderplatz in Berlin in December 2003 during an action dubbed 'We sold our shirts for education', in which some 30 students took part to protest against planned cuts in the education budget.

A demonstrator faces a water-cannon spray during a protest against the Third Summit of the Americas in April 2001 in Quebec City, Canada.

A protestor against globalization at the G8 Summit in Edinburgh in July 2005.

of Bulgaria. Posing in a larger-than-life banner hung outside the National Art Gallery in Sofia, the three beauties stared back at passers-by with a suggestion that when the large pink ribbon covering the women in the banner in just the right places came down, the public would be in for a nude shock.

As it turns out, when the pink ribbon was pulled down, the bare-shouldered bare-legged smiling women in the poster – television star Natalia Simeonova, pop diva Maria Ilieva and film actress Koyna Rousseva – were holding up pink tees with a breast cancer message printed on them.

Will the public or the paparazzi ever tire of sexy or the hint of nudity or actual nudity? No – and I am not suggesting they do. Only that this type of campaign risks becoming cliché. If I were head of a large organization with a goal to raise awareness in eye-popping ways, I would hire the brightest, most innovative and creative minds in the advertising world, and let them create something intelligent and fresh and new. But for now, Pamela Anderson and Avon know what works – and they work it.[42]

While nakedness has been used as an effective tool for showing moral outrage at serious abuses of human, animal and environmental rights, the extent of its use in the English-speaking world now means that we have entered an era in which serious campaigns run the risk of losing their impact if the use of nakedness is not carefully managed.

When Spencer Tunick joined forces with Greenpeace in 2007 to highlight the extent of global warming, the resulting 'body landscape', achieved its goal of drawing attention to the issue, and yet his carefully choreographed photographs of 600 volunteers standing on the Aletsch glacier in Switzerland fail to convey the depth of the tragedy about to occur. Greenpeace said the aim of the pictures was to 'establish a symbolic relationship between the vulnerability of the melting glacier and the human body',[43] and yet when a protest becomes a work of installation art, aesthetic appreciation replaces outrage and we are left with an admiration for the work which risks overriding any sense of concern we might have for the issue it is attempting to address.

In addition to the problem of art depriving a campaign of political impact, other threats to the most effective use of naked protest lie in the problems of hijacking and bandwagoning, a neologism in use in the world of politics and marketing. Two recent examples of campaigns which could be accused of these appropriations come from the worlds of commerce and religion.

An Airline Hijacks the Power of Naked Protest, A Cult Jumps on the Bandwagon

While Lush can avoid the accusation of hijacking since its naked packaging campaign promoted the non-commercial aim of sustainability, Aer Lingus's call for 1,000 naked participants to gather by the London Eye for their St Patrick's Day launch of cheap airfares in 2009, is a clear example of commercial interests making use of a tool successfully developed by the protest movement, and of depriving it of its integrity in the process. While naked protesters rely on their nudity being a symbolic demonstration of their desire to uphold the 'naked truth', the advertising world spins the truth so that the word 'naked' is used to gain attention, while in reality participants are not fully undressed. In the Lush campaign, staff wore aprons, in the Aer Lingus campaign participants were asked to wear shamrock designs. In reality, many stripped off when they were far from the sight of the police. Although the airline achieved publicity for their stunt, someone in the marketing department had forgotten that London in March is hardly ever warm. Despite this 400 people showed up and the sun did shine.

A more bizarre example of appropriating a tool of protest which feels uncomfortably like jumping on the bandwagon, comes from the Raëlian cult, who achieved worldwide fame when a group associated with them claimed to have produced 'Eve', the first human clone, in 2002. A 2007 article entitled 'Who Are the Raëlians, and Why Are They Naked?' begins: 'A journalist once shouted "The Raëlians are great material: They're sexy, good-looking nudists, and they worship space aliens!" If that doesn't get your attention, you're probably dead.'[44] The cult certainly provides plenty of material for the journalist and the curious, and is adept at staging events that gain good press coverage, even though their 'Mega-Orgy' in 2008 in Tel Aviv had to be cancelled due to public pressure and threats against the owner of the orgy's venue. The Raëlian spokesperson explained that the purpose of the proposed event was 'to put into practice' the saying 'make love, not war'. They wanted to 'try and bring world peace through mass orgasm . . . this by experiencing consensual sex and natural, uninterrupted pleasure.' He went on to point out how the words war, violence and murder have become more legitimate than sex, orgasm and pleasure, when 'It should be the other way around. Several years ago an Iraqi boy whose limbs were amputated was shown on TV and everybody treated this as if it was okay, but when Janet Jackson exposed her breast during the Superbowl the American nation was appalled.'[45]

However reasonably the Raëlians argued their case, they were not popular in Israel, having failed to realize that the symbol of their space-age religion was decidedly inappropriate for a Jewish state, since it depicted a swastika emerging out of a Star of David. Even though it was clear that the swastika, with its long tradition of use by Hindus, Buddhists and Jains, was not being used as a Nazi symbol, the Israeli government refused permission for the Raëlians to open one of their 'embassies' that they are establishing world-wide to welcome the aliens when they arrive.

The Raëlians are also unlikely to have endeared themselves to many who support naked protests, when in July 2003 in response to a Bare Witness photograph of naked bodies spelling out 'No GM', 300 Raëlians stripped to create their own message: 'We Love GM'.

Regardless of whether such an event was a genuine protest or 'awareness-raising' exercise, as opposed to a cynical attempt to grab publicity in the wake of another group's successful campaign, the fact remains that nakedness is still an effective tool for gaining attention and publicity. The English-speaking world may be harder to shock these days, some Cassandras may be sick of nude protests, but most of us will continue to be curiously amused, and will continue to pay attention to anyone who takes their clothes off in public and waves a banner with a message we can read. Why is this so? How many nude bodies do we have to see before we are immune to their effect?

The answer seems to be that we are fascinated by the naked protest because of its inherently paradoxical nature. Human beings are at their most vulnerable when naked but, when engaged in a protest, are also strangely powerful. They represent fearlessness, courage, the naked truth, the newborn child, the lover, the dead body stripped of all it owned. By standing with nothing they say everything about the human condition. When it comes to a political statement less is indeed more.

4

The Prime Minister of Britain
has Nothing to Conceal

Government, like dress, is the badge of lost innocence.
—Thomas Paine, *Common Sense*

In Plato's *Gorgias*, Socrates speaks of a legend that he has decided to accept as the truth. In the old days souls were judged at the end of their lives by Cronos, who sent the good to the Isles of the Blessed, and the bad to the unpleasant prison of Tartarus. The process was flawed, however, since the souls were judged just before they died and while still clothed. Zeus fixed the problem by arranging for people to be judged naked once they had died – by judges who were also naked. Nothing got in the way of the truth.

Socrates acted on his principles, and in *The Apology*, like a judge who, gazing into the souls of the newly dead, needs to be naked himself, he strips before the Athenians to confront them with the truth about their injustices. Further west the same idea was being used by clan chieftains and kings in Ireland, who would stand naked before their people to prove that they were unblemished and that they would engage in no dissembling. To stand naked before someone is the simplest way of showing you have nothing up your sleeve, and there is something reassuring and wholesome about a politician who is unashamed to be seen in the nude.

When Churchill was visiting the United States and staying at the White House, president Roosevelt once found Churchill striding back and forth across his room completely naked, puffing on a cigar as he dictated to a male secretary. As Roosevelt tried to beat a hasty retreat, Churchill called him back, saying 'The prime minister of Britain has nothing to conceal from the president of the United States.'[1]

The charm and directness of that incident stands in stark contrast to the extraordinary behaviour of Lyndon Johnson, who in an interview with a handful of journalists, unzipped his flies and showed them his penis to explain why America was still at war and continuing to bomb Vietnam.[2] The directness and naturalness of politicians who happily announce that they are naturists, such as Bernard Jenkin MP or Liberal Democrat councillor Helen Swain in the UK, stands in similarly marked contrast to the behaviour of US Representative Mark Foley, who in 2003 ran a campaign to close down a naturist summer camp for teenagers in Florida, warning that this might expose them to paedophiles. Governor Jeb Bush's general counsel responded to Foley by explaining that Florida permitted child nudity in the absence of lewdness, and that his counsel was 'unaware of any reports of criminal acts, child abuse, neglect or exploitation' at the camp. Foley later resigned after it was revealed that he had been importuning underage pageboys in Congress with sexually explicit emails.[3]

Although objections to nakedness can sometimes be born out of a conscious or unconscious desire to protect oneself from urges that may prove uncontrollable, or that one's conscience finds deplorable, they are just as likely to be born out of concerns for propriety, in the belief that nakedness equates with shame or wantonness in the minds of most people, even if this may not be the case in one's own mind. This was almost certainly the motivation behind former British prime minister Tony Blair's request to remove from the public gaze a painting of his wife posing in the nude for the artist Euan Uglow when she was a trainee barrister. Cherie apparently enjoyed life modelling so much that she acted as a model for two years for Uglow at his studio in Clapham, and admired the artist sufficiently to name her first son after him.

The resulting picture was only exhibited once in 1983, but Tony Blair then exerted his influence to ensure its return to obscurity. According to gallery owner Will Darby,

> The portrait of Miss Booth hasn't been shown for nearly a quarter of a century because it was Euan's wish that it would never be shown after the Blairs entered public life ... Everybody in the chambers knew what she was doing. There was

no secret about it. The embarrassment came from Tony Blair who was very worried after he took office that this picture would come out. As a favour to his close friend Derry Irvine, Euan agreed not to display it while he was Prime Minister. Cherie remained a great friend of Euan's until he died. She will be laughing her head off now that it's come out. She won't be ashamed at all.[4]

Being a Catholic, Cherie had no reason to feel ashamed. After all, in 1981 Pope John Paul II had declared that: 'Because God created it, the human body can remain nude and uncovered and preserve intact its splendour and its beauty.'[5] Now that Tony Blair has left office and become a Catholic he may feel more relaxed about the picture, though he will never be able to enjoy a charcoal drawing by Michael Sandle that depicts him and Cherie in the nude that was exhibited as the centrepiece of the Royal Academy's Summer Exhibition in 2007. Titled *Iraq Triptych*, the three-panel picture won the exhibition's Hugh Casson prize for drawing. In a parody of medieval paintings of Adam and Eve being banished from Paradise, Tony and Cherie stand naked on the steps of 10 Downing Street, while the side panels show Iraqi civilians being abused by British troops.

Naked in Parliament

Thomas Paine's essay *Common Sense*, which advocated America's independence from Britain, was first published anonymously in 1776. Paine had only recently arrived in America, but his essay, just fifty pages long, captured the mood of the colony struggling to find its own identity, and became an instant bestseller. In it he managed to sum up the corrosive potential of government in a masterpiece of incision: 'Government, like dress, is the badge of lost innocence.'

As Paine's influence grew, and his *Rights of Man* was published in 1791, a satire on his ideas appeared the following year on the streets of London entitled 'Buff, or a dissertation on nakedness, a parody on Paine's *Rights of Man*'. The anonymous author amused himself by

Part of the centerpiece of *Iraq Triptych* by Michael Sandle RA, which won
the Hugh Casson prize for drawing at the 2007 Royal Academy Summer
Exhibition. The large three-panel work, in its medieval imagery and structure,
is clearly a reference to the banishment of Adam and Eve from Paradise.
It shows the naked figures of Cherie and Tony Blair outside No 10, flanked
on one side by a pile of Iraqi corpses, and on the other by a British soldier
beating hooded Iraqi prisoners, based on Corporal Donald Payne who
admitted inhuman treatment of Iraqi people at a court martial in 2006.

transposing Paine's ideas of freedom with the concept of nakedness, thereby transforming 'the grand chorus of the Rights of Man' into 'a canzonetta on Nakedness'. 'Buff' is now almost forgotten by history. The *Rights of Man* has proved to be one of the most influential documents ever written.

The essayist Thomas Carlyle, however, was not a fan of Paine, writing that he was a 'rebellious staymaker . . . who feels that he, single-handed, did by his *Common Sense* pamphlet, free America; that he can and will free all this world — and perhaps even the other.'[6] But he too allowed himself to play with the concept of nakedness in a political context when in his 1833 *Sartor Resartus* he imagined a naked Westminster:

> Lives the man that can figure a naked Duke of Windlestraw addressing a naked House of Lords? Imagination, choked as in mephitic air, recoils on itself, and will not forward with the picture. The Woolsack, the Ministerial, the Opposition Benches — infandum! infandum! And yet why is the thing impossible? Was not every soul, or rather every body, of these Guardians of our Liberties, naked, or nearly so, last night; 'a forked Radish with a head fantastically carved'? And why might he not, did our stern fate so order it, walk out to St Stephen's, as well as into bed, in that no-fashion; and there, with other similar Radishes, hold a Bed of Justice?[7]

In 1986 Harold Bloom, writing on Carlyle, suggested his approach 'would do wonders' for American society:

> Envision a House of Representatives and a Senate required to deliberate absolutely naked (presumably in a sufficiently heated Capitol). Clearly the quality of legislation would rise, and the quantity of rhetoric would fall. Envision professors, quite naked, instructing equally naked classes. The intellectual level might not be elevated, but the issue of authority would be clarified. Envision our president, naked on television, smilingly charming us with his customary amiable incoherence. We might be no less moved, but reality would have a way of breaking in upon him, and even upon us.[8]

The idea that nakedness could improve the world of politics has been adopted by a number of politicians in recent years, most notably in Catholic countries, perhaps as a result of Pope John Paul II's 'Theology of the Body', which assures the faithful that the human form is indeed 'made in the image of God'.

The most widely publicized naked politician is undoubtedly Hungarian-born Ilona Staller, who rose to fame in the 1970s as the model, singer and porn star Cicciolina ('The Little Fleshy One'). In 1979 she stood unsuccessfully as a Green Party candidate for the Italian Parliament, but in 1985 switched her allegiance to the Radical Party, campaigning for human rights and against world hunger, nuclear energy and NATO membership, and was elected to the Italian parliament in 1987. When she was not re-elected at the end of her term, she formed a new party, along with her manager and a fellow porn star, as a parody of traditional political parties. The 'Partito dell'Amore' advocated the legalization of brothels, better sex education and the creation of 'love parks'.

Despite the parodying and posturing, Ilona Staller is clear about her values and is still active in the political field after a high-profile divorce from the artist Jeff Koons. She is a pacifist who opposes the death penalty, nuclear power, censorship, the fur trade and vivisection. She has proposed a tax on cars to fund environmental defence, and supports the decriminalization of drugs, and complete sexual freedom, including the right to sex in prisons. Despite these laudable goals, she has been unable to attract sufficient support in her attempts to run for mayor of Milan or to join the Hungarian parliament.

In comparison with Ilona Staller, the world's other 'naked politicians' seem positively bland, but like 'Cicciolina', who used to pose in election campaigns wearing nothing but a boa constrictor, what they hold in common is the belief that using images of themselves in the nude will help to attract voters. Like Irish kings they are essentially trying to prove that they have nothing to hide. In 2006 Alberto Rivera, leader of the newly formed Catalan Citizens' Party in Spain, ran a poster campaign of himself in the nude. The message that ran alongside the handsome Rivera, his hands crossed in front of his genitals, read 'Your party has been born. We only care about people. We don't care where you were born. We don't care what language you speak. We don't care what clothes you wear. We

I will give you 40,000 blowjobs

Tania Dervaux of the NEE, a political protest group formed in Belgium in 2005, posing in a parody of a political poster in response to parties' unrealistic claims to solve unemployment in the 2007 Belgian general election.

care about you.' In its first elections the party succeeded in securing three deputies at the regional Parliament of Catalonia.

Observing Rivera's success, 58-year-old ex-conservative party spokesman Juan Barranco in Madrid decided to pose naked for a poster when running as an independent candidate in the spring of 2007. His advertising agency managed to convince him that rather than using a balloon to hide his genitals, the photograph should feature just the upper half of his torso, with his hands held out to the camera to illustrate the slogan 'con las manios limpias' (with clean hands). By the summer the idea had been carried on the wind to Mexico, where posters of mayoral candidate Wilfrido Salazar Rule appeared all over the city of Zacatecas showing him in a playmate pose on his stomach, beside the headline 'Completamene transparente' (completely transparent).

The chutzpah of these political candidates has also been shown by local councillors in New Zealand and Britain. In 2001 18-year-old Paula Gillon made New Zealand history by being the youngest person to become a councillor, after a successful poster campaign in which she appeared scantily clad with the headline 'The Naked Politician'.

In 1979 Brighton councillor Eileen Jakes was instrumental in persuading her fellow councillors to allow a naturist beach in the town by showing photographs of herself sunbathing topless in Ibiza.

The February 1993 cover of the Italian *L'Espress* magazine showing liberal Deputy Vittorio Sgarbi posing nude, with another naked Italian politician, Sen. Luciano Benetton, in the inset in a reproduction of his advertising poster.

In 2004 *The Independent* reported that:

> Eileen Jakes, now 72, still lives on Brighton seafront. And she still has that all-over tan. But it's not from Brighton's nudist beach. 'I have a house in Spain near a naturist beach,' she tells me. 'And my friend in Brighton has a very enclosed garden.' She whispers: 'So why would I go and lie on the shingle? Anyway, you can take your top off almost anywhere, now.'[9]

The reporter, Katy Guest, concluded her article by writing:

> Yes, the beach is full of gay men ('Do you think we'd take our clothes off if they were straight?' giggled Carla from Essex), but once you get over the slightly hurt feeling of being naked and completely ignored, it's weirdly liberating. A quarter of a century on, we may not have attained Swedish-style enlightenment with regards to the naked body but Eileen Jakes does seem to have been on to a good thing.

Councillors Gillon and Jakes used photographs of themselves proactively. Other councillors have not been so lucky when pictures of themselves in the nude have been publicized by others without their consent. The openly gay Liberal Democrat councillor Charles Anglin achieved unfavourable publicity in 2006 when the photographs he had posted on a gay dating site were discovered by a local journalist, despite responses from the public that showed that many were not as shocked as the journalist had hoped: 'As a Lambeth resident I don't give a monkey's what he gets up to in private, I just wish he would arrange for my rubbish to be picked up.'[10]

Helen Swain, a naturist mother of three children, was the target of an anonymous leaflet dropped through the letter-boxes of voters in Mirfield, West Yorkshire, when she stood as a Liberal Democrat councillor in 2002. The leaflet showed a photograph of her taking part in a nude television game show that Channel Five had broadcast two years earlier. *Naked Jungle*, which featured nude contestants pitting themselves against an assault course and a nude presenter, Keith Chegwin, was only screened for one series, despite the fact that it gained the highest rating of any entertainment programme on Channel Five that year, attracting two million viewers. The same prurience that drove the *Daily Mail* to attack the programme as 'plumbing new depths of indecency', and Culture Secretary Chris Smith to criticize the programme in the House of Commons, drove Helen Swain's attackers, even though it seemed

'Naked Cowboy' Robert John Burck launches his campaign to run for mayor of New York in 2009. For over ten years Burck has played daily in Times Square wearing only boots and underpants.

Two women have attempted to rival the Naked Cowboy in Times Square. Lisa Holmund, pictured here, began appearing as 'the Naked Cowgirl' in Times Square in 2005. A few years later the self-proclaimed 'Queen of Times Square' and ex-stripper Sandy Kane, having noticed Holmund's frequent absences, took up her guitar and charged tourists $2 to take pictures with her. 'I have been naked for years', Kane said. 'This is tame for me.'

Wszystko dla przyszłości

Partia Kobiet
Polska jest Kobietą

i nic do ukrycia

The Polish Women's Party (Partia Kobiet, PK), campaign poster, October 2007, for the parliamentary elections.

clear that the public was amused rather than outraged by the programme. A Channel Five spokesman said: 'We're very surprised Keith Chegwin's private parts have generated so much interest. We received a handful of complaints about the show, most of which were not serious, and the ITC [Complaints Authority] received just one.'[11]

The Polish Women's Party

Though appearing naked is a popular strategy in Catholic countries, its success is not always guaranteed. The most ambitious use of nakedness to gain attention and votes occurred in Poland in 2007, with the launch of the Partia Kobiet (The Women's Party). Inspired perhaps by the success of 'The Calendar Girls', which demonstrated female solidarity so clearly in its group photographs (see p. 226), the poster for the party was launched with a statement from its president, Manuela Gretkowska: 'We are beautiful, nude, proud. We are true and sincere, body and soul. This is not pornography, there is nothing to see in terms of sex, our faces are intelligent, concerned, proud. We do not have our mouths open nor our eyes closed . . . All that interests us is the future, the position of women in society. We will open the archives of the former secret communist agents, we will make known their corrupt affairs.'

Despite the publicity gained from their launch, the party won only 0.28 per cent of the national vote in the general election and gained no seats. Perhaps voters agreed with British political blogger Guido Fawkes when he commented: 'This poster for the upcoming Polish elections on behalf of the Women's Party has the slogan: "Everything for the future . . . and nothing to hide." Which, typically of politicians, is a barefaced lie since they seem to be hiding behind a poster.' It is more likely, though, that voters simply didn't like the party's proposals for women's rights that ran contrary to Catholic doctrine, which still dominates Polish society.

The President and the Baptism of Intimacy

Candidates trying to make it to the top may try to get there in the nude, but once they've got there, do they have to put their clothes back on? Now that Alberto Rivera is successful, and receiving death threats as a result, there are no more naked poster campaigns, and none of the politicians who have used naked photographs have maintained nudity as a permanent image or strategy. How a politician conducts themselves in water, however, seems a different affair altogether, at least in the USA, where the president can confidently swim in the nude without any adverse publicity. Perhaps inspired by founding father Benjamin Franklin, who preached the 'gospel of ventilation' and often took 'air baths' in the nude, the precedent was set early in the nineteenth century by the sixth president, John Quincy Adams, who enjoyed skinny-dipping in the Potomac most mornings at 5 a.m. Like US Defense Secretary Robert McNamara (1916–2009), who once said 'I like to run down to the beach and have a little swim in the nude in the morning', his motives were clearly not social. Theodore Roosevelt, however, enjoyed taking the whole Cabinet with him down to the Potomac for a skinny-dip.[12] And in the 'Camelot years' at the White House, John F. Kennedy enjoyed holding lunchtime naked pool parties with two young female staff aides, nicknamed Fiddle and Faddle, joined sometimes by his brothers Bobby and Teddy.

JFK's successor, Lyndon B. Johnson, continued the tradition. LBJ was a domineering man who made staff talk to him while he sat on the toilet, and who often referred to his penis as 'Jumbo'. When visitors came to the White House he frequently invited them for a swim, bullying them if they showed a reluctance to be seen naked. One visitor was the evangelist Billy Graham, who happily joined the president in the water. Nancy Gibbs and Michael Duffy wrote: 'After a visit in the Oval Office, Johnson proposed a swim in the White House pool. That no one had brought a bathing suit was no deterrent; in years to come the president would often interrupt meetings to suggest a swim and needle anyone who was reluctant to strip naked and dive in a baptism in intimacy.'[13]

The same ease with nakedness and with bodily functions was not on display recently in Ireland, when the prime minister Brian

Painting of Italian Prime Minister Silvio Berlusconi and his favourite Minister Mara Carfagna by the artist Filippo Panseca. The painting sparked controversy when it was exhibited at the 'Art & Savonnerie' exposition in Fortezza del Priamar in April 2009.

Cowen became the unwitting subject of two Banksy-style 'guerrilla art' events. In both cases an oil painting of a naked Brian Cowen, the Taoiseach of Ireland, was found hanging in a public gallery, sparking an incident dubbed 'Portraitgate' by the media. On 7 March 2009 the 35-year-old artist Conor Casby succeeded in secretly hanging his picture of the Taoiseach in the National Gallery in Dublin alongside portraits of Irish worthies, including W .B. Yeats and Bono. The painting depicted Mr Cowen from the waist up, clutching a toilet roll, and carried a caption that mentioned his nickname 'Biffo':

> Brian Cowen, Politician 1960–2008. This portrait, acquired
> uncommissioned by the National Gallery, celebrates one

of the finest politicians produced by Ireland since the foundation of the state. Following a spell at the helm of the Department of Finance during a period of unprecedented prosperity, Brian Cowen inherited the office of Taoiseach in 2008. Balancing a public image that ranges from fantastically intelligent analytical thinker to Big Ignorant Fucker from Offaly, the Taoiseach proves to be a challenging subject to represent.[14]

Although the picture was discovered within an hour of its hanging, a second appeared the next day at the Royal Hibernian Academy. In it a naked Cowen, again revealing only the upper half of his body, was depicted holding his underpants. Before it was realized that the painting was unsolicited, a visitor had offered to buy it. The artist was soon discovered and interviewed by the police.

The Right to Be Naked

What a singular fact for an angel visitant to this earth to carry back in his note-book, that men were forbidden to expose their bodies under the severest penalties!
—Henry David Thoreau, *Journals*

Presidents can skinny dip, councillors can appear nude on a television game show or in a poster campaign, but can you or I take a nude dip in a nearby lake or in the sea without fear of breaking the law? Can we collect the milk bottles from outside our front door without having to get dressed? Could we perhaps cycle to work or stroll to our local shop in the nude?

In England and Wales, simply being naked is not in itself an offence, and it seems that in all these cases you could only be successfully prosecuted if it could be proved that you had the intention to offend someone by your behaviour. From country to country, and sometimes from region to region within a country, the situation changes. In most of Europe the naked body is not in itself considered indecent in law, and yet appearing naked in public is subject to sanctions. There are exceptions, however, such as within the city of Barcelona, where public nudity is permitted.

In most of the United States being naked in public is an offence subject to a fine or imprisonment, but not in Vermont, for example, as residents discovered in the summer of 2006 when teenagers in Brattleboro began stripping off to sunbathe in the Harmony Parking Lot in the middle of the town. In Australia the situation varies from state to state, while in New Zealand public nudity is not illegal. Even so, wherever it is not a crime to be seen in the nude, such as New Zealand, Britain and much of Europe, the indecency laws are often framed in such a way that one can still be challenged or arrested by the police, even when the law is technically on one's side. Whatever the legal position is elsewhere, only the foolhardy would attempt to test the law in the Middle East or in any Muslim country.

It would also be a mistake to try hiking, or indeed doing anything in public in the nude in Scotland, where Stephen Gough, now known around the world as 'The Naked Rambler', has achieved notoriety for being imprisoned repeatedly over the last few years for 'breaching the peace' by refusing to wear clothing. His first arrest occurred after he tried to complete a hike which started in Land's End in June 2005 and was due to finish in John o'Groats until he was arrested under Scottish law.

The 'Naked Rambler' story represents only the most recent episode in a human rights struggle whose roots lie in America and Europe in the nineteenth century. At the heart of this struggle is the premise that being able to choose, at any given moment, whether or not one's body is covered is a fundamental human right. In most of the world we do not have that freedom, and risk arrest if we choose to exercise it in public. Most people accept this fact without a moment's thought, but every so often its existential implications have astonished or outraged particular individuals sufficiently to move them to write about this or to campaign for 'body freedom', as it is now called.

In the nineteenth century, for many – particularly women – the struggle for body freedom was more modest in ambition, and revolved not around the right to be naked, but the right to wear clothing that was not restrictive. But even then, as reformers in

Naked British ramblers Stephen Gough and Melanie Roberts at Land's End in Cornwall in June 2005 in thick fog preparing to start their walk to John o'Groats on Scotland's north coast. Gough, an ex-Royal Marine, has been in and out of Scottish prisons ever since for breaches of the peace resulting from his refusal to wear clothes when in public.

America and Europe argued for dressing in a more comfortable way, there were some who wanted to dispense with clothing altogether. Enthusiasts of both persuasions could be found in New England in the 1850s. As the temperance activists Libby Miller and Amelia Bloomer promoted their 'rational costume' of loose trousers, gathered at the ankles and topped with a short skirt, Henry David Thoreau was undertaking his famous experiment in Concord, Massachusetts, living the simple life by Walden pond in a wooden house he had built on his friend Emerson's land. There he enjoyed skinny-dipping and developed his appreciation for the wilderness, writing afterwards:

> Today, wilderness is usually considered to be something good and in need of preservation. The beauty and awesomeness of it dominate our attention. We are attracted by wilderness, the Otherness of it, the sense it is something inevitably outside of us. Always beyond us, it is what is ultimately real. We cannot adequately appreciate this aspect of nature if we approach it with any taint of human pretense. It will elude us if we allow artifacts like clothing to intervene between ourselves and this Other. To apprehend it, we cannot be naked enough. In wildness is the preservation of the world.[15]

Later, in the 1870s another New Englander, the poet and Democrat Walt Whitman, was taking the lead from fellow poet John Donne, who in 1598 had written: 'Full nakedness! All joys are to thee.' Whitman decided to try living the simple life, out in the country and free of clothing. In his entry 'A Sun Bath – Nakedness' for his autobiographical work *Specimen Days* he wrote:

> I sit here in solitude with Nature – open, voiceless, mystic, far removed, yet palpable, eloquent Nature. I merge myself in the scene, in the perfect day. Hovering over the clear brook-water, I am sooth'd by its soft gurgle in one place, and the hoarser murmurs of its three-foot fall in another. Come, ye disconsolate, in whom any latent eligibility is left – come get the sure virtues of creek-shore, and wood and

field. Two months (July and August, '77) have I absorb'd them, and they begin to make a new man of me. Every day, seclusion – every day at least two or three hours of freedom, bathing, no talk, no bonds, no dress, no books, no manners . . . Never before did I get so close to Nature; never before did she come so close to me . . . Nature was naked, and I was also . . . Sweet, sane, still Nakedness in Nature! – ah if poor, sick, prurient humanity in cities might really know you once more! Is not nakedness indecent? No, not inherently. It is your thought, your sophistication, your fear, your respectability, that is indecent. There come moods when these clothes of ours are not only too irksome to wear, but are themselves indecent.[16]

Whitman's writing, along with that of the Concord Transcendentalists, Emerson and Thoreau, inspired a number of Utopian communities on the east and west coasts that began experimenting with new ways of living, which often included clothing reform and nudism. Meanwhile, on the other side of the Atlantic, the clothing reform movement was gathering momentum, and in 1881 the Rational Dress Society was formed in London to protest 'against the introduction of any fashion in dress that either deforms the figure, impedes the movements of the body, or in any way tends to injure the health. It protests against the wearing of tightly-fitting corsets; of high-heeled shoes; of heavily-weighted skirts, as rendering healthy exercise almost impossible; and of all tie down cloaks or other garments impeding on the movements of the arms.'[17]

The Origins of Organized Nudism

As corsets – worn by women, including those who were pregnant, and by fashion-conscious men – began to be shed in favour of undergarments such as knitted wool 'union suits', there were some who found even these improvements insufficient, particularly in the sweltering heat of India, where Englishmen were still required to wear shirts, ties, jackets and hats. In Bombay in 1890 three Englishmen decided to rebel against the dress codes of the British Raj. In secret they formed the Fellowship of the Naked Trust and began to meet together in the nude. The motives of their fellowship were, as they wrote:

> Physical – because given a suitable temperature, it is good for the body to be exposed to the air, and because no costume that has ever been invented is equal in comfort to perfect nakedness. Moral – because the false shame of our own bodies and morbid curiosity as to those of the opposite sex which result from always wearing clothes, are the chief sources of impurity. Aesthetic – because the human body is God's noblest work, and it is good for everyone to gaze on such beauty freely.[18]

Although the Fellowship lasted only two years and consisted of just three members, it is historically significant as the first organized nudist movement, pre-dating by three years the earliest German publication on the nudist idea, Heinrich Pudor's 1893 *Nackende Menschen: Jauchzen der Zukunst* (Naked Mankind: A Leap into the Future) and by thirteen years the founding of the first nudist groups in Europe: Freilichtpark (Free-Light Park) near Hamburg, and the community at Bois-Fourgon in France, which both opened in 1903.

Ideas never emerge out of a vacuum: the three founders of the Bombay fellowship were undoubtedly influenced by the writings of English enthusiasts of nakedness in the same way that the founders of the Utopian communities in America had been influenced by the Transcendentalists. The Fellowship's prime mover, Charles Crawford, wrote a series of letters to the poet and socialist philosopher Edward Carpenter to tell him about their initiative. Carpenter, sometimes referred to as 'the gay godfather of the British left', espoused a form of mystical socialism and was a key figure in the founding of the Fabian Society and the Labour party. He lived openly with a male partner, and was moved both by Indian mysticism and humanitarian ideals. A vegetarian who campaigned against air pollution and vivisection, and who introduced sandal-wearing to the British, Carpenter embraced many of the concepts that have become cornerstones of the contemporary alternative culture, at the heart of which lies a sense of reverence towards the Earth, sexuality and the body.

Fellow socialist George Orwell disliked Carpenter, referring to those who were in tune with his ideas as 'the sort of eunuch type with a vegetarian smell, who go about spreading sweetness and light . . . readers of Edward Carpenter or some other pious sodomite and talking with BBC accents.'[19] Carpenter was not alone in being a target for Orwell's cruel satire, which also attacked the Utopian ambitions of those socialists who had created Letchworth Garden City in the early years of the twentieth century as a new kind of town which would combine the advantages of city and countryside. In *The Road to Wigan Pier* he described the new city as a magnet for 'every fruit juice drinker, nudist, sandal wearer, sex-maniac, Quaker, nature cure quack, pacifist and feminist in England'.[20] The nudists in Orwell's list came from 'The Cloisters', a Theosophical centre in Letchworth that was inspired by the Arts and Crafts Movement. In an extraordinary building, now used by local Freemasons, residents lived a wholesome life, which involved as much exposure as possible to the benefits of fresh air and sunshine. In a building first seen in a dream by the school's founder, quantities of Swedish marble decorated a large room open to the air, an outdoor swimming pool, cloisters and towers. Residents slept in hammocks that descended from the ceiling, and could enjoy nude bathing or a drink at the nearby Skittles – England's only alcohol-free pub – or a meal in the food reform restaurant of The Simple Life Hotel. Many undoubtedly were grateful for the sandals Carpenter had introduced. Their feet could breathe at last, and as they lay in their hammocks they could read his inspiring *Civilisation: Its Cause and Cure*, which evoked a vision of a sensuous mysticism and a return of paganism to humanity:

> The meaning of the old religions will come back to him.
> On the high-tops once more gathering he will celebrate
> with naked dances the glory of the human form and the
> great processions of the stars, or greet the bright horn of
> the young moon which now after a hundred centuries
> comes back laden with such wondrous associations – all the

yearnings and the dreams and the wonderment of the generations of mankind – the worship of Astarte and of Diana, of Isis or the Virgin Mary; once more in sacred groves will he reunite the passion and the delight of human love with his deepest feelings of the sanctity and beauty of Nature; or in the open, standing uncovered to the Sun, will adore the emblem of the everlasting splendour which shines within. The same sense of vital perfection and exaltation which can be traced in the early and pre-civilisation peoples – only a thousand times intensified, defined, illustrated and purified – will return to irradiate the redeemed and delivered Man.[21]

Cec Cinder, whose *The Nudist Idea* offers the most comprehensive history of the nudist movement, believes that Carpenter would have been seen by history as the 'Father of nudism' if he had not chosen to champion homosexual rights. Between 1890 and 1895 Carpenter wrote a number of essays on sexuality which included his opinions on both subjects, but on attempting to publish them in one volume, titled *Love's Coming of Age*, he discovered that the recent trial of Oscar Wilde had so terrified publishers that his book could only be printed without the controversial material. Later he wrote: 'The Wilde trial had done its work, and silence must henceforth reign on sex-subjects.' Cinder suggests that Carpenter might well have produced a book devoted to nudism if this incident had not occurred.

The distinction of being seen as the father of nudism went instead to the German Richard Ungewitter, who in 1906 published *Die Nacktheit* (Nakedness), which became a bestseller.[22] Ungewitter's book extolled the health benefits of nudism and proposed a vision of an ideal society in which men and women could enjoy each other's company in the nude, while gymnasia trained their children in physical and moral development similarly free of clothing. Ungewitter's book fell on fertile soil, and soon its sales had reached 90,000 copies. In reality, the concept of a 'father' of the nudist movement is misleading, since nudism emerged as a result of the work of numerous individuals, who in turn were influenced by wider forces. In the final decade of the nineteenth century, as

Carpenter in England extolled the virtues of a life close to the primal forces of nature, in Germany the idea of *Nacktkultur* (Nudism) had already emerged within some of the reform movements, known collectively as Lebensreform (Life Reform), which sought to encourage a healthier way of living. In particular, two movements, the Wandervögel (Migratory Bird) and Freikörperkultur (Free Body Culture) had already begun to propagate the idea that it was good to expose the body to air and sunshine. The Wandervögel, a popular movement of German youth groups started in 1896, wanted to break free from the perceived hypocrisies and repression of their elders, to get back into contact with nature and the simple pleasures of life. As precursors of the scouting movement, they encouraged the development of youth leadership and of hiking, and often on summer walks would sunbathe and swim in the nude. The Freikörperkultur movement (often abbreviated to FKK) arose at around the same time, and was similarly inspired by the idea of getting closer to nature by spending time outdoors free of clothing. By the following decade, with the founding of the first nudist club and the publication of Ungewitter's book, nudism was finally established as a movement in its own right.[23]

In the same period, a Swiss doctor, Auguste Rollier, had started to experiment with the health benefits of exposing the body, and had begun treating tubercular patients first with 'skybaths' of indirect sunlight, and then with direct sunlight, with extraordinary success. At first he exposed only parts of the body, but soon discovered that naked sun-baths worked best. By 1923 he was treating nearly a thousand patients in 37 clinics, and his methods were being copied all over the world. His success supported the contention of nudists that outdoor nakedness promoted health and should be encouraged.

The early German nudist apologists, such as Ungewitter and the less articulate Heinrich Pudor, were fatally tainted, though, as were so many in that era, with a rabid anti-Semitism that found its way into their writings. Ever since the beginnings of the Lebensreform movement, many enthusiasts of clothing and diet reform, eugenics and the benefits of gymnasia had found common cause with nudism, and once the First World War ended, these ideas gathered momentum in the fervent atmosphere of the Weimar

Republic, with nudism reaching the peak of its popularity during this time. In the process, the image of the healthy Aryan became for many an ideal that required not only frequent doses of fresh air, sunshine, a vegetarian or 'reform' diet, and exercise in the nude, but also the toxic notion of 'racial hygiene'. Nudism could help to purify the racial stock by curing and preventing disease, and by helping the healthier Germans it produced make better mate selections.

Darwin's theory of evolution had inspired eugenics, which ran like a seam through the Lebensreform movement. Even though racist and anti-Semitic ideas, fuelled by eugenic theory, circulated amongst the FKK, the Wandervögel and the nudist camps, these groups were also breeding-grounds of progressive thinking that attracted socialists, liberals, pacifists, Marxists and many Jews. The ideas of the reform movements that were based on a 'return to nature' and on natural health methods were carried to the United States, particularly California, by some of the thousands of German immigrants, many of whom were Jewish, who arrived in America before the Second World War. They promoted vegetarianism, raw food diets and nudism, and became prototypal hippies – a term first used in the 1930s. The keenest gravitated to the canyons of

Seven of California's 'Nature Boys' in Topanga Canyon, August 1948. They were the first generation of Americans to adopt the 'Naturmensch' philosophy and image, practising nudism and living in the mountains and sleeping in caves and trees, sometimes as many as fifteen of them at a time.

America's west coast, where they lived in caves or in trees, ate raw food and lived the simple life. Typical of these 'Nature Boys', as these followers of the 'Naturmensch' philosophy became known, was Eden Abhez, born into a poor Jewish family from Brooklyn, whose song 'Nature Boy' became a Nat King Cole hit.[24]

Back in Germany, as fast as nudism was appealing to progressive thinkers, it was also attracting the condemnation of the Catholic church. When Hitler was appointed Chancellor in January 1933, he succeeded in appeasing the Catholics and dismantling at one stroke a network that harboured many of his enemies by outlawing nudism. In March Hermann Göring issued an edict that:

> One of the greatest dangers for German culture and morality is the so-called nudity movement. Greatly as it is to be welcomed in the interest of the public health, that ever wider circles, especially of the metropolitan population, are striving to make the healing power of sun and air and water serviceable to their body, as greatly must the so-called nudity movement be disapproved of as a cultural error. Among women nudity kills natural modesty; it takes from men their respect for women, and thereby destroys the prerequisite for any genuine culture. It is therefore expected of all police authorities that, in support of the spiritual powers developed through the national movement, they take all police measures to destroy the so-called nude culture.[25]

Within a few months, however, the situation was to change. A nudist Nazi, Karl Buckmann, worked behind the scenes, and as Marxist groups found their properties shut down and confiscated by the police, a state-sponsored national nudist organization – purged of dissident elements – was created, The Battle Ring for National Free Physical Culture,[26] as part of the National Association for Public Health. By the summer over half the clubs were back in operation and by the beginning of 1934 the police were instructed not to interfere with acknowledged nudist groups. Even so, accounts suggest that the Gestapo repeatedly investigated and harassed these groups, still fearful that they harboured subversives and Marxists.[27] However much the Nazis decided that in the end the nudist movement could be tolerated, and could even further the aims of racial perfection, the fundamental right simply to be naked if and when one chose to be was respected no more in Nazi Germany than in any other part of the world.

The Progressive Movement in Britain

In the year that Hitler and Göring banned nudism, George Bernard Shaw wrote to the secretary of the Sun Bathing Society, whose patron was the Countess of Mayo, at their offices in Upper Norwood, London. He was anxious to clarify his relationship with the nudist movement, and to offer his qualified support. He declared that while he was not a 'complete nudist . . . I am strongly in favour of getting rid of every scrap of clothing that we can dispense with.' He went on to say: 'I object also to the excessive use of clothing to produce idolatry, and stimulate sexuality beyond their natural bounds. And of course I know the mischief done by making us ashamed of our bodies.'[28]

Just as in Germany nudism had become part and parcel of a wider reform movement that sought to change society, and for this reason had attracted progressive thinkers of every kind, so the same process had occurred in Britain. The establishment of the first nudist club in the country coincided with the rise to power of the first Labour government in 1924 – the year in which C. H. Douglas published his influential *Social Credit*, which suggested a complete reform of the monetary system, and the year after Dr Auguste Rollier's book *Heliotherapy*, which advocated the health benefits of nude sunbathing, had been published for the first time in English. Prominent socialists such as H. G. Wells and Havelock Ellis, though not card-carrying members of the nudist movement, were – like Bernard Shaw – sympathetic to nudism and were not averse to shedding their clothes to swim or sunbathe with family and friends.

By this time the health benefits of air and sun baths had become so widely recognized that a new organization, The Sunshine League, whose inaugural meeting was held at Carnegie House in Piccadilly in May 1924, attracted Alexandra, the Queen Mother, as its first patron. The league's journal was edited by the surgeon Sir Arbuth-not Lane, who mustered an advisory council of over a hundred distinguished names, including Asquith, Lloyd George, the Earl of Oxford and Julian Huxley. The moving force behind the league was Caleb Saleeby, a medical doctor, eugenicist and keen propo-nent of heliotherapy, whose book on the subject, *Sunlight and Health*, had been published the previous year along with the English edition of Rollier's work. Although the Sunshine League was not overtly campaigning for nudism, Saleeby confided to friends that the idea behind it was to stimulate the nudist movement under the guise of a conventional sunbathing organization. Only a month after its founding, however, another organization sprang up, The Sun Ray Club, whose moving force was not so interested in compromise.

Forty-two-year-old Captain H. H. Vincent BA, BSc., believed that nudists should follow the lead shown by the suffragettes, whose militant action had won the franchise for women in 1919. In a talk just prior to the founding of The Sun Ray Club, Vincent proposed a protest march in defence of nudist rights through Hyde Park. No-one took up the call to arms, but Vincent soon discovered, as protesters have today, that just the threat of a naked protest is sufficient to generate publicity. From May onwards the British public could obtain light relief from reading about the achievements of the new government by turning to those pages of their newspaper that dealt with the new 'sensation': nudism. In January 1925 the story was still providing material, with *The People* running the headline 'SUN-BATHERS WANT TO STARTLE LONDON — PROPOSED HYDE PARK MARCH OF 2000 NAKED MEN AND WOMEN'.[29]

The only record of a nude 'protest' in the park from that time reveals not only the gap between the vision and any attempt to enact it, but also the degree of prudery that existed. In 1927 the Captain was arrested as he sunbathed bare-chested in Hyde Park and was fined for indecent exposure. The magistrate told him: 'I am going to hold, rightly or wrongly, that to expose the upper part of your body is indecent. I think it is likely to shock persons of ordinary sensibility.'[30] Vincent would have found comfort in the words of modern body freedom activist Terri Webb, who campaigns for the right to be naked in public in the USA, and who said in 2002: 'To be offended by the visual appearance of another person is prejudice, akin to racism. The right to exist, uncovered, should hold precedence over the right not to view [nudity].'[31]

Although Vincent seems to have been a lone voice crying in the wilderness, with his fellow nudists remaining content to undress only in private, his initiative stands as the first widely publicized attempt to place the right to be naked in public on the political agenda: calling into question whether anyone, least of all a government, has the right to dictate whether or not a person is clothed.

Since even suggesting the idea of nakedness could provoke offence, most English nudists at this time described themselves either as 'sunbathers' or as 'gymnosophists', from the Greek *gymnos* (naked) and *sophia* (wisdom). The latter euphemism had the additional benefit of conferring classical dignity on the activity, and of suggesting that nudists were naked for philosophical reasons.

In the year Vincent was arrested in the park, the American sociologist Maurice Parmalee made use of this term when he published *The New Gymnosophy*, the first book in English to present nakedness as a way of life. Havelock Ellis, a sexologist and supporter of eugenics, agreed to write the introduction, but in it he made it clear that,

> I have not myself the slightest intention of following Dr Parmalee's example in joining any of the societies for the practice in common of the principles of gymnosophy. I am pleased that such societies exist; I can see that they perform a valuable function. Personally, however, I am well content to continue to follow an old practice of simply encouraging the practice of nakedness privately and among personal friends. I find, increasingly, that that is what others also are doing, on simple hygienic, moral, or aesthetic grounds, for themselves and their children.[32]

By the 1930s nudism had reached the height of its popularity in Britain. The 1933 summer edition of *Sun Bathing Review* carried not only George Bernard Shaw's letter to the society's secretary, but an excerpt from Dora Russell's lecture on sex education, delivered at a meeting of the World League for Sexual Reform, an article on 'The Unpleasantness of Clothes', and a message of congratulations

Members of the National Sun & Air Association gathered at the fireside during their annual conference at Friern Park in North Finchley, May 1938. The association was founded in 1931 with 30 members; by 1937, it had a membership of 2,350.

on the founding of the review that year from Dr Rollier in Switzerland, whose success with tuberculosis patients had by now achieved worldwide recognition. A brief report from abroad announced that "News from Germany tends to confirm reports of interference in nudist activities . . . those who have recently visited Germany have been unable to join nudist groups.'

In the same edition there were reports from a number of schools in the progressive education movement that regularly exposed their pupils to the elements. Pinehurst school in Heathfield, Sussex, which offered boarding facilities to boys and girls from 3 to 12 years old, announced that in their 26 acres 'the children live and work out of doors whenever the weather is favourable'. The principal, Miss B. Reid, reported that 'In the summer term the school assembles at 9am, and all the children sunbathe on the tennis lawn until 9.30, running about completely naked.' Two other sunbathing sessions followed during the day, with children having three to four hours exposure daily. On days when it rained, when it was not too cold, 'the children have an air and rain bath and thoroughly enjoy this'. Having run the school for eight years Miss Reid reports that they have entirely avoided the influenza, whooping cough and measles epidemics that have occurred around them, with pupils suffering from nothing more than the common cold.

The principal at Bedales school in Hampshire reports that they have been pioneers of sunbathing, and that ever since the school was founded in 1893, one hour a day has been set aside for this activity. When swimming together boys and girls wore costumes, but each day they also swam in separated groups: 'then costumes though allowed are not encouraged; the great majority prefer to bathe without them.'

Subsequent editions of the review included advertisements for Children's Delight, a school at Birling Gap near Eastbourne, which welcomed pupils from the age of one, and Rocklands school in Hastings, which offered 'reform food dietary, open air and sunshine'. Fellow advertisers offered confidential developing and printing services for 'your sun bathing snaps', the monthly journal *Gymnos* – 'For nudists who think' – and 'perfectly safe' sun lamps to maintain your tan through the winter.

For the nudist who wanted to meet with others during the winter, the Lotus League was always a possibility. The spring 1934 edition of the review proclaimed:

Activities are now in full swing at the splendid new premises at North Finchley. Indoors, members play Badminton and other games in the commodious sports room. There, also, the highly efficient and popular lady instructress gives classes in physical culture, with musical accompaniment, twice weekly. Excellent refreshments (non-alcoholic) are available throughout each meeting, in the luxurious lounge. The accommodation includes: Billiard room, three bath rooms, separate heated dressing rooms, and a room where members may benefit by the health-giving rays of the Ultra-Violet Lamp in comfort, under the personal supervision of one of the directors. Boxing instruction is given by a well-known ex-champion boxer. There is a dormitory for the use of gentlemen and another for ladies . . .

Membership of the league was only open to those who successfully passed a personal interview.

Members could also visit and correspond with an increasingly international network of nudists. In 1930 the first International meeting of nudists was held in Frankfurt, with three thousand participants and delegates from Britain, France, Austria, the Netherlands, Switzerland and Greece. Clubs had already been started further afield too – in Canada in 1918, in Australia in 1926, and in the United States in 1929.[33]

In 1934 *Health and Efficiency*, a magazine that is still published today as *H&E Naturist*,[34] suggested a new term, 'naturism', to replace 'nudism'. This was not adopted generally until the 1960s, by which time nudism as an organized activity in Britain, and most other countries, was already on the decline. As this 'social nudism' carried out through clubs and organizations waned, however, the practice of nude sunbathing, swimming and holidaying began to grow in popularity. With the advent of the package holiday, anyone who wanted an all-over tan found it easier to fly to resorts abroad rather than risk the changeable British weather. And with the arrival of the Pill and Flower Power there were also other territories to conquer.

Why Don't We Do It in the Road?

The main hang-up in the world today is hypocrisy and insecurity. If people can't face up to the fact of other people being naked, or whatever they want to do, then we're never going to get anywhere. People have got to become aware that it's none of their business and that being nude is not obscene. Being ourselves is what's important. If everyone practised being themselves instead of pretending to be what they aren't, there would be peace.

—John Lennon

Human rights and liberation movements took on a new impetus as the period of post-war austerities gave way to the more liberal atmosphere of the 1960s. The rights of women, children, indigenous peoples, animals, the disabled, prisoners, and eventually in the late 1970s, the Earth, all began to be championed on both sides of the Atlantic, and in other parts of the world.

At the festivals of Woodstock and Stonehenge, and at the famous hippy 'Be-in' at San Francisco's Golden Gate Park in 1967, the keenest participants took their clothes off to dance and spend time naked to celebrate their sense of joy and freedom, but also to deliberately challenge the Establishment, and at the height of Flower Power, in 1968, John Lennon and Yoko Ono appeared naked on their *Two Virgins* record album, upholding the individual's right to simply be 'themselves' – naked or otherwise.

It took another thirty years, though, for individuals and organizations to arise to defend this right. In particular it took the reincarnation of Captain Vincent in the form of 26-year-old Vincent Bethell, who in 1998 decided it was time for direct action when his letters to the Home Office asking why he was not allowed to be naked in public received no reply. In a series of actions over the next few years, which the Captain would undoubtedly have loved to have initiated himself, Bethell, sometimes accompanied by others, began holding naked protests in Piccadilly Circus, outside

Vincent Bethell is arrested outside the Law Courts in London's Strand in 1999 during his 'Freedom to be Yourself' campaign, which protested for the right to be naked in public.

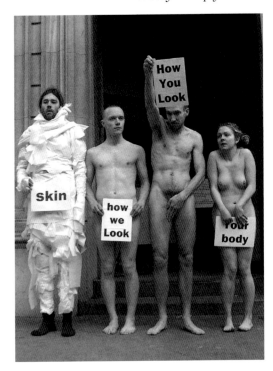

In January 2001 four members of the 'Freedom to be Yourself' campaign stood in the freezing cold outside Bow Street Magistrates Court in London's Covent Garden to protest on behalf of their colleague Russell Higgs who was in court after being arrested for handcuffing himself naked to the gates of Downing Street. Higgs claimed that 'Naked protest is a direct political and philosophical action, highlighting the absurdity of our social programming and the uniformed state that enforces it.'

Buckingham Palace, the Houses of Parliament, the Old Bailey, the National Gallery and St Paul's Cathedral, and during the Trooping of the Colour. At each protest he displayed posters and dished out leaflets carrying his message: 'The freedom to be yourself – protest naked for the right to be naked in public.' Bethell, once an art student in Coventry, also paid his respects to that patroness of the nude protest, Lady Godiva, by staging a protest walk in Coventry from the fountain to her statue.

Despite being repeatedly arrested and fined, Bethell continued his 'Freedom to Be Yourself' campaign, telling the Birmingham magistrate who denied his appeal in 2000 against a fine of £75 for indecent exposure: 'It is outrageous that because someone doesn't like the way that I look, they can say that I'm indecent.' Outside court he told journalists: 'People can see I'm a rational, lucid man who has never had a psychotic moment. The suffragettes had a hard time and had to die for their cause. I'm trying to generate a situation where nakedness in public is deemed to be acceptable.'[35] Both Vincents had evoked the image of the suffragettes, but despite

Bethell's, and more recently the 'Naked Rambler' Stephen Gough's campaigns, the suffragettes' success has eluded them. Even though they have received support from members of the public and fellow protesters, theirs have been essentially lone campaigns. Most nudists, keen to be seen as 'normal' members of society, have failed to support the campaigns, with Mark Nesbit, past editor of *H&E Naturist*, being the exception when he said: 'It takes some balls to do what he does. One of the things he highlights is this real lack of freedom we actually have in Britain. The laws prohibiting nudity in Britain are arcane and the British attitude to nudity is very odd.'[36]

Although being naked in public is not in itself an offence in Britain, police can evoke the Sexual Offences Act of 2003 if they believe it can be proved that you intend to offend someone by your behaviour. (The practice of naturism is, however, specifically excluded from this Act, thanks to the lobbying of the organization 'British Naturism', who gave evidence before a Home Affairs Select Committee of the House of Commons.) Since it is hard to prove anyone's intentions, the police are more likely to turn to the Public Order Act of 1986 to suggest that your conduct is disorderly, threatening, abusive, or is insulting behaviour, likely to cause alarm, harassment and

A protestor for the 'Right to be Naked in Public' campaign being chased by a policewoman in the fountain outside Buckingham Palace in London in June 1999.

A British policewoman chasing after a group of naked street boys by the Serpentine in Hyde Park, London, in 1926.

distress. Under this law you can only be arrested if you continue your behaviour after you have been warned by a police officer. Quickly slipping into something comfortable should render you immune to arrest, but this was not the case in 2006 when naturist campaigner Richard Collins protested against the Iraq war by cycling around Piccadilly Circus in the nude, holding a placard saying 'Naked for Peace'. The charge against him was dropped, but he was held in custody for over six hours, and as an article in *H&E Naturist* stated: 'Unfortunately it's a widespread cynical practice for the police to arrest someone they don't like on some dubious pretext, hold them in the cells overnight, and release them without charge in the morning.' Although local police in Cambridgeshire now let Collins cycle in the nude in his locality, no-one in England can be sure that they are truly free until the law is properly tested in a court of sufficient status to set a legal precedent. *H&E* believes that is unlikely for some time: 'the grey areas suit the authorities in England ... and on that basis I think it unlikely you'll ever see a Collins or a Gough in a higher court in England. This is a war of attrition more likely to be won by pushing the boundaries on a wide front, rather than a single decision in the House of Lords.'[37]

Even in the United States, which has seen more campaigning teamwork than Great Britain, the body freedom movement has found it hard to gain ground. Although according to a 1983 Gallup poll, about 72 per cent of the public in the USA approves of clothing-optional beaches (as does about 82 per cent in the UK),[38] fundamentalist Christian groups still fight to change the designation of these beaches. The Free Beach Movement has campaigned for over thirty years to keep beaches open to nudists, and in one memorable letter to the *Boston Globe* in 2002 an activist member of the movement, evoking the numerous court cases involving the sexual abuse of minors within certain churches, wrote: 'Let's re-open designated skinny-dipping beaches and ponds, but not before we have the legislation in place that no religious facility can be built within 2,000 feet of a Naturist beach. While we have never had a child molested at a Naturist beach, we are concerned about the negative secondary effects of some religious facilities.'[39]

Body freedom activists on the west coast of the United States have become adept at creating 'happenings' that combine performance art with celebration and protest, and over the years have managed to craft numerous pithy slogans to convey their message: 'Why hide your appearance?' 'Question Shame.' 'The human body: legalize it!' 'Don't arrest me – I was born this way!' 'Body shame is not a family value!' 'Government has no business setting dress codes – period.'

Despite the creativity and the verve which US campaigners put into their cause, they still represent a minority of the population. Of all human rights movements, the campaign for the freedom to be naked in public is perhaps the most doomed to failure, and it seems highly unlikely that a society will ever exist on earth that will tolerate granting that one freedom universally to its citizens. Californian Stuart Ward makes a thought-provoking and humorous attempt at depicting such a world in his novel *Strange Days Indeed: Memories of the Old World* – a fictional memoir written in the year 2061 which explores why we used to always cover our bodies and why we ate animals. In the old days, before humanity threw off the fetters of clothing, 'Life was a masquerade; costumes were compulsory.'[40] A sober look at our world suggests, however, that the masquerade will continue for some time. As Susan Stanton writes

Twenty-year-old Andrew Martinez cashing a check at his local Bank of America in 1992. Martinez achieved fame at the University of California, Berkeley, where he was known as The Naked Guy. His frequent naked appearances led to the University banning public nudity in 1992, and to the city council banning it in 1993.

in *Being Naked*: 'There is nothing mysterious about the human body. It is the human attitude toward the human body that is mysterious and bewildering.'[41]

There is, however, an irony that redeems this situation. The taboo against nakedness provides us with the thrill and the opportunity for transgression. Nakedness often engenders powerful feelings precisely because it is forbidden, and the naked human body will continue to retain its power as a political weapon for as long as it is considered unacceptable and shocking to expose it in public.

5

The Death of Shame

At Seaton while Dora was sitting on the beach I had a bathe. A boy brought me two towels as I thought, but when I came out of the water and began to use them I found that one of the rags he had given me was a pair of very short red and white striped drawers to cover my nakedness. Unaccustomed to such things and customs I had in my ignorance bathed naked and set at nought the conventionalities of the place . . .

—Revd Robert Francis Kilvert, *Diary*, 24 July 1874

So far, in this brief history, we have looked at serious reasons for getting naked: to find God, perform magic, or achieve mystical states of awareness; to gain votes or protest against injustice. But what about getting naked for fun and profit?

The male students and dons at Oxford certainly knew it could be fun when they frequented 'Parson's Pleasure', a section of the River Cherwell that runs through the University Parks, which for many years allowed nude bathing only for men. To preserve decorum, women were advised either to avert their eyes as they glided past, or to disembark and to walk along a path flanked by a fence that skirted the site. Their male companions could then haul their punt over a set of rollers and collect them further along the river. For a brief period an attempt was made to provide an area for female and family bathing too. 'Dame's Delight' was established on the river in 1934, but swimming costumes were needed there, and the area was closed in 1970. In 1991 'Parson's Pleasure' was closed too, and the fence dismantled, putting an end to a centuries-old Oxford tradition that was enjoyed by the author C. S. Lewis, amongst many others.[1] The most well-known story associated with the site recounts the time, probably in the 1940s, when a group of female students apparently floated slowly past with their gaze not averted at all, to the embarrassment of the naked dons sunning themselves on its banks. The brightest amongst them, Maurice Bowra, later to be knighted and once described by Elizabeth Longford as 'Voltaire and the Sun-King all rolled into one', quickly covered his face with a handkerchief, while the others (reported variously as Isaiah Berlin, or Hugh Trevor-Roper and John Sparrow) hastily scrambled for towels to cover their genitals. When asked why he had done this, Bowra replied 'I don't know about you, gentlemen, but in Oxford, I, at least, am known by my face.'[2]

The lengths taken to protect the bathers at Parson's Pleasure may seem surprising to us now, but its patrons had good reason to feel nervous. In 1930 a mob attacked a group of nudists who had taken to swimming and sunbathing beside the Welsh Harp reservoir in Hendon, shouting: 'Not even cannibals would lie about in that condition! Hottentots would behave with more decency: you are a rotten lot of dogs!'[3] The police were called, and this dark episode in the history of British nudism is known as the 'Welsh Harp incident'.

Parson's Pleasure by William Roberts, 1930.

Around this time even using the word 'naked' was problematic. Just after the Second World War, the BBC's guide for comedy writers and producers, known as the 'Little Green Book', warned that the word should never be used as a punchline to a joke. Such attitudes naturally had no effect on the more liberal and bohemian elements of society. The nudist movement was at the height of its popularity, with the 'Hertfordshire nuderies', as they were known, boasting as many as six resorts just a few miles away from Hendon, where a decade or so earlier the Welsh Harp incident had occurred. At Sandy Balls in Hampshire, adult members of the Order of Woodcraft Chivalry, a youth movement created in 1916 as an alternative to the Scouts, sometimes met together in the nude, following the advice of the gifted writer, artist and naturalist who inspired their movement – Ernest Thompson Seton – who believed that being naked in nature was one of the 'seven secrets of outdoor living'.[4] Across the border in Surrey, the distinguished architect Oliver Hill was in the habit of persuading guests to jump into his blue Rolls-Royce coupé with pink trim, leaving his house at Valewood Farm, near Haslemere, with its musical lavatory-paper dispenser, peacocks and parrots, to join him for naked picnics in the countryside.

A Change in the Climate – The Streakers Arrive

While eccentricity and prudery existed side by side during this time, nudity and commerce only really knew each other at the sleazy end of town – in strip joints, pin-up magazines and seedy cinemas. By the end of the century, however, they had become fast friends as the media, big business, the advertising and music industries and even the world of fundraising for charity realized that more nakedness often meant more money.

This realization was the product of a fundamental change in Western society's attitudes to sexuality that occurred as a result of three powerful influences: the theories of Freud, which revolutionized our way of thinking about human motivation, the impact of two world wars that overturned a social order that had become stifling, and the sexual liberation of the 1960s, brought about by the invention of the birth-control pill and the rise of feminism.

Sigmund Freud's *On the Interpretation of Dreams* was published on cue at the very beginning of the twentieth century. In it he proposed his theory that sexual repression caused neurosis. Sixty years later, when humanity had been exposed to the horrors of the two wars, and when the threat of nuclear annihilation hung like the sword of Damocles over it, sexual freedom seemed not only psychologically sensible, but also one of the few antidotes available to counteract the existential despair of the nuclear age.

Being naked is often an act not only of celebration, but of defiance: of the individual claiming their right simply to be, in the face of potential obliteration or of tyranny. Despite this, however much the sexual revolution may have been driven at an unconscious level by the defiance of a species facing the possibility of its extinction, at a conscious level the motivation was far simpler: the sheer pleasure of being able to express oneself freely and without inhibition was at last recognized as the birthright of every individual.

This right was exercized with exuberance by students on university campuses in the United States during the 1960s, who started running in the nude in public places for the sheer fun of it. They soon became known as 'streakers'. This activity had been occurring intermittently on American campuses since the nineteenth century, with the first recorded incident in 1804, when a student and future US Congressman, George William Crump, was suspended for one term for running naked through Lexington, Virginia. By the 1960s the time was ripe for a rise in the popularity of such escapades, with more and more students joining in the runs. By 1967 they had become so frequent that a commentator listed the social problems at one university – Carleton College – as 'the large number of departing female students, the rise of class spirit, low grades, streaking, destruction, drinking, and the popularity of rock dances.'[5]

By 1972, after a decade of teasing the campus police with their nude excursions into public places, University of Notre Dame students organized a 'Streakers' Olympics', and the following year 500 students at the University of Maryland took part in a 'mass nude run' that broadcast the term 'streaking' across the world when Associated Press reported the event. In 1974 streaking reached its height of popularity, with 1,543 students joining a mass nude run at the

Participants in the 1999 'Naked Mile' mass nude run of students that used to take place on the last day of classes of the winter semester at the University of Michigan, Ann Arbor. Since 2000 pressure from the police and the university has resulted in the tradition being abandoned.

University of Georgia, and 1,200 at the University of Colorado. Over a dozen American universities, including Harvard, Princeton and Tufts, now have a 'tradition' of streaking, developed usually in the 1970s or '80s. Each combines bravado and irreverence in a unique way, as in the University of Virginia, where before graduating, both male and female students run naked from the steps of the Rotunda and across a wide lawn to kiss the buttocks of a statue of Homer, then sprint back to the Rotunda to peer at the marble statue of the school's founder, Thomas Jefferson, through the keyhole of its door, before retrieving their clothes.

In Britain streaking began in a more individualistic form. Like Americans, the British had seen images of young people baring all at rock concerts like Woodstock and Hyde Park from 1969 onwards, and, emboldened by the spirit of the times, took to making solo dashes in public places. Sally Cooper's run across Richmond

A passing *Daily Mail* photographer scooped the attempted arrest of Sally Cooper when she ran across Richmond Bridge on 17 March 1974 to become the first streaker in Britain to achieve widespread publicity. After this photo was taken, the dog bit Ms Cooper and in the ensuing confusion she managed to escape.

Bridge in March 1974 was the first to achieve widespread publicity. As she ran, completely naked except for her jewellery, a policeman spotted her and in attempting an arrest pinned her against a wall. His dog then bit her bottom. A passing *Daily Mirror* photographer recorded the incident, which soon made news around the world.

Events that year unfolded rapidly on both sides of the Atlantic. The following month a male streaker created the most memorable moment in the history of the Oscar awards when he ran across the stage flashing a peace sign to the audience at the 46th Academy Awards ceremony in Los Angeles, just as David Niven was introducing Elizabeth Taylor. Quick as a flash Niven quipped: 'Isn't it fascinating to think that probably the only laugh that man will ever get in his life is by stripping off and showing his shortcomings?' There are some suggestions that the whole event was a stunt stage-managed by the show's producer, Jack Haley, Jr.

A few weeks later in Britain, Michael O'Brien, a young Australian accountant watching the rugby match between England and France at Twickenham, accepted a bet to run naked across the pitch. In a stroke of visual genius the arresting bobby placed his helmet over O'Brien's groin, providing the world press with photographs that could safely be printed. The bearded streaker had stretched out his arms, apparently to indicate the limits of the dash he intended to make, but his Christ-like face and head tilted as in many depictions of the crucifixion created an image which offered powerful resonances. If the photo of Sally Cooper showed the policeman and his dog as agents of repression, the photos of Michael O'Brien portrayed the police as Roman soldiers leading Christ to the cross, with the added twist that on some photographs O'Brien and a policeman are smiling at each other. The officer insists that O'Brien was saying 'Give us a kiss'. Now back in Australia, O'Brien denies this, and takes a dim view of streaking. In a recent television interview, in response to being told he had started a worldwide trend, he replied:

> That's my only regret . . . I do feel very very guilty about that. The stupidity that went on for years and years later . . . going onto live games, running onto racing tracks, it's just sheer stupidity. If Ian Bradshaw hadn't got that photograph

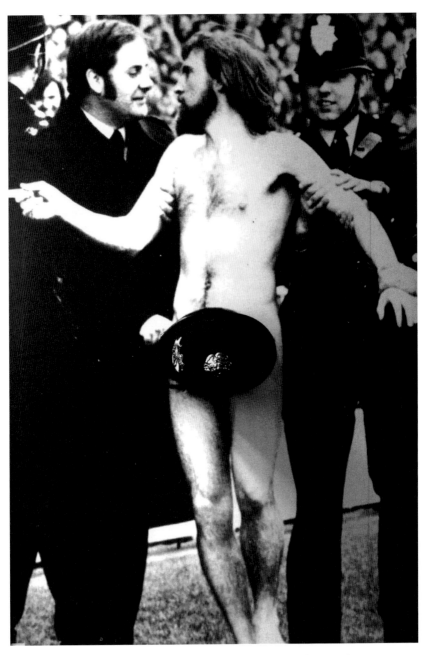

Australian accountant Michael O'Brien arrested on 20 April after streaking at Twickenham during the 1974 England vs France Rugby International. The police helmet was later sold at auction for £2,400 and went on display with a life-size copy of this photograph at the Rugby Club of London.

it probably would never have happened. There were no TV cameras at the games in those days, so I would have had a clear run, nobody but the 48,000 people in the park would have ever known about it . . . but Ian had a new camera and he just picked it up and went click click click, got the photo and the rest is history.[6]

The Australian authorities share O'Brien's view and after seven separate streaking attempts during a one-day cricket match in 1996 introduced a fine of $5,000 for pitch invasion. Potential streakers, who previously only had a public indecency fine of $150 to fear, now had to think carefully before taking the plunge – and very few have done since. In addition, any pleasure that streakers may have obtained from knowing that their exploits were being shown on television was removed when broadcasters made a decision in the 1980s to stop showing any streaks at sporting events, in an attempt to discourage them. When you are watching sport on television these days, if the view ever changes suddenly to detailed shots of the sky or anywhere rather than the pitch, while the soundtrack reveals a crowd roaring and cheering, you can be pretty sure some-one is streaking, and you are being denied the free entertainment.

Broadcasters and sportsmen may dislike streakers (in one inci-dent the cricketer Greg Chappell struck a streaker with his bat and was charged with assault) but the majority of the public love them. This is how the author of a website devoted to streaking explains it:

There's something about running madly around in the alto-gether in front of other people that is inherently humorous. Perhaps it is the infectious glee exhibited by the often drunk runner, the absurdity of the small battle between unclothed bravado and half-smiling authority, or the shock of seeing bare flesh in an ocean of clothing. Certainly it is the sight of jiggling rude bits and flabby pale behinds gadding wantonly about in the fresh air before being tackled ungracefully by puffing policemen. Streaking is an important activity. In a time when the media teaches us to believe in the perfect beauty of the human species, it is a reminder of what is normal for most of us. It thumbs its nose (or other

A streaker vaults over the stumps in mid-play at Lord's cricket ground, London, in August 1975.

appendages) at outdated public exposure laws in the true anarchic tradition of flaunting authority. It represents what we may have looked like 50,000 years ago while chasing mammoths. It livens up the cricket.[7]

In 2007 a Magistrates' Court in Liverpool accepted the fact that streakers provide entertainment and refused to grant an ASBO (Anti-Social Behaviour Order) to Merseyside police who wanted

A streaker is
removed from the
pitch by a player at
the Molde Stadium,
Norway, in July
2000.

to curb the antics of inveterate streaker Mark Roberts, who at the
age of 42 has clocked up 380 streaks on two continents. *The Independent* reported that 'there is barely a sport that he has not disrupted.
He has been seen cantering along the course during Ladies' Day at
Ascot, prancing through the Crucible Theatre during the 2004
world snooker final, dashing down the fairway during the Open
Golf Championship, with "19th hole" emblazoned on his back, and
vaulting the net during a women's doubles match at Wimbledon,
wearing nothing but a message saying "Only balls should bounce".'
After weighing the evidence, District Judge Nick Sanders pronounced: 'What Mr Roberts does may be annoying but, in my
opinion, it does not amount to antisocial behaviour.' The judge may
have been swayed in his verdict by the wit of Roberts's lawyer, who
defended the behaviour of his client, arrested after he ran around

the green at the Open Golf Championship, just as Tiger Woods was about to tee off, with a toy squirrel covering his genitals and a golf ball between his buttocks. His lawyer declared: 'My client has turned over a new fig leaf. He accepts that some people might be offended. But this is good, old fashioned British fun.'[8]

While streakers continue to entertain or annoy us, the phenomenon actually peaked over thirty years ago in 1974, although in the years that followed a number of spectacular streaks continued to maintain a tradition that seems particularly concentrated in Britain and America. Erica Roe's 1982 topless streak during an England vs Australia rugby match at Twickenham has become one of the most iconic. Photographs of her being tackled by the police again provided powerful images of youthful enthusiasm and joie-de-vivre battling against the forces of authority and repression. It was the perfect picture to represent the rise of women's confidence, showing a goddess offering us her breasts at the very moment the agents of patriarchy struggled to hide them. Ms Roe, who claimed alcohol as the inspiration for her attempt, apparently secured over £80,000 in television and modelling contracts after her appearance.

Streakers had become such a feature of games in England that in 2004 a 'Streaker set' was marketed for table football enthusiasts for 'tactical delay to play'.

Erica Roe enjoys a cigarette and the attentions of two policemen, having streaked topless at an England vs Australia Rugby Test Match at Twickenham in 1982.

The Urge to Be Seen – Exhibitionism and Flashing

Bishop Berkeley worried that if he wasn't looking at the world, it might disappear. I worry that if the world isn't looking at me, I might. Or at least I used to.
— Kathleen Rooney, *Live Nude Girl: My Life as an Object*

Some people dismiss streakers, naked protesters and even nudists and life models as 'exhibitionists' without fully appreciating that we are all, to a greater or lesser extent, motivated by exhibitionism. We learn to be that way in order to stay alive. A baby needs to be seen and to be noticed by its mother, and this need continues to operate in us throughout our lives. As evidence of this, in the past one of the greatest punishments was ostracism, and today one of the most effective ways to hurt someone lies in simply ignoring them – failing to acknowledge even their existence. Every human being is motivated by this deep desire to be seen, to have attention paid to them, to be noticed and to be heard.

If, deep down, we all want to be the centre of attention, what better way to fulfil this need than to stand, naked and in silence, before the concentrated gaze of a group of people for several hours? Accounts given by life models show that this activity could represent a healthy and adaptive way not only to receive attention, but also to engage in a deeper process. When Sarah Phillips interviewed models for her book *Modeling Life*, many of them explained how their work developed their self-awareness, and how vital it was to 'be present' during a session. One model told her that, for him, modelling was a 'devotional act' in which 'I can witness the spirit in my body and the way in which that is manifest.'[9]

Life modelling can result in a heightened awareness of one's sensuality and a deep sense of appreciation and fulfilment that comes from feeling metaphorically 'caressed' by the gaze of the artists around one. The writer Kathleen Rooney's memoir of six years as a life model, *Live Nude Girl: My Life as an Object*, reveals the rich vein of experience that can be tapped by someone willing to explore its effects on their psyche, which include: 'A spine-tingling combination of power and vulnerability, submission and dominance.' She goes on to describe the very first moments of a session:

Standing as a potent symbol of freedom and personal empowerment, a singer at the
V Festival in Chelmsford, Essex, August 2004, raises her microphone as the crowd cheers.

American artist Skip Arnold specializes in using his own naked body as art: standing as a statue or squatting as a gargoyle on buildings, sitting in a perspex box in a gallery, or here lying face down in June 2002 at the Art Basel 33 exhibition in Switzerland.

An inflatable naked self-portrait of Polish artist Pawel Althamer exhibited in the Palazzina Appiani Sports Arena in Milan, June 2007. The artist wrote: 'it is a major achievement to realise that the body is only a vehicle for the soul. I feel like a cosmonaut in the suit of my own body. I am a trapped soul.'

The first thirty seconds of nudity are always the most jar-
ring, charged for me and for those who are looking at me . . .
The disrobing is a gentle shock, a surprise, a kind of eye-
wash, and the instant is electrified, more vivid than those
which preceded it and those that will come after. My nudity
might seem unreal, as if it can't really be happening, as if
this strange other person can't possibly be presenting herself without a stitch and letting her body be drawn. So too
might my nudity feel hyper-real, as if this person is the
most three-dimensional object in space, vulnerable in her
nakedness, but powerful in her command of the entire
room's studious and uninterrupted attention . . .[10]

Exhibitionism is a term used in common parlance to denote
'showing off', but it is clear from the accounts of models that much
more than the simple desire to display or be noticed is driving their
behaviour. Exhibitionism, however, is not just a derogatory term
used in everyday language. It is also a term used in psychiatry to
describe a psychopathology. The vast majority of exhibitionists, or

A policeman advising model Anne Bruzac to get dressed in London's Carnaby Street
in 1977.

There are many ways to fulfil a tendency to exhibitionism. A driver with a customized car displaying a photograph of her body, 1980.

Nudity can be tiresome in the cold or rain. Here a designer has attempted to at least partly solve the problem by designing a transparent raincoat.

'flashers' as they are popularly called, are male and are almost invariably driven by the desire to expose just one part of their body: their genitals. Feeling weak and inadequate, exhibitionists are turned on by shocking and frightening their victims. Their kick comes from the sense of power this gives them, although they are usually so filled with guilt and internal conflicts that this kick is short-lived and they almost always flee the scene soon after their exposure. Commonly the habit develops into an obsessive-compulsive disorder that requires the behaviour to be repeated more and more frequently. Although the majority of flashers do not physically molest their victims, they sometimes masturbate in front of them. Sadly recidivism is high: up to 50 per cent of men arrested for exhibitionism are re-arrested within two years, and there is no consensus amongst the psychiatric community as to the pathology's aetiology, although it is sometimes associated with brain damage or schizophrenia. Nor is there an effective cure, or a clear understanding as to why the problem afflicts men almost exclusively.

However much critics of streaking may want to suggest that streakers are just flashers who play to a bigger crowd, leaving aside the fact that plenty of women enjoy streaking, there is as much

Spoof flashers at the 32nd Annual Village Halloween Parade in New York, October 2005.

difference between a streaker and a flasher as between a naturist and a streaker. Naturists make a lifestyle choice: they prefer living without clothes and just want to be left in peace to swim, sunbathe and socialize in the nude. They have no desire to shock people or to achieve five minutes of fame by sprinting across a rugby pitch. In contrast, streakers are 'up for a lark' and are probably born entertainers, or drunk, and are no more driven by the desire to live in the nude as they are to frighten people with their genitals.

The Desire to See – The Voyeur in Us All

The desire to see and to be seen is one and the same.
—Tertullian

Alongside our innate urge to be seen lies our need to see. There is a natural voyeuristic tendency in all of us that in some cases can become distorted, resulting in the psychiatric pathology in which the sufferer can only achieve sexual arousal or satisfaction by watching other people undressing, naked, or engaged in erotic acts.

The interest in observing another person or being observed naked is not in itself considered pathological, and a healthy relationship can often include times in which lovers take pleasure in simply watching each other being naked or engaging in sexual activity. As with exhibitionism this only becomes pathological when it becomes obsessive or the only means whereby an individual can achieve satisfaction.

The exhibitionist and voyeurist tendencies within one individual can even be satisfied simultaneously when observer and observed become the same person through the use of a mirror, and the photographer Uwe Ommer has created a book based upon this idea. Ommer gave friends and models cameras and invited them to enjoy photographing themselves in the nude using an actual mirror, or the camera itself as a way of mirroring their image.[11]

The use of a mirror or camera to enjoy observing oneself in the nude could simply be a symptom of narcissism, but it can equally represent a creative response to an individual's need to develop pride and confidence in their own body, and at the same time an

A semi-nude woman can be seen doing chores through a window on 'The Voyeur Bus' in Times Square in New York City in November 2000. The bus was travelling around America to promote the First Amendment right of free speech.

economical way to satisfy both the need to see nakedness and be seen naked. Such an activity may even have at its heart the conscious or unconscious desire to attain self-realization, and can be used as the basis of a meditation in which the process of self-reflection is enhanced by being physically enacted.[12]

Any doubt that we are not naturally voyeuristic as well as exhibitionistic is called into question by the popularity of sites such as Jennicam – a website which ran for seven years that allowed the public to view the everyday activities of a young woman, Jennifer Ringley, thanks to first one, and then a set of webcams she placed in her home. Viewers could, for example, watch eight hours of live transmission of darkness as she slept, hours of views of an empty room when she went out, but they could also occasionally catch glimpses of her in the nude, or even having sexual intercourse or masturbating. Soon three to four million visits a day were being made to her site, she was featured in *The Wall Street Journal*, and appeared on the *David Letterman* show. Hailed by some as a conceptual artist, Ringley claimed that she improved her self-image and body image by running the site and later appeared nude in the magazine *Celebrity Sleuth*. Now in her thirties, she is reported to be enjoying the experience of privacy.

The avenues that people find to fulfil their desires are myriad, and the urge to be seen naked or to see nakedness can lead to behaviour that seems disturbing to some and liberating to others. The arrival of the internet and digital media have created a host of new ways for these desires to find expression. The voyeur can look at nakedness and erotic activity of every kind from the privacy of their own home. The exhibitionist can display themselves to the world with the click of a mouse. For a brief period eBay sellers could amuse themselves by dabbling in 'reflect-o-porn' – posting photographs of shiny goods for sale that just happened to be reflecting an image of their naked owner. This avenue of pleasure has now been closed, but there are plenty of other opportunities for the internet poseur. Those who enjoy the thrill of being observed in public places can post their photos on public nudity sites, while those who would like to be watched, perhaps even examined or humiliated in the nude by clothed members of the opposite sex can explore the busy world of CFNM (Clothed Female Naked Male) or the less popular world of CMNF. Men with iPhones can post photos of themselves in the nude with their phones on a dedicated website, or they can forget the phone and most of the body and allow the whole world to gaze at their 'divinity', as Salvador Dalí termed his best friend, by posting a photo of their penis on other sites.

The more socially inclined might prefer a visit to the virtual reality of Second Life, where you can choose to roam its world naked. Many venues will bar you, but fly to 'Nude Island' and you could find yourself being propositioned in a cave or on the beach. You can keep up to date with current events by watching the internet TV channel 'Naked News', which hosts news anchors who strip while announcing the latest disasters. You can videochat in the nude, you can enter the 'nudist blogosphere', or post a naked vlog from the waist-up on Youtube, or the waist-down on one of the new porn sites that host videos from members of the public, and which are now so popular they threaten the porn industry's film-makers as much as the internet now threatens the conventional film industry, television companies and the music business.

The gift of the internet has been DIY (Do It Yourself). It is the individual who has benefited more than the giants of the corporate world. Just as you can now publish your own book or start a shop or

Naked News, based in Toronto, broadcasts news and current events programmes to more than 135 countries and claims an audience of 25 million weekly viewers. To launch its European expansion, presenters Lily Kwan and Sam Page posed topless for photographers in London in August 2004.

record label from your own computer, so you can make your own material that features nudity and watch others' home-grown attempts for free. As a result the distinction between a normal or natural tendency to exhibitionism and voyeurism and their darker manifestations in psychiatric pathology has become blurred. What is liberating for one person can easily become addictive for another, or even for the same person when the ease of the internet means that an experience that was initially cathartic, or simply undertaken out of curiosity, can enter the service of a neurosis and become a compulsion.

Unhealthy attitudes breed in an atmosphere of ignorance and secrecy, and although the internet has greatly helped to dispel ignorance by disseminating information and satisfying our curiosity about the human body, it has also fostered the corrosive effects of secrecy and shame by enabling people to hide behind virtual masks and prey on others. Even so, as Ruth Barcan explains in *Nudity: A Cultural Anatomy*: 'As a technology, the Internet helps fuel moral change, since it encourages both anonymity (and hence experimentation) and community (which encourages both the sharing of interests and a consequent push towards moral normalization).'[13]

The real advance in liberating our attitudes and redressing centuries of repression has come, however, not from the internet but from the world of the arts.

The Theatre and the Death of Shame

We live in an atmosphere of shame. We are ashamed of everything that is real about us; ashamed of ourselves, of our relatives, of our incomes, of our accents, of our opinions, of our experience, just as we are ashamed of our naked skins.

—George Bernard Shaw, *Man and Superman*

In Germany naked people managed to get on stage at the beginning of the twentieth century. For six years, from 1907, Karl Vanselow held *Schonheitsabends* (Beauty Evenings) in Berlin that presented lantern slides of nude men and women to the accompaniment of a live string orchestra. Further slides of famous nude paintings then heralded the arrival of naked dancers, who at one time included Isadora Duncan. By 1913 Vanselow had spent a fortune defending his right through the courts to hold these evenings, and although he had won every battle with organizations such as the Cologne Morality Association, he was in poor health and died the following year at the age of 38.

Isadora Duncan was naturally drawn to Vanselow's productions because she believed in the sacredness of the naked human body and its importance to the expression of art. A believer in the reality of the Greek deities and an advocate of dress reform, she wrote: 'the noblest art is the nude. This truth is recognized by all, and followed by painters, sculptors and poets. Only the dancer has forgotten it, who should remember it, as the instrument of art is the human body itself.'[14] In private she danced in the nude, saying 'Dancing naked upon the earth I naturally fall into Greek positions.'[15] In London she danced for Lawrence Alma-Tadema, whose paintings of nudes in idealized classical settings were once thought kitsch and are now highly valued. And it was Alma-Tadema who showed the young Isadora the museums of London and led her to study the positions of figures on Greek vases.

Frozen images of naked bodies, as if on a vase, were all that were allowed on the British stage until 1968. Only women could be seen naked in the theatre and then only if they remained motionless, which is why Mrs Henderson (played by Judi Dench in the 2005 film *Mrs Henderson Presents*) had to direct her girls at the Wyndham Theatre to form *tableaux vivants* – an idea also used by Vanselow in Berlin, who called these artificial poses *Lebende Plastiken* (Living Sculpture). The same concept applied in striptease clubs and to the nude revues at the Folies Bergère in Paris, and elsewhere, where dancers and strippers would endlessly tease before freezing in position when dropping the last stitch.

Even when actors remained motionless, the Lord Chamberlain, then responsible for censorship, still felt obliged to step in on occasion. In 1957 the nude Britannia in John Osborne's play *The Entertainer* was scrutinized but allowed. A naked male figure was different, though, and ten years later a nude statue of Lyndon Johnson was forbidden in the play *Mrs Wilson's Diary*. A year after that everything changed, with the Lord Chamberlain being stripped of his powers to stop others stripping, when the new Theatres Act was introduced which abolished censorship of the stage.[16]

The Musical that Changed Everything

The year 1968 has become known as 'the Year of Revolutions' – it was the year of the Prague Spring, of student protests around the world, of the Paris riots, of the assassinations of Robert Kennedy and Martin Luther King. And it was the year a musical opened on Broadway that was to act as a catalyst for much of the nudity that exploded on to the stage from this time onwards – it was called simply *Hair*. An exuberant celebration of hippie ideals, created at a time when America was still fighting in Vietnam, it had a simple political and social message: stop fighting wars, make love as often as possible and get high. As an insight into the supremacy of the image over the word, the musical is remembered more for its brief nude scene than its provocative lyrics in its song 'Sodomy'.

The musical's creators, Gerome Ragni and James Rado, got the inspiration for the nude scene from seeing two naked war protesters in Central Park. Scott Miller explained its relevance to the musical in *Rebels with Applause: Broadway's Ground-Breaking Musicals*: 'nudity was a big part of the hippie culture, both as a rejection of the sexual repression of their parents and also as a statement about naturalism, spirituality, honesty, openness, and freedom. The naked body was beautiful, something to be celebrated and appreciated, not scorned and hidden. They saw their bodies and their sexuality as gifts, not as "dirty" things.'[17]

Even though the musical broke new ground by including nudity, the naked scene still followed the familiar pattern of a frozen tableau. Those actors who wished to participate undressed behind a screen and then emerged to sing of 'beads, flowers, freedom, and happiness' while standing motionless as floral patterns were projected on to their bodies. The moment was over so quickly, the lighting so dim, that Jack Benny was heard asking: 'Did you happen to notice if any of them were Jewish?'

Despite the coyness of the nudity, *Hair* was conveying ideas that resonated with the spirit of the time, and later that year the show came to London's West End and was soon being produced in Europe. With the abolition of theatre censorship in Britain that year, male nudes could now be seen on stage, and the musical was a huge success, even though some critics complained about the 'much-touted nudity, which seemed to take place in semi-darkness'.[18] Charles Marowitz wrote 'If one is going to show butts, boobs and assorted genitalia in a show like *Hair*, it must be, like everything else in the show, in a blaze of abandon.'[19]

The cast of the London production apparently had the greatest difficulty in freeing themselves sufficiently of inhibitions to appear naked even in the dim lighting. In France they had no problem; in Germany early productions of the scene were played behind a sheet entitled 'Censored' until permission was granted by the authorities, who were shamed into acquiescence when a local *Hair* spokesman declared that his relatives had been marched nude into Auschwitz. Of all the casts, the Germans were perhaps the most sensitized to the political implications of nakedness. The singer and songwriter Donna Summer, who was in the German production, commented: 'it was not meant to be sexual in any way. We stood naked to comment on the fact that society makes more of nudity than killing.'[20]

The cast of *Leve-Toi et Viens* (Get up and Come) the French production of the musical *Hair* at a performance in Paris in July 1975.

Audiences in San Francisco were happy to enter into the spirit of the moment – they loved the nakedness and even meditated with the cast before the show – while in Norway protesters formed a human barricade in an attempt to prevent performances. In Sweden the cast was reluctant to undress, while in Denmark they didn't think there was enough nakedness and chose to walk down the aisle in the nude during the prelude.

In the world of films the taboo against seeing full-frontal nudity was also broken in the Year of Revolutions. Nudity had arrived on the screen in Britain in the 1950s with naturist films such as *Naked as Nature Intended*, which featured wholesome men and women playing with beach balls or sunbathing in environments plagued with bushes and trees which foiled every attempt by the camera to reveal them totally nude. But in 1968 Lindsay Anderson's *If . . .* and the Swedish film *Hugs and Kisses* showed full-frontal nudity, while in the following year Ken Russell's *Women in Love* showed two naked men wrestling. Either the rot had set in or the fun had just begun.[21]

Mick Jagger, Anita Pallenberg and Michele Breton, in a scene from the film *Performance*, 1970.

Nakedness on the London Stage

When people speak of nudity in theatrical performance, they tend to refer to actions in which actors expose their genital organs to the audience. Even to an entirely female audience, female performers who expose their breasts will appear more 'naked' than male performers who expose their bare chests. Nudity in performance refers to the exposure of the most erotically exciting and excitable sexual identifiers of the body, with exposed genitals being the most complete 'proof' of the body's vulnerability to desire and the appropriating gaze of the Other. However, this view of nudity entails some difficulties in relation to theatrical practice. For instance, some performers have used flesh-colored body-stockings to simulate nudity, while others have used prosthetic genitals or breasts as part of a costume which in fact conceals the body of the performer. Consider also those theatrical scenes in which the spectator knows the actor is really nude but cannot see this nudity 'sufficiently', because clever light and shadow 'veil' the body.

—Karl Eric Toepfer, *Nudity and Textuality in Postmodern Performance* [22]

However briefly glimpsed, however poorly lit, the nude scene in *Hair* was enough to help light a torch of freedom that still burns today. In June 1968, just a few months after *Hair* opened in

New York, the Royal Shakespeare Company broke the taboo on female nudes moving on stage. The new Theatres Act that allowed this would not be passed until September of that year, but the ice was melting and the RSC decided they could risk a Helen of Troy who was not only naked but mobile.

Producers and directors soon realized that nakedness sells tickets, and a trend developed for nude cameo scenes, preferably undertaken by famous actors: Diana Rigg and Keith Michell engaged in a nude love scene in Ronald Millar's *Abelard and Heloise* at the Wyndham Theatre in 1971. In the same year theatregoers could see naked rugby players in the showers in David Storey's *The Changing Room* at the Royal Court. A few years later Peter Shaffer's play *Equus* was staged at the Old Vic, with its revival in 2007 receiving much publicity due to the fact that the role of the young man, who plays a sex scene naked, was taken by the seventeen-year-old Daniel Radcliffe, who had played the lead role in the *Harry Potter* films. Similarly, Nicole Kidman's brief display of nudity in *The Blue Room* in London and New York in the late 1990s caused great media attention, as did Kathleen Turner and then Jerry Hall, a few years later, when they disrobed as Mrs Robinson in a production of *The Graduate* in London.

It was only the nude scene in *The Romans in Britain* directed by Michael Bogdanov at the National Theatre in 1980 that ran into any trouble, and that was not because of the nakedness of the druids on stage, but because of the simulated act of homosexual rape one of them was obliged to suffer, which offended campaigner Mary Whitehouse sufficiently for her to undertake a private prosecution under the Sexual Offences Act.[23]

Today nakedness has found its legitimate place in the theatre, at least in much of Europe and on the liberal east and west coasts of the United States. It may sometimes be used gratuitously to fill the house, but if theatre is to portray life, of which nakedness is an integral part, it cannot help but include it. As the critic Michael Billington writes: 'We should treat it as a dramatic imperative or as something designed to give erotic pleasure . . . we should accept that nudity can be a deeply pleasurable spectacle.'[24] In pointing to the value of depicting both the naked and the erotic on stage, the Comédie-Française actor Alexandre Pavloff explained: 'We used to

Naked druids in a scene from the play *The Romans in Britain* by Howard Brenton, directed by Michael Bogdanov at the National Theatre, London, October 1980.

hide our bodies but they are part of us and we cannot exclude them from art. We talk openly about eroticism nowadays, everyone, not just actors or dancers. As we reveal our bodies, we reveal our souls.'[25]

Naked Dance

> Well, it would be awkward, wouldn't it, with all those bits and bobs
> bobbing and bitting around all the time.
> —Sir Robert Helpmann[26]

The Australian dancer and choreographer Robert Helpmann's concern that dancers and audiences in classical ballet might find total nakedness awkward is clearly widely held, since little use has been made of total nudity on the ballet stage. There have been exceptions, though, such as the naked dancing included in the Royal Danish Ballet's production of *The Triumph of Death* in 1971, and the Russian National Ballet's production of *Romeo and Juliet* in 2005.

Actor Sonia Segura gets the thumbs up from assistant director Valentina Carrasco after her performance of typing on a keyboard naked in a giant fish tank at a press call for Spain's controversial La Fura Dels Baus theatre company's production of *XXX*, a modern adaptation of the Marquis de Sade story 'Philosophy of the Bedroom', in Melbourne, February 2004.

Helpmann's concern was also voiced by Kenneth MacMillan when he apparently said 'The problem with nude ballet is that when the dancer stops, not all of the dancer stops', but this failed to deter the marketing manager of the English National Ballet when he persuaded the males of the company to strip for the ball scene in *Swan Lake* at the Albert Hall in 2002. The giant poster advertising the event featured a triple-entendre headline: the dancers were draped around the waist with the flags of the eleven World Cup countries and it read: 'Spot the Ball?'

Nakedness in ballet may still be rare, but when it comes to contemporary dance there has been even more nakedness over the last fifty years than there has been in the theatre. And, again, it was the sexual revolution of the 1960s that acted as the catalyst for this phenomenon.

Although dancers such as Isadora Duncan, at the end of the nineteenth century, and Rudolf Laban, at the beginning of the twentieth, had experimented with dancing naked when not on stage, it was only in the 1960s that public performances featuring nude dancers became possible, and again it was the revolutionary currents of the time that acted as the catalysts for this phenomenon. In Japan student riots and the questioning of authority led to the development of a radical form of contemporary dance that came to be known as *butoh*, in which naked or semi-naked dancers, often covered in white body make-up as in traditional Japanese dance, expressed intense emotions and were fearless in confronting taboos.

In the West, the same impulse to break with tradition and explore new frontiers led Anna Halprin, believed by many to be 'the mother of postmodern dance', to bring her dance troupe to New York in 1967 to give a performance which finished in a blaze of yellow light with the dancers cavorting naked in a pile of brown corrugated paper. Clive Barnes explains what happened next:

> For this they were hauled up in a New York court on either obscenity or public decency charges. I was subpoenaed as a witness, and a bushy-tailed assistant DA asked, 'Mr. Barnes, did you find the naked women sexually stimulating?' I replied no. He then looked piercingly at the presiding judge, and, presumably noting my English accent and charming

lisp, asked, in tones of Perry Mason-like triumph, 'Did you, by chance, find the naked men stimulating?'[27]

The court may have succeeded in stopping Halprin for a moment, but naked dance was here to stay, and New York became one of the most significant centres for the genre. In 1968 Merce Cunningham rejected the advice of Andy Warhol to use naked dancers in Cunningham's production *Rainforest*, and resorted to skin-coloured unitards. Within a few years, though, completely nude performers were being increasingly seen on stage, as in Yvonne Rainer's *Trio A*, which featured dancers wearing American flags like bibs in a production that explored a debate about the desecration of the flag. One of the dancers, David Gordon, later recounted his feelings about the show: 'I was 35 years old and I did not love my body. I pulled my pants and underwear down and put them in a pile like an obsessive little creature, tied the bloody flag around my neck and went out there to do it . . . I was doing somersaults buck naked with a flag around my neck. It was the most terrifying and embarrassing experience, and I never did it again.'[28]

A dancer who was not terrified of appearing nude on stage, the Venezuelan-born Javier De Frutos, who trained with the London Contemporary Dance Theatre, helped to familiarize English audiences with nudity when he returned from working with Merce Cunningham in New York in the 1990s. De Frutos quickly became known for his exciting choreography and frequent appearances in the nude.

By the new millennium more and more contemporary dance productions in New York and around the world began to use naked dancers, prompting Gia Kourlas, in his 2006 essay 'The Bare Essentials of Dance', to explain the current resurgence of productions involving nudity: 'Contemporary dance and nudity are hardly strangers, but in many recent performances skin has practically taken the place of costume. At the moment, the upsurge isn't rooted in sexual liberation, as it was when nude bodies appeared onstage in the 1960s, or in political defiance, as when they re-emerged in the 80s. Instead, choreographers are baring it all as a way to reveal something essential about human experience. The nudity on view is tough and raw yet unmistakably vulnerable.'[29]

RoseLee Goldberg, the founding director of Performa, a New York-based organization devoted to research and performance by visual artists, suggests that the latest interest in nakedness amongst choreographers may represent a desire to return to basics: 'It seems like every now and then we need to remember that choreography is about the body.'[30] This view is shared by a leading proponent of nude dancing in France, the dancer and choreographer Boris Charmatz, whose troupe regularly perform naked.

The obvious criticism that nudity is simply being used as a gimmick is swiftly dismissed by Steven Heathcote, principal dancer at the Australian Ballet, when he says: 'For me, nudity in performance of any kind is all about context. It's very obvious when nudity is gratuitously included . . . when appropriately used, however, it can create a sense of vulnerability and intimacy for audience and performers alike.'[31]

The creation of this sense of vulnerability and intimacy represents one of the most effective uses of nakedness on stage. Maria Ede-Weaving, a member of the audience at a performance in 1997 by the physical theatre group DV8 entitled *Bound to Please*, describes her reaction:

> It was a contemporary piece that dealt with the taboo of love between an older woman and a younger man. The female dancer was in her sixties, maybe older. There was a key moment when she appeared alone and naked with a bowl of water and began to simply wash herself. In our culture, the very act of a woman of her age stripping naked in public might sadly for some have been a challenge, particularly in the wider context of the dance piece where the sexual interaction between her and the young man was so powerfully explored. In this one simple moment of her being alone and naked, utterly exposed to the audience with all its potential prejudices and negative preconceptions, her body expressed such moving tenderness, poignancy and power. It was an incredibly intimate moment. There we all were, a theatre full of clothed strangers watching what felt like, to me at least, the unveiling of someone's soul. It made me feel very tearful and not a little naked myself. I keep

Members of the Canadian dance group Dave St-Pierre and Compagny performing in the KraftWerk in Wolfsburg, Germany, in May 2005, in the production *La Pornographie des Ames* (The Pornography of Souls).

thinking of Blake's notion of the body being an extension of the soul, and it seems to be that in true nakedness, physical and psychological, the soul speaks. It doesn't matter how much we use our emotional and intellectual defences to cover up or hide ourselves, the body seems reluctant to join in with the lie. We can deny what we feel and yet our bodies are shaped by what we have experienced, sculpted by our emotions, and so to undress is to expose our story. When someone has the courage to stand truly naked before us, the courage to share that story, something deep within us has the potential to be unveiled too.[32]

Opera in the Buff

If opera ventures increasingly down this path, it will have to grapple with the same questions of relevance, gimmickiness and sensationalism that have dogged theater, film and dance.
—Anthony Tommasini, *Take it Off, Brünnhilde: On Opera and Nudity*

Tommasini's remark in the *New York Times*, made in response to the sight of naked flesh in the 2009 production of Strauss's *Salome* in New York, cuts to the heart of the debate about the use of nudity on stage. Is it really justified? Is it just being used to titillate and to get people on to seats? To ask these questions, though, suggests that art should ignore financial realities and shun attempts to seduce or excite its audience. Titillation and economic motives alone do not make good art, but they do not have to be antithetical to it either.

It is true that producers sometimes have to work hard to attract new audiences since opera is often perceived as a hopelessly anachronistic art form that will eventually become as extinct as the dodo. The temptation to use nudity to demonstrate that it is alive, well and relevant is clearly present, but in opera, of all media, artistic sensibilities are finely tuned and the results have been impressive.

The 'Dance of the Seven Veils' in Strauss's *Salome* is an obvious candidate for some legitimate titillation as veil after veil can be removed to reveal the soprano in all her glory. At the Metropolitan opera house in 2004 and again in 2009 it was Karita Mattila who stripped naked to offer a portrayal that was in one critic's words: 'emotionally intense, vocally molten and psychologically exposed'.[33] At the Opera di Roma in 2007 audiences were promised a fifteen-minute prologue that would display 'due Salome al prezzo di una. E tutt'e due nude' (Two Salomes for the price of one, and both nude). Soprano Francesca Patanè was accompanied in this prologue by the actress Maruska Albertazzi who promised to appear 'sara nuda, completamente depilata' (I will be naked, completely hairless).[34] Audiences were not disappointed.

There is a refreshing honesty in the Opera di Roma publicity that some might find too brazen, preferring instead the understated approach of Glyndebourne, whose naked Sierva Maria in the 2008 production of Peter Eotvos's *Love and Other Demons* was so cunningly lit that only those in the first few rows of the stalls could possibly determine whether she too was 'depilata'.

There are some operas, though, that cry out for a good display of naked bodies: Verdi's *Rigoletto* is one of them, and David McVicar's 2000 production for the Royal Opera House in Britain made full use of nudity and of simulated sex acts, as did the Dutch Opera Spanga's film version, set in the 1960s, and released on DVD in 2003. The Moldovian Chisinau Touring Opera's 2006 version, following in their wake, received considerably less critical acclaim.

Of all the arts, some of the greatest risks in the use of nakedness have been taken in opera – perhaps to overcome the stigma of
inaccessibility, perhaps simply because, of all art forms, opera can 'get
away with it' since it is seen as so sophisticated. The most provocative productions have emanated from Austria. In 1995 a Viennese
artist, Hermann Nitsch, was commissioned by the Vienna State
Opera to design the sets and costumes for Massenet's *Hérodiade*, in
which the heroine lets her veil fall beside the decapitated head of
John the Baptist. Over 40 complaints were received by the opera
house, not because of any nudity, but because of Nitsch's copious
use of red paint and simulated blood.

Nitsch's full use of nudity came instead in his Das Orgien Mys-
terien Theater (Orgy Mystery Theatre) productions, which have
included naked women strapped to horses and crucifixes, the
slaughter and disembowelling of animals, and audiences being
sprayed with blood. In one six-day event, held at his castle in 1998,
the audience experienced the slaughter of three bulls (which the
audience then ate), marching bands, Gregorian music, church bells,
and synthesizer music playing while an army tank burst onto the
castle grounds and was doused with blood and roses.

In comparison, Austrian director Johann Kresnik's production
of Verdi's *A Masked Ball* for the Erfurt theatre in Germany 2008

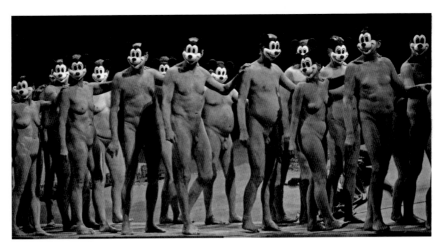

Actors wearing Mickey Mouse masks perform on stage during a rehearsal of Giuseppe
Verdi's opera *A Masked Ball* directed by Austrian Johann Kresnik, in April 2008 at
Erfurt, Germany.

seems almost bland. It featured many naked young women, a female singer wearing a red swimsuit, sporting a Hitler moustache and performing Nazi salutes, and 35 naked pensioners wearing Mickey Mouse masks, cavorting amongst the ruins of Ground Zero at the World Trade Centre. Kresnik, a Marxist, and well-known in the German-speaking world for his prediliction for lavish displays of nudity and provocative, anti-capitalist productions, said: 'The naked stand for people without means, the victims of capitalism, the underclass, who don't have anything anymore.'[35]

As Kresnik's production opened in Erfurt, The Royal Opera House in London began planning its first nude charity calendar on behalf of Macmillan Cancer Support. The result, 'A World Stage Revealed', a calendar for 2009, shows their five male Carmen dancers in the Full Monty finale position with hats on their groins, Emma Turner of Stage Management boldly posing on the roof of the opera house, clutching at a scarf to hide her pudendum, and dancer Zenaida Yanowsky showing us her naked pregnant belly. Despite its cloaking of groins and nipples, the calendar is symptomatic of the times. Nakedness is no longer the province of hippies or the wild artistic left. It's mainstream and has gone upmarket.

Nude Orchestras and Shameless Rock Stars

Orchestras have tended to steer clear of nude performances, so it took a Japanese pornography producer Zenra to create The Stark Naked Orchestra. Zenra, who specialize in making films of naked women participating in everyday tasks normally undertaken clothed, brought together a group of twenty young female musicians who performed to an audience in a concert hall during which they were filmed for a DVD which is widely available on the internet.

Orchestras might be shy, but such a trait is rarely possessed by rock musicians. Jim Morrison is famous for having once produced his penis onstage in Miami in 1969, and Courtney Love has flaunted her breasts while playing live, but more meaningful exposures have also occurred. In 1993 the band Rage Against the Machine protested against censorship by the Parents Music Resource

A 'Body Festival' organized by Japanese artist Yayoi Kusama in New York, *c.* 1967.

Center by standing onstage naked in Philadelphia for 15 minutes with duct-tape on their mouths, and Alanis Morisette presented the 2004 Juno awards in a nude suit complete with nipples and pubic hair attached by velcro which she then removed, to protest against United States censorship. In the video of her hit 'Thank You' Morisette walks naked through city streets and a supermarket, and sits beside clothed passengers on a train, while conveying the song's mystical message inspired by her recent visit to India.

Iggy Pop, Ozzy Osbourne, Robbie Williams, Queens of the Stone Age and the Red Hot Chili Peppers have also enjoyed stripping on stage, with the Chilis making imaginative use of their socks, but not all stars want to be completely nude while singing – they prefer to save the nakedness for photo-shoots for album covers and magazine features, or in the case of Madonna, for a book entitled *Sex* featuring her in naked and erotic poses. The trend for using nudity on album covers started in 1968 with John Lennon and Yoko Ono looking innocent on their *Two Virgins* cover, and the

Actress Davorka Tovilo arrives for the 'ECHO' German Music Awards at the Estrel Convention Centre in Berlin, Germany, April 2005.

models for Jimi Hendrix's *Electric Ladyland* not looking innocent at all. The following year saw Jane Birkin lying provocatively on a bed for the cover to her and Serge Gainsbourg's 'Je t'aime . . . moi non plus', the Welsh rock band Man in the buff for their album *Revelation*, and a photograph of a topless pubescent girl on the cover of the first album produced by Eric Clapton's new band, Blind Faith. This caused a storm of controversy, but has become one of the most well-known album covers as a result. From the 1970s onwards there have been so many images of nakedness used in this way that there are now websites devoted to the genre. The trend shows no sign of abating, though: in 2009 the newest rising stars, Lady Gaga and Beth Ditto, both posed naked for magazine covers, while their contemporary Lily Allen continued to resist the temptation and sang instead about the shamelessness of following this trend.

Oh! Calcutta!

When the producers of *Hair* came up with the idea of a twenty-second naked scene forty years ago, they must have had no idea of the impact they were helping to create. Not only did famous actors, opera divas and pop stars begin stripping on stage, but a whole rash of musicals featuring nudity broke out on Broadway and in the West End.

The year after *Hair* made its debut, a musical comedy revue entitled *Oh! Calcutta!* hit the off-Broadway stage and flung wide the door nudged open by *Hair*. Created by the theatre critic Kenneth Tynan, it was made up of sketches written by Tynan, Samuel Beckett, John Lennon, Sam Shepard, Edna O'Brien and Jules Feiffer. The lyrics and message of *Oh! Calcutta!* were the same as those of *Hair* – the sexual revolution had arrived. The difference was that the cast of ten stripped and remained naked for much of the show. When it opened in London, Scotland Yard sent two undercover agents to assess whether the law was being broken. They reported that John Lennon's 'Four in Hand' sketch about masturbation was 'dirt' and found a sketch called 'Delicious Indignities' 'pathetic, unjustifiable, appalling pornography',[36] although they did concede that it was acted well by Cherie Blair's father Anthony Booth.

When the British are uncertain about whether or not obscenity is occurring they turn to headmasters or headmistresses for guidance. When Eric Gill carved a naked figure of Ariel for the BBC on Broadcasting House, questions were raised about the size of the boy's penis. Was it not too large? An ex-headmaster was consulted for his professional opinion, after which Gill was asked to trim the offending organ. When the Director of Public Prosecutions received the police report on *Oh! Calcutta!* they sought the advice of

Hippy festival-goers enjoy the sunshine and good vibes at the second Glastonbury Fayre (later known as the Glastonbury Festival) organized by Arabella Churchill and Andrew Kerr at Worthy Farm, Pilton, Somerset, June 1971.

two eminent headmistresses, together with a professor of law and a vicar from Feltham, to help them decide whether the show could be deemed obscene. Surprisingly the experts were of one opinion, voiced by one of the headmistresses, Dame Margaret Miles, who said that the revue 'recognised the greater honesty, openness and freedom with which sex is viewed at the present time'.[37]

Oh! Calcutta! was an enormous success, running in London for over 2,400 performances, and in New York for over 1,600. In 1976 it was revived on Broadway and ran for 13 years. The same fate did not await the many musicals that attempted to convey the same message of sexual liberation and bask in the same success as Hair and Oh! Calcutta! In 1971 a musical called Stag Movie opened in New York which featured the naked and vivacious Adrienne Barbeau, whose acting was described as 'strenuous and acrobatic'.

A woman triumphantly displays herself at the Woodstock Festival held at White Lake, Bethel, in upstate New York in August 1969.

John Lennon and Yoko Ono pose naked for the cover of the 23 November 1968 issue of *Rolling Stone* magazine.

Jimi Hendrix, Noel Redding and Mitch Mitchell pose for a portrait with two barebreasted women in October 1968 in Hawaii.

Marilyn Manson at the Huntridge, Las Vegas, in the mid-1990s.

As one critic remarked: 'Unlike *Oh! Calcutta!*, it had a plot, it was witty, and it had gay and bisexual characters who were integral parts of the story'.[38] It only lasted 5 months before closing, but another just as audacious production opened that same year: *The Dirtiest Show in Town*, which featured straight, gay and lesbian characters and the entire cast writhing in a naked orgy at the climax of the evening.

The next year the 'wild musical revue' *While Crazy Now*, which featured songs such as 'Get Naked' and 'Dirty Mind', survived for

Nick Oliveri of Queens of the Stone Age performing – prior to his arrest – at the third music festival 'Rock in Rio' in Rio de Janeiro, Brazil, January 2001.

A scene from Kenneth Tynan's avant-garde revue *Oh! Calcutta!* at the Roundhouse, London, July 1970.

only one performance, and by 1974 the genre had peaked in *Let My People Come*. Billed as a 'sexual musical' it kicked off with lyrics that encouraged listeners to liberate their genitalia. Although it ran off-Broadway for over a thousand performances, it is all but forgotten.

There's a limit to how much you can exploit a theme, and when nudity returned in a new guise to the musical stage in the following millennium it was conveying a different message altogether.

6

The Hero's Return

Full nakedness! All my joys are due to thee,
As souls unbodied, bodies unclothed must be,
To taste whole joys.
—John Donne

A taboo acts like a perimeter wall that preserves a status quo that only the criminal, mad or subversive dare transgress. For the first sixty or so years of the twentieth century a steady pressure had begun to build in Western culture that challenged conventional sexual mores and the taboo against the display of nakedness. By 1968 this pressure had built to such a degree that the wall collapsed. The influences of Freudian psychology, and to a lesser degree the sunbathing and nudist movements, the rise of feminism, modernism and secularism and the invention of the birth control pill, all helped to bring it down, and the first to climb over the rubble into the new territory were the artists – musicians, actors, film-makers and pop stars – for whom display was their medium. A few years after Marshall McLuhan proclaimed 'the medium is the message' it became clear that the naked body provided the perfect example of this dictum. In the right context, simply undressing was all you needed to do to convey the message of the age: liberation.

When the wall collapsed there were plenty of objections, and although theatre censorship was abolished in Britain that year, Scotland Yard was still seeking to protect the nation's morals – *Oh! Calcutta!* was investigated and the reel of Andy Warhol's film *Flesh* was confiscated as soon as it arrived in Britain.

The first over the top in that extraordinary year of change, and in the year that followed, were cultural icons of their day: John Lennon and Yoko Ono, Ken Russell, Kenneth Tynan, Samuel Beckett, Jim Morrison, the cast and producers of *Hair*. Of course subversives had already been working behind the lines: Yoko Ono, for example, had filmed the naked bottoms of 15 people on a treadmill in 1966 and then those of 364 'swinging Londoners' in 1967, and in the USA, although the news-stand magazines *Penthouse* and *Playboy* only dared reveal pubic hair on women in the early 1970s, Ilsley Boone had won a ruling in the US courts in 1958 that his nudist magazines, available only by post, could show the pubic hair of both sexes.[1] In that same year in London Paul Raymond had worked out how to circumvent the silliness of strippers having to freeze in a tableau when they were completely nude. By licensing his premises as a private club rather than a theatre, his women were free to move.

The Mood Changes

In the 1980s in Europe and the USA, the exuberant use of nakedness to denote freedom from outmoded restrictions and the sheer joy that came with being able to be openly sensual was tempered by the arrival of AIDS. In art and on stage the harsh realities of the risks involved in sexual permissiveness meant that nakedness now began to be used to symbolize not only liberation and sexual pride, but also human vulnerability. The arrival of this darker but more mature era can be sensed in the photograph Annie Leibovitz took of John Lennon and Yoko Ono for the cover of *Rolling Stone* magazine just a few hours before he was shot in December 1980. Naked and curled like a foetus against the body of Yoko, clothed in black, it seems as if he is trying to return to the womb of the Great Mother. Five months later the first cases of AIDS were reported in Los Angeles, and while the nude continued to be portrayed in celebration of its beauty and sexual power, most notably in this era by Robert Mapplethorpe, whose male nudes caused controversy even after his death, others – like film-maker Derek Jarman – took the opportunity in their depiction of nudes to explore the relationship between the body and suffering.

The Flesh Sculptures of Spencer Tunick

In 1986 a young American photographer, Spencer Tunick, on a visit to Britain, photographed someone nude at a bus stop and then a series of nudes at Alleyn's School in London. From photographing individuals, Tunick moved on to working with groups, most often outdoors, and in urban settings. By 1994 he had taken photographs at over 65 sites in the United States and abroad, and his work had become not only photography but also a series of highly publicized installations which later he began to describe as 'flesh architecture', explaining that 'I aim to get a sculptural feel for groups of bodies, as well as create performance art.'[2]

In tune with the times, Tunick's photographs spoke not only of the beauty of the human form, but also its vulnerability. As the spectre of a 'plague' haunted the collective consciousness, some of his photographs of massed naked bodies lying inert in arid industrial landscapes were reminiscent of those images of bodies found in the mass graves of concentration camps. Even when Tunick ventured into the natural environment and photographed groups lying by the sea or snaking in a river of flesh we were reminded of dead shoals of fish and images from Rachel Carson's *Silent Spring*.

By the end of the century, perhaps due to the richness of associations evoked by his work, perhaps due more simply to its risqué novelty, the interest in Tunick's art had grown sufficiently for him to feature in an award-winning TV film, *Naked States*, which documented a road trip that he and his girlfriend made through America. In each state models were solicited, most memorably at a bikers' convention, and shoots in outdoor locations organized and filmed.

As Tunick's success has grown, his installations have grown in size too, evoking wonder in their celebration of the human form and the way in which 'bodies extend into and upon the landscape like a substance'.[3] The resonances in some of his earlier work to images of dead bodies has given way to representations of humanity that have done more to make nudity acceptable in widely different contexts than any other artwork or social movement. The website dedicated to a documentary on his work *Naked World* suggests that his installations 'which do not underscore sexuality become abstractions that

Thousands of volunteers pose for the American installation artist and photographer Spencer Tunick at Maria Cristina avenue in Barcelona, 8 June 2003.

challenge or reconfigure one's views of nudity and privacy'.[4] In cities across the world he has filmed and photographed his flesh sculptures often using thousands of people: 2,000 in Amsterdam, 2,754 in Cleveland, Ohio, 7,000 in Barcelona, 18,000 in Mexico City. In 2003 160 volunteers in London were photographed on the steps of County Hall in London to mark the opening of the Saatchi

Gallery. After shoots models normally dress immediately, but in this case they were invited to remain undressed and to join the first visitors to the gallery. By this time Tunick's work had become so well known that in the same year the London store Selfridges hosted a Tunick installation and *The Guardian* ran a spoof campaign, 'Say No to Nudity', in which groups of people posed for Tunick-style pictures on Brighton beach – but fully clothed.

In 2005 almost 1,700 volunteers were involved in a Tunick installation for the Baltic Centre for Contemporary Art, posing on the quaysides at Newcastle upon Tyne and Gateshead, and – in Tunick's first night shot – on the Gateshead Millennium Bridge. By 2009 Tunick had completed his second project in association with Greenpeace, creating a nude installation in a vineyard in France to draw attention to climate change.

The Full Monty

Accepting the limitations of broad-brush presentations that miss the finer details and contradictions, if the 1980s represented a time when the use of nakedness in popular culture and art achieved a maturity and introduced a sense of vulnerability into the more youthful and ebullient expression of nudity that had emerged in the 1960s and '70s, it was in the '90s that a new, more considered and socially responsible consciousness was born.

Four initiatives helped to shape this new face of nakedness. They were inspired by a photographer, a chef, a group of women from that bastion of middle-class England, the Women's Institute, and a film. In the final years of the millennium, Spencer Tunick, Jamie Oliver, the Calendar Girls and *The Full Monty* began to change the way we relate to nudity.

Spencer Tunick's photographs, showing nakedness in public places as evocative and unsexualized, began to be noticed from the mid-1990s, forming a backdrop to the change in attitudes that the other three initiatives helped to provoke. The 1997 British film comedy *The Full Monty* told the story of six unemployed men in Sheffield who form a striptease act and in the process gain the admiration and respect of their families and local community. Three years earlier, the British film industry had been rescued from a period of stagnation by *Four Weddings and a Funeral*, whose success was now rivalled by *The Full Monty*. To date both films have each earned over $257 million, with *The Full Monty* gaining the BAFTA Award for Best Film and four Academy Award nominations. The film's success had, as Kelly Farrell wrote in the journal *Men and Masculinities*: 'an unprecedented impact on British popular culture. Suddenly, "ordinary" men across Britain felt that taking their clothes off in public was not only possible but something to aspire to.'[5] In the wake of the film's popularity, the Prime Minister Tony Blair visited the job centre featured in the film, and promised 'to go the full monty' in the fight against poverty, suggesting that the film's message was that 'people must believe in themselves and get up and show they can do something'. A few months later The Prince's Trust organized a *Full Monty* party in Sheffield, and Prince Charles danced for the cameras in a queue at the job centre in imitation of one of the most endearing scenes from the film. He also admitted that he liked the film so much he had seen it twice.

Kelly Farrell believes that 'there was much more at stake in *The Full Monty* than the state of individual masculine identities: the film made working-class male subjectivity available for appropriation for national purposes as both Prince Charles and Tony Blair used it as a vehicle for their own political ends. The working-class men in the film became convenient metaphors for an invigorated postimperial identity while preserving the status quo of British class

A scene from the 1997 British comedy film *The Full Monty*.

A stripper performs in a working-men's club in Northern England in 2000.

divisions.'[6] Whether or not this was the case, the film achieved its impact by offering a comedy that explored serious issues: unemployment, depression, impotence, fathers' rights and suicide. The decision of six men to become strippers could have seemed trivial and exhibitionistic. Instead it was portrayed as heroic and socially responsible. As it did this, however, it used the theme of nakedness to seduce and excite the audience while displaying very little of it. Male striptease acts had been around for some time, and at hen parties in Britain male strippers would often go 'the Full Monty', but on a large commercial scale, acts like The Chippendales, anxious to keep within the law, worked with the belief that success comes from selling the sizzle rather than the steak, and would cover their genitals with their hands when, at the final moment, they removed their pants. *The Full Monty* followed suit, and in the final moment of the film, when the Sheffield men rip off their thongs, the audience is denied a sight of their groins. The stage lighting is conveniently arranged and the film ends in a blaze of spotlights.

The Power of the Word

Not being fully naked and yet using the idea of nakedness to tantalize and convey meaning was taken even more literally a few years after the film came out by Jamie Oliver, whose series *The Naked Chef* first appeared on television in 1999. While Oliver has never appeared nude in his shows or in his books, the use of that title was a stroke of genius, helping Oliver, who had just started his career, to stand out from the crowd: he wasn't just 'a chef' he was '*the* chef', the naked chef, with all its associations with sauciness, directness and excitement, giving him an instant 'brand name' to exploit. If he had been 'The Nude Chef' he might have felt obliged to disrobe, but by being 'naked' all he had to do was be transparent, cheeky and down to earth.

Authors and publishers, aware of the power of words, already knew just how effective the term could be in a book title. The success of Norman Mailer's *The Naked and the Dead*, published in 1948, was followed by a flurry of titles in the 1950s, including *The Naked Sun* by Isaac Asimov, *The Naked Land* by Hammond Innes, *Naked Lunch* by William Burroughs, and *The Naked Island*, a book by Russell Braddon about Japanese atrocities in World War II, which sold over a million copies in Britain. In the 1960s Desmond Morris's *The Naked Ape* and Quentin Crisp's *The Naked Civil Servant* were both bestsellers, but it was not until the 1990s and the following decade that the word became so popular in titles that today thousands can be found listed on the internet. Some of these are clearly about nudity, such as *Naked Girls Smoking Weed*, *Naked Places: A Guide for Gay Men to Nude Recreation and Travel*, and *Girls, Money and Sexy Snaps: What Really Happens When A Girl Strips Naked For A Photographer?* Many, however, such as *The Naked Public Square: Religion and Democracy in America* and *Naked Pilot: The Human Factor in Aircraft Accidents*, use the term metaphorically – as Jamie Oliver does.

Calendar Girls

Part of Oliver's appeal lay in the fact that he was 'an ordinary lad' – the boy next door – and his 'nakedness' equated with him

The 'Calendar Girls': The Rylstone and District Women's Institute Charity Calendar, May 2002.

being 'real'. If nakedness had associations to posing, that idea was on its way out, helped ironically by a group of women who did exactly that – posing for a charity calendar in the same year that *The Naked Chef* television series was launched. The women were all members of the Rylstone Women's Institute in North Yorkshire. In 1998 one of their husbands died of cancer at the age of 54, and they decided to pose naked for a fund-raising calendar, unaware of the fact that they were about to become a major cultural phenomenon that would result in their story being made into a successful film and a West End musical. By 2009 they had raised over £1.5 million for leukaemia research, and their website was offering a new calendar for 2010, Calendar Girls preserves and chocolates, and the opportunity to meet them for a glass of Pimm's and a raffle at a hotel in Sheffield, home of the *Full Monty* story.

Like the *Full Monty* strippers, none of the Calendar Girls was pictured totally naked – plants and watering cans were strategically placed – but this was not important. The public was getting used to seeing images of people who were not clothed, who were not models, and who looked 'ordinary'. They were also getting used to the idea of nakedness as an activity that could be fun, and socially useful, even heroic, as opposed to seeing it as an indicator of perversion.

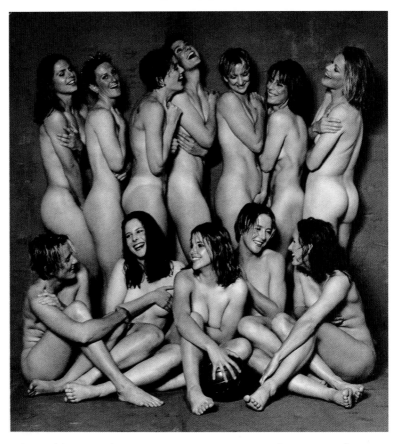

'The Matildas', Australia's women's soccer team, pose in Sydney in November 1999 for a calendar to promote women's soccer in Australia.

And, thanks to Jamie Oliver, they were getting used to the word being used to describe someone who is honest and unpretentious.

The Calendar Girls' success gave birth to a trend: creating a 'naked calendar' for fund-raising became so widespread amongst groups in Britain and America that a television documentary exploring the phenomenon was aired in 2008, and a website called 'Naked Charity' was established to list the number of nude charity calendar projects. In 2009 you could track the year with images of naked clowns to support multiple sclerosis research; naked folk musicians to contribute to their health care; or naked bikers to raise funds for a pet rescue service in Maryland. You could buy the Naked Knitting calendar to support the Christie Hospital in Manchester,

Ballet dancer Zenaida Yanowsky photographed for December in the Royal Opera House calendar for 2009, 'A World Stage Revealed', in aid of Macmillan Cancer Support.

Celtic and Rangers football supporters pose for groundbreaking photographs at Hamden in September 2007 in Glasgow, Scotland. The photographs were created to help support anti-sectarianism and show two of the world's most traditionally antagonistic clubs united in harmony.

or the Turn the Other Cheek calendar, produced by veterinary students at Cambridge University.

The film *Calendar Girls*, though not as successful as *The Full Monty*, grossed nearly $100 million at the box office, undoubtedly helped by the inclusion of Helen Mirren and Julie Walters in the cast. Helen Mirren, who once said, 'I'm a nudist at heart', when teased by an American talk show host responded, 'You Americans are so prudish. I went to Hungary when communism was still active. There's a park in the middle of Budapest, and they had a little section for nudist sunbathing right in the middle of the city. And you could walk past it. It wasn't like it was hidden behind greenery or fences. You could see everybody naked just by taking a walk in the park. It's very common in Europe, and Americans can't seem to get their heads around it.' She finished her riposte with a line worthy of the woman who won an Oscar for Best Actress playing the Queen of England: 'In America, you put swimming costumes on, don't you? Hmmm.'[7]

In 2009 the *Calendar Girls* musical opened in the West End after a regional tour and Jerry Hall, who last appeared naked on stage in 2001 in *The Graduate*, joined the cast. *The Full Monty* was also turned into a musical in the USA in 2000, where it ran on Broadway for two years. It also played in the West End for a shorter time to a mixed critical reaction and in nearly a dozen other countries.

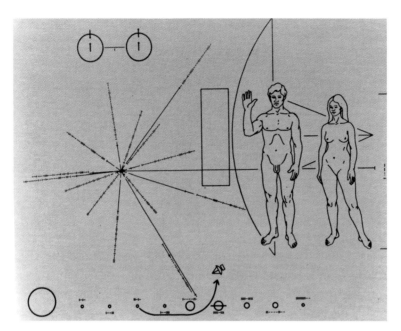

The NASA 'Universal Message of Friendship' that was displayed on the 1970s Pioneer 10 and 11 spacecraft, and was designed to convey fundamental information about Earth for any alien civilization that might one day intercept them. The images of the waving naked male and his companion were clearly designed to be informative even though visiting aliens would be unlikely to encounter people looking like this unless their craft landed in a nudist resort.

A new generation of x-ray scanners are being introduced at airports which conduct a virtual strip search and show a clear outline of passengers' genitals. Critics are concerned about exposure to radiation and violations of privacy. In 2009 they were introduced into US, Dutch and British airports.

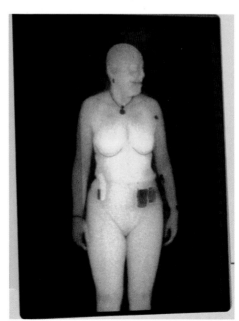

Nakedness Post-9/11

The four initiatives discussed in the previous section were all begun just before the end of the century. As the new millennium dawned their influence steadily grew. As the tragedy of 9/11 marked the beginning of an era of fear and curtailment of civil liberties, displaying oneself naked came to represent the opposing sentiment of trust and the idea of the simple and basic freedom to exist in the world without any restrictions. As *The Full Monty* and *Calendar Girls* showed images of ordinary people stripping for socially responsible causes, the newspapers, television and internet carried images of people stripping to protest against war and injustice. After centuries of repression and shame, the display of nakedness was starting to gain the moral high ground – at least for those for whom the sight of naked protesters or charity fund-raisers evoked a respect they denied to the likes of Bush and Blair posing in their bomber jackets as Afghanistan was attacked.

The moral objection to public displays of nakedness comes from the belief that such behaviour is shameful or immodest, but since the 1960s the force of this objection has been eroded in European and liberal American culture. Instead, objections are often raised on practical or aesthetic grounds: seeing others naked can violate our visual sensibilities or standards of hygiene.

The fact that the area of the body that often excites the most interest, that the *Full Monty* builds towards and then never shows, that the Calendar Girls hide behind vases, is both the seat of our greatest sensual pleasure and the area involved in excretion presents a conundrum memorably expressed by W. B. Yeats when he wrote 'And Love has pitched his mansion in the place of excrement.'[8]

The issue of maintaining standards of hygiene while being naked is effectively handled in nudist resorts by asking patrons to use towels when using public seating and by designating areas 'clothing-optional', which means that it is not compulsory to be nude. Such simple solutions do not prevent predictable remarks about nudists and food or hot drinks, which have provided on at least one occasion a publicity opportunity for a supermarket chain. Public Relations officers are often accused of practising the 'dark arts' of media manipulation, and the inside story of one such incident reveals how the common objection to nakedness as being unhygienic was apparently used by Tesco supermarket to excuse themselves from a venture they mooted purely for the purpose of publicity. When the company announced that it was considering running a naturist shopping evening at their store in Hastings in 1999, they received massive publicity. British campaigner Mary Whitehouse denounced the plan as 'cheap and disgusting', and the store admitted that their health and safety experts had voiced a major concern about the risk of bodily contact with fruit and vegetables. Although the story was presented as coming from nudists who wanted to shop au naturel, notes written by the Public Relations officer of the Central Council of British Naturism reveal that the idea was dreamt up by Tesco:

> Early in January their publicity department phoned to see if we would consider a nude shopping evening. They were told it would not work, but nevertheless they said it would be good publicity for us both and they were putting out a press release next day; which they did. I was surprised to find out they had done their homework and chosen Hastings, because that was where the first naturist beach was. The story having broken the phone went mad, 36 inter-

A department store in Vienna launched a promotion in February 2000 offering a 5000 Austrian *schillings* voucher to the first people to enter the store naked.

views in the first 48 hours, early morning and late evening, which meant 4am and two after midnight. In most cases these were going out live and I was able to tell listeners that we had no intentions of going shopping in the nude, but that there are many ways in which we are hoping to extend nude living in Britain.[9]

The shopping evening never occurred. The PR team at Tesco were just amusing themselves playing with the media and the public.

Other nude shopping ventures, however, really have taken place. In 2003 a new Lisbon clothing store was swamped with eager customers when they offered two free items of clothing to anyone who shopped in the nude. Until 2005 Gaslight Music – a record store in Melbourne – used to hold annual nude shopping days, and in 2006 nude shoppers promoted 'West End VIP – Very Important Pedestrian – Day' in Regent Street and Oxford Street in London.

The Tesco stunt that played with a joke about nudists and unprotected fruit may have helped to get media coverage, but the associations between nakedness and hygiene run deep, and reflect both logical considerations and the illogical. The fear of exposing or seeing those parts of the body that excrete substances does not apply to the mouth, nose or ears, but for some it applies to the female nipple. While it is now acceptable in much of the West to expose cleavage in public places, the simple suggestion of a nipple can cause outrage, as it did in 2004 in the United States, when millions of television viewers saw a nipple-shield on Janet Jackson for less than a second. During a concert in Houston, singer Justin Timberlake tore off part of Jackson's costume mid-performance, revealing her right breast, which was covered by a large metallic-looking star. CBS, who televised the event, now dubbed 'Nipplegate', were fined $550,000 by the Federal Communications Commission for its 'indecency violation'.[10] Minutes after the incident, veteran British streaker Mark Roberts, wearing only a g-string, with 'SUPER BOWEL' and an advertisement for an online betting website written on his chest, ran around the pitch. He was fined $1,000 and is banned from visiting the USA.

Despite all the gains in relaxing attitudes to nudity made by Spencer Tunick, *The Full Monty* and *Calendar Girls*, the Nipplegate affair

The sight that resulted
in a $550,000 fine for
CBS: Justin Timberlake
rips clothing from
Janet Jackson to reveal
her breast as they
erform during the
half-time show at
the Texas Super Bowl,
February 2004.

offers a startling reminder of the power of conservatism in the
United States, showing to what extent the puritan roots of American prudery have managed to retain their grip on a country in
which topless bathing is still prohibited in most states, and in which
women have had to fight to gain the right to breast-feed in public.

Although the British attitude to nudity is more relaxed than in
America, the Calendar Girls still considered it wise not to promi-
nently reveal their nipples, as if recognizing that they too represent
the mystery indicated by Yeats, that the body is a gateway between
the inner and outer worlds, able to make substances appear, fluids
that can create and destroy, make children, and feed or infect others. Every night, across the world, hundreds of thousands of men,
and a lesser number of women, scan the virtual world to gaze in fas-
cination at close-up images of that part of the body out of which
they emerged into the world, or at pictures of that other part of the

body which pumped half their genetic code into their mother's wombs. And every day, across the world, sanctions are maintained to control this behaviour.

Nakedness as Ugly

The dance between revelation and concealment drives our world. Lovers are lured by the unknown in each other, God plays hide and seek with the mystic, politicians agonize over the need to know, and scientists push forever against the moving wall marked 'Unknown'. Utter nakedness may feel good to those who have discovered the joys of skinny dipping, sunbathing or just spending their days in the nude, but those who observe them often say that they find their nakedness unattractive or not sexually exciting. When everything is revealed, the fun is up, the chase is over, and there is no more mystery. From this perspective it is only in the world of performance or art – erotic or otherwise – that full nakedness can be conveyed as alluring. The fact that it usually requires clothing for the body to be tantalizing has clearly been grasped by Jamie Oliver, the Calendar Girls and the makers of *The Full Monty*. They have all been successful precisely because they have understood this phenomenon and have maintained the mystery.

The lack of mystery that is found in a nudist resort offers one explanation for why nudism will always remain a minority activity, and is usually portrayed as either absurd or quaint, as it was in the 2006 British comedy film *Confetti*, which featured a nudist wedding and was filmed partly at one of Britain's oldest naturist resorts. Even when the American comedian David Sedaris admits in his 1997 best-selling set of autobiographical essays, *Naked*, that his week in a nudist resort ended with him resenting the constriction of clothes, he comments that 'It is ironic that nudists are just about the last people you'd ever want to see naked.' It takes a journalist, Zoe Williams, to point out that nudism lacks vanity,[11] and the philosopher Alain de Botton, in his documentary *Status Anxiety*, to include naturists as part of a generalized Bohemian movement that began in the nineteenth century, and that has included Romantics, Surrealists, Dadaists, hippies and punks, all of whom 'didn't much care about money or convention' and who 'stand outside the bourgeois mainstream and live for a set of new independent values'.[12] Naturists, in their very rejection of much of the value of clothing, offer a lifestyle that has the potential to transcend a preoccupation with appearances. A nudist with spiritual aspirations finds themselves in the unusual position of being able to enjoy an enhanced sensual life combined with a type of asceticism that frees the ego of its preoccupation about how its body appears to others. By surrendering the mystery of clothes they surrender to a deeper mystery.

The fashion collection 'Il Sarto Immortale', 1994–7, by Leipzig artist Alba D'Urbano featured her own naked body printed on clothing.

Marc Quinn's 15-foot high statue of a naked and pregnant thalidomide woman, displayed on the 'fourth plinth' at Trafalgar Square, London, in 2004.

How to Look Good Naked

The way in which complete nudity can convey a deeper mystery that lies beyond the dialectic between clothing and nakedness has been shown not only by nudists, but also by installation and performance artists such as Spencer Tunick, the Neo-Naturists and Vanessa Beecroft, who makes striking and controversial use of live female models. Meanwhile, the recent success of the British TV series *How to Look Good Naked* makes alchemical use of the common belief that most of us are less attractive when undressed.

In 2006 the fashion stylist Gok Wan shot to fame by presenting a series of programmes on British television in which he took women who believed they were unattractive, and who were dissatisfied with their body image, and promised to make them feel good about how they looked. Citing research that 81 per cent of women in Britain felt ashamed of their bodies, Gok Wan was able to build on a growing dissatisfaction with the promotion of idealized female bodies. Businesses such as The Body Shop and Dove had already been engaged in helping to change public opinion for some years, and

The microwear one-piece string bikini at $44 is apparently a popular choice when a swimming costume must be worn.

Sacha Baron Cohen, better known as Borat or Ali G, poses in Berlin in June 2009 for his new film *Brüno*, wearing a carefully 'manscaped' woollen bodysuit.

Dove's 'Campaign for Real Beauty', whose goal was to 'free the next generation from self-limiting beauty stereotypes', had planned to reach 5 million young women by the end of 2010. By 2009 their video had been viewed by over 10 million YouTube viewers.

The success of Gok Wan's formula relied on him enhancing his subjects' confidence and appearance so that when they were revealed, almost completely nude, to the tumultuous applause of family, friends and the public, they had accepted their body shapes and had not undertaken cosmetic surgery or tried to lose weight. When asked how she found parading on a catwalk with virtually nothing on, one of them replied 'liberating and strangely exciting', with a sense of confidence that was 'sky high'. The series has been so successful that Polish, French, Swedish and Belgian versions have been produced, and the US version, fronted by *Queer Eye for the Straight Guy* presenter Carson Kressley, has been promoted on the Oprah Winfrey show.

Nine life-size statues by Antony Gormley, famous for his *Angel of the North*, were exhibited in London in 2007 as part of his exhibition at the Hayward Gallery, entitled 'Event Horizon'. The figures, based on the sculptor's own body, were placed on rooftops facing the gallery, with one on Waterloo Bridge, shown here, and with a rooftop statue also visible.

Zhang Dali's *Chinese Offspring* exhibited at the Saatchi Gallery in London in November 2008. Fifteen life-size cast resin figures hang from the ceiling, each sculpture a representation of a migrant construction worker. The figures are hung by their feet to denote their vulnerability and economic entrapment.

Banksy's work often uses the naked body to create an intentionally dramatic effect. Here, painted on the wall of a sexual health clinic in Bristol in June 2006, he depicts a man coming home to discover his partner's infidelity.

How to Look Good Naked has reinforced the message of body-acceptance given by *Calendar Girls*, *The Full Monty* and Spencer Tunick's models – all of whom display the sort of 'ordinary' bodies possessed by the majority of the population. As a result, it is harder today to invoke an objection to nudism on the basis of the supposed unattractiveness or ordinariness of the bodies on view.

In 2008 German film director Niko von Glasow took the concept of granting the right to feel good about your body to a new level when he made a film about twelve victims of thalidomide, including himself, who reveal themselves naked in a way that is profound and moving. The award-winning *NoBody's Perfect* follows the director's search for eleven people who will join him to pose naked for photographs that will be shown in a book and an exhibition. In an interview with *Stern* magazine he explained: 'I tried not to be voyeuristic. It could have been a freak show, so it was important to ensure the protagonists kept their dignity.' The documentary also follows von Glasow's futile attempts to show his photographs to members of the Wirz family, who own the company that manufactured the drug.

NoBody's Perfect, and Marc Quinn's 15-foot-high statue of a naked and pregnant thalidomide woman, displayed on the 'fourth plinth' at Trafalgar Square in 2004, have shown that in the right context the taboo on depicting the disabled in the nude can be broken, and that doing so can help us question what it means to be embodied and alive.

Smoothies, Brazilians and Manscaping

The taboo against nudity is in reality a set of sanctions that relate to specific areas of the body, such as its front or back, chest or groin. The taboo against exposing the chest, for example, exists in certain cultures only in relation to women. In the Victorian age, for a woman to exhibit a naked ankle was considered immodest, while today on most beaches it is considered acceptable to sunbathe totally naked apart from the slightest bikini, or on topless beaches, simply a 'monokini'. During the 1980s, as swimwear started to cover less and less skin and the thong-style Brazilian tanga was

Ian and Barbara Pollard, authors of *The Naked Gardeners*, who often work unclothed in their garden, Abbey House Gardens in Malmesbury, Wiltshire, which is open to the public. They also hold clothing-optional days when members of the public can shed their clothes to wander the grounds.

introduced, women began to remove some or all of their pubic hair, making a behaviour that had been confined to a minority increasingly widespread, particularly among younger women.

The minority who had begun depilating their pubic area before the arrival of skimpy swimsuits were either those driven by the desire for greater erotic pleasure, with the personal letters pages of men's magazines often carrying enthusiastic accounts of their experiences, or nudists who may have been seeking enhanced sexual pleasure, but who were also driven by the desire to be 'nuder than nude'. In the 1960s and '70s 'smoothies', as they quickly became known, may have appeared odd to their naturist colleagues who sensed a violation of a basic tenet of nudism – that it is 'natural' – but as the subject became more openly discussed, with 'Brazilians' and bikini-waxing being advertised in high street beauty parlours, and with celebrities such as Elton John openly chatting on television about their pubic shaving, by the end of the century smoothies

From 1978 until 2006, a group of radical London artists calling themselves the Neo-Naturists performed and created in the nude. The Binnie sisters and Wilma Johnson, joined later by Turner Award-winning Grayson Perry and others formed the group. Here Christine Binnie is painted and photographed by Wilma Johnson at St Martin's School of Art, London, in 1980.

Body-painting gives people the opportunity to appear in the nude in public while feeling, or giving the illusion, that they are somewhat clothed. The World Bodypainting Festival is held annually in Austria, and nude or semi-nude painted bodies are becoming a frequent sight at music festivals. Here at the Burning Man Festival in Nevada in August 2000, participants prepare to go on display.

of both genders had become a common sight in nudist resorts and magazines. In the wider world the depilating of some or all of the male pubic area was no longer deemed the province of the male porn star, as 'manscaping' and 'back, sack and crack' waxing was openly discussed in magazines and on websites, and filmed in close-up for Channel 4's documentary series *Extreme Male Beauty*.

Being free of pubic hair may make one more attractive to some people, it may enhance the experience of being naked, and of sexual activity, but critics point to the way in which it can appear to 'infantilize' adults, regressing them to pre-pubescence and calling into question the motives of those who like to see pictures of depilated young men and women. The prevalence of images and films of smooth women on the internet has also meant that young women report a pressure on them to shave, to cater to their boyfriends' preferences and conform to the stereotype of attractiveness that it promotes.

While the idea of depilation has now entered the cultural mainstream, the opposing trend, that celebrates the existence of pubic hair, tends to be confined to minority websites that treat hairiness as a fetish. This imbalance has been partly fuelled by commercial interests. No money can be made on encouraging people to leave parts of their body alone, but it can be made on selling skin care and shaving products.

Aware of the way in which pubic depilation was becoming more popular in the opening years of the twenty-first century, Saatchi & Saatchi in New Zealand created a 'Nothing to Hide' campaign in 2007, which capitalized on the associations between hairlessness, aesthetics and hygiene. The viral video that they released on to the internet, for the Irish Elave cosmetics company, showed smooth women and men working naked in a laboratory and introducing their products to the viewers. The campaign reportedly increased sales by 500 per cent, with Saatchi & Saatchi stating that on creating the ad the film crew were also naked to make the actors feel more relaxed.

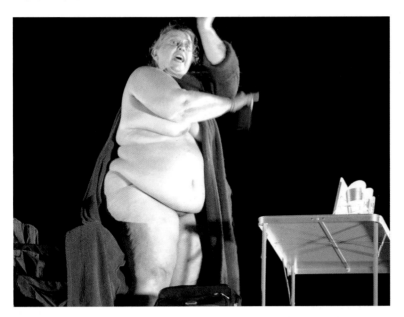

The 'One & Other' event in London's Trafalgar Square, a 'live artwork' initiative of Antony Gormley carried out for 100 days between July and October 2009, invited members of the public to occupy the fourth plinth for an hour. 2,400 people were picked at random from 35,000 applicants. Seven men and five women chose to undress on the plinth, including Suzanne Piper, editor of *Naturist Life*, seen here.

In a more elliptical campaign, the 'Viral Factory' in Santa Monica, California, produced a 3-minute hoax documentary in 2006 of a fashion show created by a fictional hair stylist, Stefane Monzon. As viewers watched clips from behind the scenes before the show, they soon discovered that Monzon was a stylist of pubic hair, and the resulting catwalk featured models entirely naked, sporting eccentric designs that included peacock feathers woven into their pubic hair. The film was created for the hair grooming company Remington. The playfulness and imagination used to create this film reflects the growing ease with which the more liberal wing of modern Western society has come to regard the genital area.

The Genital Liberation Movement

As symbols of power and vulnerability, with their inconvenient associations with issues of hygiene and with a type of pleasure that only too easily combines guilt with its ecstasies, the genitals have always represented the final frontier of nakedness. You are only fully naked if your genitals are exposed. That frontier might be capable of shifting a fraction for smoothies, enabling the unshaved to feel a little dressed in comparison, and it might be capable of a more significant shift to the 'final frontier' for the male if he is seen or depicted erect, but the fact remains that one is only really naked when the crotch is uncovered, which is why someone wearing just a thong is only described as naked by the media or the prudish.

Despite the powerful range of taboos and laws that have been created to prevent the display and depiction of genitals, a consideration of the way in which they have 'come out of the closet' in recent years reveals the extent to which popular Western culture has changed.

Yet again we have to turn to 1968 to discover the time in which that change began to occur. In that year, a young Chicago groupie named Cynthia Albritton hit on the idea of making plaster casts of rock stars' penises, and her first 'client', Jimi Hendrix, was happy to agree to model for her. Frank Zappa found her idea funny and believed it had artistic merit. He encouraged her to move to Los Angeles to build up a collection of casts for an eventual exhibition,

A nude encounter group psychotherapy session, run by psychiatrist Paul Bindrim, Palm Springs, California, 1968.

and although this never materialized, Cynthia Plaster Caster, as she called herself, was made the subject of a documentary and continues to sells T-shirts from her website that feature slogans such as 'Make Plaster Not War' and 'Cómo Está Your Schwantz?'

Perhaps because the penis has represented power and dominance for so long, the trajectory of its outing in recent years has been determined, as if in compensation, by humour, while more sensitive or artistic approaches seem to have arisen where the vulva is concerned, with online resources such as The Vulva Museum showing a wide range of positive representations of the female genitals, and the 1996 stage show *The Vagina Monologues*, although comic as well as serious, commanding an attention and success denied to their male imitators *The Penis Monologues* and *Talking Cock*.

Stage shows that featured men or women talking openly about their genitals represented a significant step forward in helping to create a culture of openness and honesty, with the $50 million raised for women's anti-violence groups by *The Vagina Monologues* offering concrete evidence of their potential for effecting positive change.

If talking about genitals can be of value, perhaps actually displaying them can also be useful. Performance artist Annie Sprinkle

Puppetry of the Penis auditions at the Apollo Theatre, London, in October 2004.

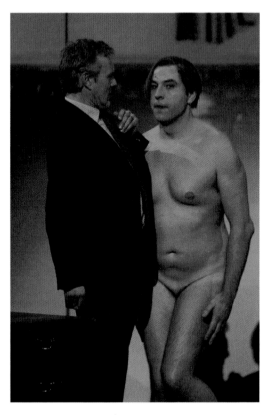

Actor and comedian David Walliams baring almost everything at a Little Britain Gala in support of Comic Relief in London, November 2006.

certainly believed this when she toured *A Public Cervix Announcement* for five years in the USA in the 1980s. In this feature of her one-woman show, she invited members of the audience to examine her cervix with a speculum. She explained: 'I'd give people flashlights, and I put a microphone there and people could comment. It was very innocent and playful. People told me it helped them relieve some shame.'[13] One reviewer, commenting on the experience after a performance wrote that, 'Sprinkle had gone beyond nakedness to a supernakedness that transcends sexuality: body interiors aren't sexy.'[14]

In the first half of the twentieth century such a performance would have been unthinkable, as would have been the idea that two men could create a successful public entertainment based upon revealing and then contorting their penises. By the end of the century, though, this is exactly what had happened. In 1997 the Australian Simon Morley created a calendar with photographs of his acrobatics, which he termed 'installations', or, more mundanely, 'dick tricks', and by the following year had succeeded in turning his unusual skill into a show called *Puppetry of the Penis*, which won the best show award at the Melbourne International Comedy Festival. It was so well received that over the coming years Morley and his fellow puppeteer David Friend found themselves touring the world for over five years. The show, which features close-ups of the contortions projected onto a giant screen behind the puppeteers, reached London's West End in 2000. By 2002 other actors had been trained to perform the show, and eight companies were staging it in different cities around the world. By 2007 it had been a hit on Broadway, had played the Edinburgh Festival for eight years in a row, and a documentary film and book had been created as spin-offs. In a playful imitation of televised selection contests, a further documentary entitled *Cock Stars* was also made of the selection process undergone by actors auditioning as puppeteers.

The Modesty Movement

Despite such openness being displayed on stages around the world, not everyone was in favour of genital manipulation or the supernakedness of Annie Sprinkle. As the trend for more

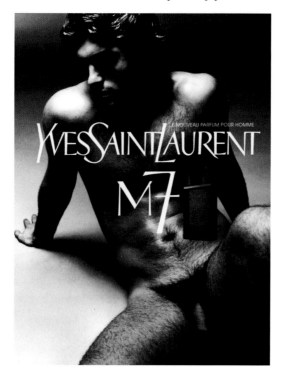

Yves Saint Laurent caused controversy in 2000 when it became the first company to use full-frontal male nudity in advertising.

revelation reached its peak at the turn of the millennium, a counter-vailing current arose, spurred on by Wendy Shalit's 1999 book, *A Return to Modesty: Discovering the Lost Virtue*, which argued for a return of traditional values, including more modest clothing and sexual restraint. Remaining confined to America, the movement has achieved only a modicum of success that has failed to cross the Atlantic. Books which promote the 'real sex' that can only occur in marriage, like *The Thrill of the Chaste: Finding Fulfillment While Keeping Your Clothes On* by Dawn Eden, and *Real Sex: The Naked Truth about Chastity* by Lauren Winner, both published in 2006, have failed to sell outside the USA, and a fashion trend to encourage young people to 'dress their age' and reject clothing designed to be sexually enticing has also failed to gain attention outside America.

A quite independent counter-current in favour of more cloth-ing seemed to arise in France in the summer of 2009 with the media reporting that young French women were reverting to the use of bikini tops, but it seems that these reports were the result of publicity generated by the historian Christophe Granger's study

Record-holding super-heavyweight weightlifter Mark Henry, photographed by Joe McNally for his 1996 'Olympic Nude Series' depicting the United States's 1996 Olympic team as a series of nude figure studies, published in *LIFE* magazine. The only time in the history of *LIFE*, the magazine ran four separate covers in one month featuring these images.

By the 1970s, some proponents of the natural childbirth movement that had begun in the 1930s were suggesting that both mother and father could be naked together during a birth to enhance naturalness and intimacy. Here Carmella and Abel B'hahn hold their newborn baby in 1986.

of the social history of the beach and the body in France, *Corps d'Eté*, fuelled by the media's desire for controversial material and perhaps by the fashion industry's desire to sell more swimwear. It will take a few more years to determine whether these reports reflect a genuine trend. Meanwhile the militant feminist group Les Tumulteuses will continue to fight for topless rights by plunging into public swimming pools without bikini tops, and monokinis will still be a familiar sight on French beaches.

While modesty continued to occupy some minds, a number of companies decided that more rather than less nakedness offered the key to commercial success: in 2000 Yves Saint Laurent used full-frontal male nudity to advertise a cologne; Abercrombie & Fitch featured 49 naked and semi-naked young models of both sexes in its 2002 clothes catalogue. By 2009 Walkers Crisps in the UK had upstaged its rival – Tyrrell's Naked Potato Chips – with a comic and erotic television advertising campaign that featured male and female actors and the footballer Gary Lineker in the nude.

The Return of the Hero

The freest people I know are those who have the least to hide,
defend or protect. Naked is powerful!
–Alan Cohen

As the first decade of the twenty-first century draws to a close, the range of freedoms granted and restrictions placed upon nakedness has never been greater. If you undress in the street in Barcelona nothing will happen. If you try the same thing in most other cities in the world you will be threatened with arrest. In one context you can stand naked in public and will be allowed to display and manipulate your genitals. In another, if you are a man even removing your shirt will result in expulsion, as in certain British supermarkets, or if you are a Muslim woman in certain countries, uncovering your face in public will result in punishment.

The greatest range of responses can be observed in the United States, where, as evidence of the resistance to nudity that still exists in American culture, an advertisement for the cosmetics firm Dove was banned in 2007 from US network television because it showed 'too much skin'. As part of Dove's 'Campaign for Real Beauty', the company had launched a 'pro-age campaign' to promote positive body images for the over-'50s, with photography by Annie Leibovitz. Despite its responsible message and lack of full-frontal nudity, the fact that the models were all naked made it unacceptable to broadcasters. By 2009, however, the film had been viewed on YouTube over 1.5 million times, reinforcing the suspicion that the US television networks were failing to keep pace with the spirit of the times.

British television, though, has shown in recent years that it is in touch with the zeitgeist. A year after launching the *How to Look Good Naked* series, programmes such as *My Penis and I* and *My Penis and Everyone Else's* explored the way in which many men are as concerned about the size of their genitals as women are with the size of their breasts. Film-maker Lawrence Barraclough's exploration of this ubiquitous male insecurity also included a 'snap your chap' project that gathered photographs from men around the world.

As part of the trend towards an increasing familiarity with psychological concepts, writers, film-makers and even business interests have come to realize that how we perceive and relate to our bodies profoundly affects our sense of wellbeing. By exploring how we feel about our nakedness and the most intimate parts of our bodies, we can access these feelings in their most direct and intense form.

In the 1960s some Californian psychologists had tried 'nude psychotherapy' for individuals, couples and groups, pioneered by Paul Bindrim, who was inspired by a remark of Abraham Maslow, the father of the Humanistic psychology movement, that nudity might be useful in sensitivity training.[15] Aileen Goodson, in her 1991 book *Therapy, Nudity and Joy*, described her experience of Bindrim's first 'nude psychotherapy marathon' in 1967, and her attempt – 20 years later – to determine its long-term effects on the participants, most of whom agreed that it had resulted in lasting and positive benefits. Bindrim was working with the idea that physical nakedness could facilitate emotional nakedness, thereby speeding up the therapeutic process. Despite the apparent success of his and others' attempts, the idea never caught on in the world of professional psychotherapy.[16] Instead it found its way into the psycho-spiritual encounter groups run by the Rajneesh (Osho) community, and nakedness in groups is still used by trainers inspired by that movement, such as Paul Lowe.[17] In addition, their experience with nude therapy, and nudism in general, influenced the work of sex therapists such as William Hartman, who wrote:

> Even though we are not nude with our clients, our work in sex therapy was directly influenced by our experiences with nudism. We became more comfortable with our own bodies and it affected our work in every way. One of the techniques we use for body-imagery work and self-concept is the exercise of standing nude in front of special mirrors, like tailors' mirrors, with the client touching and talking about every part of his or her body. Through the years these clients have indicated to us that this was a crucial and pivotal aspect of their therapy.[18]

Gok Wan in *How to Look Good Naked* uses the same technique, translated for mass consumption. The increasing openness and ease with which people could be encouraged to look at themselves, and accept what they saw, meant that by 2009 as the world was gripped by economic recession, three programmes on British television were broadcast which demonstrated the way in which an exploration of nakedness could have psychological and therapeutic value.

In March the BBC *Horizon* documentary *What's the Problem With Nudity?* explored why people tend to feel ashamed or embarrassed when they are naked. Nina Jablonski of Penn State University argued that becoming hairless represented a major step forward in human evolution. Whereas most animals have fur, we developed an upright stance and became 'naked'. By shedding fur we were able to cool ourselves more quickly and developed bigger brains, leading to the development of tools, language, and the ability to make fire. If nudity really does represent such an important factor in the development of our culture and what we call our 'humanity', then it is not surprising that it is so redolent with meaning for us, and this could explain why some studies show that people prefer hairless bodies. It also means, as radio and television magazine the *Radio Times* stated, 'that something everyone takes for granted may hold the key to the success of the entire human species.'

During the programme a psychologist, Dan Fessler, suggested that shame about being seen naked may have arisen as a way of reinforcing pair bonding, and hence more effective child care: 'Over thousands of generations, we've learned that showing off a naked body sends out sexual signals that threaten the security of mating pairs. And we've chosen to agree that that is a bad thing. Shame is the ideal emotion to enforce that code of conduct. Because it feels unpleasant, we avoid it at all costs.'[19]

The documentary then invited eight volunteers to undergo a series of experiences in the nude in the presence of each other and a team of psychologists, which concluded that our inhibitions about being seen naked are the result of social conditioning, and that we are not born with a shame of nudity, but learn it.

In *The Naked Office*, broadcast by Virgin in June, a company challenged by the harsh economic climate was invited to undergo a training process, devised by business consultant David Taylor, author of 'The Naked Leader' trilogy, which culminated in all employees being invited to spend a 'Naked Friday', working together in the nude. As inhibitions were shed, communication between workers, contentment and productivity increased significantly. In *The Credit Crunch Monty*, broadcast by Sky in July, auditions were held in Wolverhampton for six men who would train to put on a male striptease act. As dozens of men queued for the audition, the *Full Monty* story was acted out in real life for the cameras. Six were chosen and viewers watched as they were put through their paces and finally went for 'The Full Monty' – and this time they really did show all. As they danced on stage, each holding a copy of 'The Daily Crunch', with its headlines of 'More Jobs Gloom' and 'Growing Debt' they proved that more than a decade after the appearance of *The Full Monty*, its central idea was as humorous, exciting and empowering as ever. A 58-year-old electrician with six children who took part in the show explained that his girls were appalled at the thought of him stripping on stage, that his boys and 80-year-old mother loved the idea, and that his grandchildren will 'know who I am'. In that one remark he succeeded in summing up the power and the mystery of nakedness: that revelation of the body can intimate revelation of the self.

In ancient Greece nakedness was the badge of heroes – gods and statesmen were depicted in the nude and Olympic athletes competed naked. Their nakedness was, however, also symbolic of an ideal of beauty which came to dominate Western culture, and to exert its own peculiar tyranny, particularly on women. Projects like the 'Calendar Girls', *The Credit Crunch Monty* and its inspiration *The Full Monty* have brought to the world a special gift – demonstrating that each of us can be heroic, regardless of our body shape. The heroes in these initiatives are not heroic because of their physiques, but because of who they are. They are real heroes, not fictional or mythological ideals.

As the bodies of the women of the Rylstone Women's Institute or the men of recession-hit Wolverhampton are unveiled, cynics might sneer at their imperfections, but in doing so they will miss something quite extraordinary: the arrival in our world of the gods – of Everywoman and Everyman as hero, and as fully human.

Postscript

When I free my body from its clothes, from all their buttons, belts,
and laces, it seems to me that my soul takes a deeper, freer breath.
—August Strindberg

I wish I had been in Mayfair in 2006 when the Perfume Shop presented their new season of perfumes to a select group of journalists
and friends. Each was given a blindfold to wear, and then the show
began. One by one, with pauses in between to clear the air, a model
walked slowly along the catwalk – entirely naked, and wearing only
one of the season's new scents. What a temptation there must have
been to tear off the blindfold as the first model paused at the end of
the walk, the only sign of their existence emanating from the perfume
on their skin! Perhaps I could have asked for an invitation, but I
was in France, researching this book, and unaware of the fun going
on back at home.

The inspiration for writing this brief history had come a few
years earlier, after I had discovered the simple pleasures of baring all
at the age of 49. On the hottest day of the year in 2001, in researching a biography, I found myself walking around one of Britain's
oldest naturist resorts, Spielplatz in Hertfordshire, pausing to swim
in its pool, and rest in the shade of its magnificent trees, wondering
to myself 'Why has it taken me almost half a century to discover
this delightful pastime?' Although I had been brought up in a liberal
household and in the permissive environment of the 1960s, my only
knowledge of nudism had come from its caricature in a *Pink Panther*
film, in which Peter Sellers wanders through a nudist resort holding
a guitar to his waist. Although I had enjoyed skinny-dipping a few

times, I had never tried simply not bothering with clothes on a warm day, and enjoying the experience of swimming, sunbathing, eating lunch and chatting with other people, all without any clothing. The thought of 'organized' nudism had seemed odd and illogical to me: why would one go to the bother of creating clubs and resorts for such an activity? It was only when I visited one that I understood their rationale. Being naked renders one vulnerable, and it is the context in which one undresses that makes the experience satisfying or disturbing. By designating a beach, a resort, a swimming pool on a certain evening each month, as 'clothing optional' or 'naturist', a context is created which protects one from the fear of disapproval or ridicule.

I became painfully aware of the importance of context in this respect as I worked on the book. In exploring the history and development of the nudist movement I came across the existence of Cap d'Agde, known as the 'Naked City' on the south coast of France, where as many as 40,000 people at any one time stroll along beaches and visit a supermarket, restaurants, shops and a bank entirely in the nude. This seemed extraordinary to me, and I decided I should pay a visit. Having received assurances from friends that I could disrobe immediately on arrival, I found it impossible to undress in a car park surrounded by building work that was being carried out by teams of men who were naturally clothed as they operated cranes and heaved bricks to and fro. Once in the 'city', I undressed, and placing my clothes in a carrier bag, strode purposefully towards the shopping precinct, only to be confronted by two policewomen on horses who greeted me, but who confirmed my uneasy suspicion that I was now actually asleep and suffering from a bad dream. I walked into the supermarket and found I was the only person naked. The same experience occurred in the other shops, and in the one restaurant I entered. An enjoyment of the absurd was all that could save me from a mounting sense of panic. Had I profoundly misunderstood something? The sight of one other naked man told me that I, or all the inhabitants of the city, had not temporarily gone mad. Late in the day I realized the obvious: it just wasn't warm enough for most people. Only when I was back in England did I discover that there is a darker side to Cap d'Agde: conflicts between conventional naturists and visitors who are swingers or fetishists have led to accusations of

A model walks past guests during the Naked Fragrance Fashion Show hosted by the Perfume Shop at the Embassy in London, October 2006.

Seeing and being seen. At 'The Naked Truth' exhibition at the Leopold Museum in Vienna in July 2005, nude visitors were given free access to the gallery to view artworks related to nudity and art scandals in Vienna in the 1900s.

foul play as nightclubs have burnt to the ground. Old-guard nudists have been accused of being terrorists.

Taking off clothes arouses passions, and in attempting to under-stand this I continued my research. I didn't streak across a cricket pitch or pose naked for a charity calendar, nor did I try joining the mass annual mooning of Amtrak that occurs every July in Orange County California. Instead I tried dancing naked with a witch's coven, made a pilgrimage to Jain temples in India, and decided to explore the experience of being observed naked.

However much nudists may claim that they simply want to be left in peace in the nude, and have no desire to be observed in that state, my knowledge of psychology and simple observation of nud-ist magazines and of the world convinced me otherwise. Two female friends told me of their experience of life modelling, and of how satisfying they had found it. I had imagined that being a model would offer an initial experience of embarrassment, combined per-haps with a frisson of excitement, but followed by hours of boredom as one held the poses. My friends urged me to try the experience at

Peter Sellers as Inspector Clouseau on a manhunt in a nudist resort, from
A Shot in the Dark, 1964.

first hand, and to my surprise I found that it was indeed strangely
satisfying. For someone who is predominantly active in the world,
being obliged to be still and become passive – to move from being
Subject to Object – felt like balm to the soul, and the fact that I
was naked seemed to intensify the experience: I had to let go of all

263

attempts to defend my identity. Baring myself in that environment helped me gain access to a deeper sense of self. Reading two studies on the experience of life models confirmed that this feeling is shared by others. It also confirmed the picture that was starting to emerge as I wrote the book: that the experience of being naked and of being observed in that state reflects a fundamental aspect of being in the world: that we are social animals who develop our sense of self, not alone but in relationship with others. We need to see and to be seen.

REFERENCES

Introduction

1 John Berger, *Ways of Seeing* (Harmondsworth, 1972), p. 54.
2 Readers keen to explore the different resonances and meanings evoked by the two terms should refer to Ruth Barcan's *Nudity: A Cultural Anatomy* (Oxford, 2004).
3 Hemchandra, *The Jain Saga*, trans. M. M. Johnson (Ahmedabad, 2005), p. 240. See also chapter Five, ref. 12.
4 Mario Perniola, 'The Glorious Garment and the Naked Truth', in *Clothing And Nudity Zone 4, Fragments for a History of the Human Body*, ed. Michel Feher with Ramona Naddaff and Nadia Tazi (New York, 1989). www.marioperniola.it.
5 See Mario Perniola's essay 'Between Clothing and Nudity', in *Fashion: Critical and Primary Sources*, vol. I, ed. Peter McNeil (Oxford, 2009).

1 Clothed with the Sky

1 From Robert Cochrane, Evan John Jones, *The Robert Cochrane Letters: An Insight into Modern Traditional Witchcraft*, ed. Michael Howard (Milverton, 2003).
2 See estimates based on various surveys at www.religioustolerance.org.
3 The Five Acres Country Club in Bricket Wood (originally Four Acres), outside St Albans, which still exists. See www.fiveacrescountryclub.com.
4 R. Hutton, 'A Modest Look at Ritual Nudity' in *Witches, Druids and King Arthur* (London, 2003), p. 204.
5 In ibid., p. 203, Hutton introduces a further caveat: that we cannot be certain that Albrecht Dürer's drawings depict witches, even though two are commonly designated as such. One shows women in poses taken directly from classical representations of the Graces, and the other, which shows an old woman riding on a goat, 'echoes a medieval figure commonly used to personify lust, and is taken in turn from an ancient iconic pose of Aphrodite or Venus.' The pictures of two of Dürer's pupils, Altdorfer and Grien, can be positively identified as witches, however. They were working in Strasbourg where sermons against witchcraft were preached during the 1500s.
6 Interrogators were more interested in evidence of devil-worship, child sacrifice and sexual orgies. Testimony of nudity was scant, but was mentioned from time to time.
7 R. Hutton, *The Triumph of the Moon: A History of Modern Pagan Witchcraft* (Oxford, 1999), p. 147.
8 Plotinus, *Enneads*, book I, ch. 6, line 7.
9 Mark C. Carnes, *Secret Ritual and Manhood in Victorian America* (New Haven, CT,

265

1989), p. 1. Ronald Hutton suggests that although figures for Britain are not known, the American figure given by Carnes can be extrapolated. See *The Triumph of the Moon*, p. 64.

10 The use of nakedness in initiation into classical Mystery Schools was not confined to the Mithraic cult. We know that ritual bathing was a requirement in the Eleusinian mysteries and it has been suggested that nakedness was a feature of the cults of Orpheus and Dionysos. Most of the work on ritual nudity in the classical world was carried out by German scholars at the beginning of the twentieth century, with the most important book on the subject being probably one of the last books to be published in Latin, presumably to avoid upsetting the unlearned. Ronald Hutton convincingly challenges much of their conclusions in 'A Modest Look at Ritual Nudity', in *Witches, Druids and King Arthur*, pp. 195–9.

11 Abridged extract from *The Key of Solomon the King*, trans. S. Liddell MacGregor Mathers (San Diego, CA, 1998).

12 Hutton, *Witches, Druids and King Arthur*, p. 210.

13 For a review of popular customs associated with flax see Marcel de Cleene, Marie Claire Lejeune, *Compendium of Symbolic and Ritual Plants in Europe* (Ghent, 2003), p. 233.

14 Ibid., p. 391.

15 Pliny the Elder, *Natural History*.

16 Henry Cornelius Agrippa, *Three Books of Occult Philosophy*, Book 1, ch. 42.

17 *The Daily Telegraph*, 21 August 2006.

18 De Cleene and Lejeune, *Compendium of Symbolic and Ritual Plants in Europe*, p. 260.

19 Hutton, 'A Modest Look at Ritual Nudity', pp. 194–5.

20 Ibid., p. 194.

21 Gilberto de Lascariz, *Ritos Misterios e Secretos do Wicca* (Sintra, 2008).

22 See Peter Owen-Jones, *Around the World in 80 Faiths* (London, 2009).

23 At least six groups formed the Hertfordshire Nuderies: Five Acres, Spielplatz, Sunfolk, Gardenia, Sun Campers and Diogenes (which moved to its present location in Buckinghamshre in 1964).

24 Ross Nichols, 'The Jain Customs and Philosophy', in Philip Carr-Gomm, *In the Grove of the Druids: The Druid Teachings of Ross Nichols* (London, 2002), p. 79.

25 Nichols also indirectly introduced another term to Gardner that has become influential and popular: 'The Book of Shadows'. Gardner initially described the book of spells and rituals of a witch as 'Ye Bok of ye Art Magical' until he seems to have come across an article written by a friend of Nichols, Mir Bashir, entitled 'The Book of Shadows', in a journal edited by Nichols and published in 1949: *The Occult Observer*.

26 At the time of writing, for example, the detailed Wikipedia entry for 'Skyclad' fails to mention the word's derivation.

27 Adam Stout, *Universal Majesty, Verity And Love Infinite: A Life of George Watson Macgregor Reid*, in *The Mount Haemus Lectures*, vol. 1 (Lewes, 2008).

28 Ibid., p. 146.

29 See the Naturism section at www.druidry.org. Also see a more complete biography of Nichols: Philip Carr-Gomm, *Journeys of the Soul: The Life and Legacy of a Druid Chief* (Lewes, 2010).

30 Philip Carr-Gomm, *The Druid Way* (Loughborough, 2006).

31 Ronald Hutton, *The Druids* (London, 2007), pp. 168–72 and personal communication with author.

32 Diogenes Laertius, *Vitae*, trans. T. D. Kendrick, Introduction 1, p. 5.

2 Beside the Jhelum and the Jordan

1 'Shri Gurudev Mahendranath' at www.mahendranath.org.
2 The earliest written description of naked ascetics probably comes from the *Ríg Veda*, which has been dated back as far as 1500 BC, but with roots in an earlier oral tradition. A hymn in the *Ríg Veda* describes a group of naked long-haired sages undergoing ecstatic trances.
3 Others believe that Pyrrho could have spent two years with the gymnosophist sage Calanus as he travelled with Alexander, giving them enough time to learn how to communicate with each other effectively.
4 Arrian of Nicomedia, *Anabasis* (book 7, sections 1.5–3.6)
5 Plutarch, *The Life of Alexander* (section 64), in *The Parallel Lives*, vol. VII (Cambridge, MA, 1919), p. 407.
6 The full quotation reads: 'In Taxila, once, he met some members of the Indian sect of Wise Men whose practice it is to go naked, and he so much admired their powers of endurance that the fancy took him to have one of them in his personal train. The oldest man among them, whose name was Dandamis (the others were his pupils), refused either to join Alexander himself or to permit any of his pupils to do so ... These words convinced Alexander that Dandamis was, in a true sense, a free man. So he made no attempt to compel him. On the other hand, another of these Indian teachers, a man named Calanus, did yield to Alexander's persuasion; this man, according to Megasthenes' account, was declared by his fellow teachers to be a slave to fleshly lusts, an accusation due, no doubt, to the fact that he chose to renounce the bliss of their own asceticism and to serve another master instead of god.' Arrian of Nicomedia, *Anabasis*, Book 7.
7 Plutarch, *The Life of Alexander*, 6:65. Calanus is the Greek version of the sage's Indian name: Kalyan.
8 The veracity of this is disputed: Paul LeValley, citing James H. Oliver, 'The Ruling Power, A Study of the Roman Empire in the Second Century after Christ through the Roman Oration of Aelius Aristides', *Transactions of the American Philosophical Society*, n.s., XLIII/4 (1953), p. 912, writes: 'Plutarch's tale of Gymnosophists holding down a hide to demonstrate that Alexander should govern his empire from the centre has been traced back to a story about Cyrus the Great, written by Ctesias some seventy five years before Alexander ever met the Gymnosophists'. Paul LeValley, 'What Did The Gymnosophists Believe?', in *Yavanika, Journal of the Indian Society for Greek and Roman Studies*, 2 (1992).
9 See Arrian of Nicomedia, *Anabasis*, Book 7, 1.5–3.6. Plutarch, in his *Alexander*, gives a slightly different account of Calanus' end: 'At the same time, Calanus having been a little while troubled with a disease in the bowels, requested that he might have a funeral pile erected, to which he came on horseback, and after he had said some prayers and sprinkled himself and cut off some of his hair to throw into the fire, before he ascended it, he embraced and took leave of the Macedonians who stood by, desiring them to pass that day in mirth and good-fellowship with their king, whom in a little time, he said, he doubted not but to see them again at Babylon. Having thus said, he lay down, and covering up his face, he stirred not when the fire came near him, but continued still in the same posture as at first, and so sacrificed himself, as it was the ancient custom of the philosophers in those countries to do.' There are 4 different classical accounts of this moment, each with variations. While the tales of the Ten Questions posed to the gymnosophists and Calanus' use of the hide as a teaching tool may be apocryphal, the first account of Calanus' death has the distinction of being the earliest record in western literature of this practice. See Paul LeValley, 'The

Gymnosophist Legacy in India 326 BC–1604 AD',
dissertation, Florida State University (1987), pp. 6–18.

10 The Tirthankara, Mahavira, is said to have practised sallekhana at Pavapure (near modern Patna) when he fasted to death. Sallekhana is permitted once one has discharged one's worldly obligations, and it involves simply taking no food and meditating until death.

11 Hermann Jacobi, *The Golden Book of Jainism* (Twin Lakes, WI, 2006).

12 See Shri Gurudev Mahendranath, *The Naked Saints of India* at www. mahendranath.org.

13 At www.rev.net/~aloe/ajivika/.

14 *Tirthankara* means 'maker of a ford': in other words, he is the creator of a bridge between worlds.

15 'The name Digambara took some time to become established in use. Until the fourteenth century a sect called the Yapaniyas existed, which shows the original flexibility regarding sectarian affiliation. Yapaniyas were a compromise, wearing clothes only when with lay followers.' St Martin's College, 'Overview of World Religions', at http://philtar.ucsm.ac.uk/encyclopedia/jainism/digam.html.

16 Padmanabh S. Jaini, *The Jaina Path of Purification* (New Delhi, 1979), p. 40.

17 Ibid., p. 223.

18 Anguttaranikaya: 1:206, quoted in ibid., p. 223.

19 See also David Deida, *Naked Buddhism* (London, 2002).

20 *Uttaradhyayana*, XXX (6, 8).

21 Eloise Hart, 'A Lamp of the True Light', at www.theosophy-nw.org/theosnw/world/asia/reljain2.htm.

22 See www.tarunawakening.org.

23 St Martin's College 'Overview of World Religions' cites a study carried out in 1994 that estimated that in all of India there were only about 65 naked Digambara monks (http://philtar.ucsm.ac.uk/encyclopedia/jainism/digam.html). This study most likely underestimated the true number, since the Chaturmas List for 2009 prepared by the Jain Info Team at Pune lists the names and locations of 176 skyclad Jain ascetics (http://www.digambarjainonline.com/news/news17.htm). In 1986, a survey of one branch of Shvetambar ascetics alone numbered 4,360 nuns and 1,330 monks. See http://philtar.ucsm.ac.uk/encyclopedia/jainism/shvet.html.

24 See www.mahendranath.org/nakedsaints.mhtml.

25 *Nepal News Daily*, quoted at www.hotelnepal.com/nepal_news.php?id=1716.

26 Kirin Narayan, *Storytellers, Saints, and Scoundrels: Folk Narrative in Hindu Religious Teaching* (Philadelphia, PA, 1989).

27 Baba Rampuri, *Autobiography of a Blue-Eyed Yogi* (London and New York, 2005).

28 Although there are undoubtedly rare exceptions. About 10 per cent of sadhus are estimated to be female, and are known as sadhvis, and in the past some did go naked. John Oman in *The Mystics, Ascetics and Saints of India* (London, 1903) recounts meeting an almost naked sadhvi.

29 This can be observed within the Nudist/Naturist community, and on the internet. There is no parallel, for example, between the CFNM (Clothed Female, Naked Male) movement, which exists primarily on websites but also in 'live' events, and any equivalent movement devoted to the reverse activity of clothed males observing naked females. In the CFNM movement, males enjoy being observed in the nude, and often sexually humiliated, by clothed women. The sites and venues (such as strip clubs) that cater for the reverse activity seem driven not by women who wish to be observed by clothed men, but by men who enjoy observing or humiliating women by being dressed while observing them naked. In the same way, the few sites that cater for CMNF interests seem

driven by men rather than women.

30 *Naked Song* by Lalla, trans. and introduced by Coleman Barks (Varanasi, 2004), p. 19.

31 Siddhayya Puranik, *Mahadevi*, trans. G.N. B. Sajjan (Mysore, 1986), p. 12.

32 Armando Menezes and S. M. Angadi, eds and trans., *Vacanas of Akkamahadevi* (Dharwar, 1973).

33 Mark Storey, 'India's Naked Woman Poet', in *Nude and Natural*, XXI/1 (2001), p. 91.

34 *Naked Song* by Lalla,, p. 107.

35 Ibid., p. 3.

36 Jaishree Kak, *Mystical Verses of Lalla: A Journey of Self Realization* (New Delhi, 2007).

37 *Naked Song*, p. 41.

38 2 Kings 6:20, Latin Vulgate Bible (Douay-Rheims version).

39 1 Samuel 19:24. 'Naioth in Ramah', a place on Mount Ephraim, the birthplace of Samuel and Saul. Naoith signifies 'habitations', and probably means the huts or dwellings of a school or college of prophets over which Samuel presided, as Elisha did over those at Gilgal and Jericho.

40 Jim C. Cunningham, ed., *Nudity and Christianity* (Bloomington, IN, 2006), p. 282.

41 Ibid., p. 279.

42 Isaiah 20:2–4 (King James version).

43 Samuel Pepys, *The Shorter Pepys*, ed. Robert Latham (Harmondsworth, 1987), 814 (29 July 1667).

44 P. Crawford and L. Gowing, *Women's Worlds in Seventeenth-Century England* (Oxford, 2000), p. 256.

45 'The Torah indirectly alludes to Aaron's nakedness in the ceremony of his washing and investiture (Leviticus 8:6f). This rite of initiation into the priest-hood took place in about 1000 BC.' Michael A. Kowalewski, 'The Naked Baptism of Christ', in *Nudity and Christianity*, ed. Cunningham, p. 431.

46 Quotations from St Cyril and Theodore of Mopsuestia in *Nudity and Christianity*, ed. Cunningham, p. 28.

47 Jim C. Cunningham, *De Nuditate Habituque*, in *Nudity and Christianity*, ed. Cunningham, p. 28.

48 St Francis of Assisi entry in the Catholic Encyclopaedia at www.newadvent.org.

49 *The Remembrance of the Desire of a Soul* by Thomas of Celano, The Second Book, Chapter lxxxiii.

50 Karen Gorham and Dave Leal, *Naturism and Christianity: Are They Compatible?* (Cambridge, 2000), p. 13.

51 Ibid., p. 24.

52 Ibid., p. 24, quoting C. S. Lewis, *The Great Divorce* (London, 1946), p. 29.

53 Cunningham, ed., *Nudity and Christianity*, p. 32.

54 At www.jimccunningham.com/bio.

55 Karol Wojtyla, *Love and Responsibility*, trans. H. T. Willetts (New York, 1981), pp. 176–92.

56 Ronald Hutton, 'A Modest Look at Ritual Nudity' in *Witches, Druids and King Arthur* (London, 2003), pp. 201.

57 Ibid. p. 202.

58 John 19:23–26 (Young's Literal Translation).

59 John 20:7 (New International Version).

60 See www.jam-montoya.es.

61 See www.cosimocavallaro.com.

62 Pope John Paul II, *Theology of the Body* (Slough, 1997), p. 76. Christopher West, writing on a website dedicated to John Paul's *Theology of the Body*, states: 'The TB calls us to look deeply into our own hearts, to look past our wounds and the

scars of sin, past our disordered desires. If we're able to do that we discover God's original plan for creating us as male and female still "echoing" within us. By glimpsing at that "original vision," we can almost taste the original experience of bodily integrity and freedom – of nakedness without shame. And we begin to sense a plan for our sexuality so grand, so wondrous, that we can scarcely allow our hearts to take it in.' At www.theologyofthebody.net/index.php?option=com_content&task=view&id=27&Itemid=48.

63 'Naked on the Cross' by Michael A. Kowalewski, in *Nudity and Christianity*, ed. Cunningham, p. 349, quoting St Jerome, Epistle 58, *Ad Paulinum*.
64 'Naked Eye' words and music by Jill Cunniff © 1996, reproduced by permission of EMI Music Publishing Ltd, London W8 5SW.

3 Naked Rebellion

1 Many naturists include a further motivation which is 'social', arguing that being naked in social settings with others is psychologically and even politically more healthy than being clothed.
2 Tony Hancock in the 'Twelve Hungry Men' episode of *Hancock's Half Hour*.
3 'The Body as Weapon', *The New Internationalist*, 371, September 2004.
4 At www.haaretz.com/hasen/spages/986110.html.
5 At www.bsa.govt.nz/decisions/2005/2005-029.htm.
6 At www.truthorfiction.com/rumors/a/ashcroft-breast.htm.
7 At http://breastsnotbombs.blogspot.com.
8 At http://breastsnotbombs.blogspot.com/2005/12/decent-thing-to-do.html.
9 T. E. Turner and L. S. Brownhill, 'The Curse of Nakedness: Nigerian Women in the Oil War', in *Feminist Politics, Activism and Vision: Local and Global Challenges*, ed. L. Ricciutelli, A. Miles and M. H. McFadden (London, 2004), pp. 169–91. For an exploration of the role of women in naked protest see also Barbara Sutton, 'Naked Protest: Memories of Bodies and Resistance at the World Social Forum', *Journal of International Women's Studies*, April 2007, and B. Hooks, 'Naked Without Shame: A Counter-Hegemonic Body Politic', in *Talking Visions: Multicultural Feminism in a Transnational Age*, ed. E. Shohat (Cambridge, MA, 1998), pp. 65–74.
10 At www.peaceonearth.net/womenforpeace.htm.
11 At www.baringwitness.org.
12 See www.redefiningseduction.com.
13 At www.justgiving.com/wank4peace.
14 Reuters report, 'Yoko Ono to Go Naked for Peace in Paris', 14 September 2003.
15 In 'Canticle of the Creatures', St Francis wrote: 'All praise to you, Oh Lord, for all these brother and sister creatures.'
16 At www.runningofthenudes.com.
17 Alix Sharkey, 'The Fur Will Fly', *Seven Magazine*, 6 July 2008.
18 Dan Mathews, *Committed: A Rabble-Rouser's Memoir* (New York, 2008).
19 At www.treespiritproject.com/Mission.
20 Adapted from ibid.
21 At www.worldnakedbikeride.org.
22 Simma Holt, *Terror in the Name of God* (Toronto, 1964), pp. 107–39.
23 In *Terror in the Name of God* Holt writes: 'It is estimated that in the last forty years, a total of 1,112 depredations by Sons of Freedom have cost Canada's tax-payers a minimum of $20,124,185 in actual destruction and for police and court costs. This figure does not include the thousands of dollars spent to police, shelter and feed those involved in hundreds of demonstrations, nude parades and hunger strikes' (p. 8). In just one summer (in 1929) 28 schools were the subject of arson attacks by the Sons of Freedom (p. 66.)

24 *H&E Naturist*, February 2007, p. 12.
25 At http://news.bbc.co.uk/1/hi/world/americas/2966496.stm.
26 *H&E Naturist*, July 2007, p. 13
27 Victor Allen, *The Movement of the 400 Pueblos of Veracruz: When Your Body is Your Only Weapon* (Bloomington, IN, 2009). See www.400pueblos.com.
28 *H&E Naturist*, May 2004, p. 12.
29 http://benjamingedan.blogspot.com/2008/11/bearing-it-all-to-ban-botnia.html.
30 At www.annoticoreport.com/2009/03/actress-gets-naked-in-milan-exchange-to.html.
31 *The Villager*, LXXV/12 (2005), at www.thevillager.com/villager_119/talkingpoint.html
32 The only naked protest in the Middle East recorded on the internet concerns a student who stripped nearly naked in a supermarket in Tel Aviv in 2008 and again in 2009 to protest against the sale of bread and other leavened grain products in the shop during Passover. At http://english.siamdailynews.com/asia-news/western-asia-news/israel-news/hareidi-strips-naked-in-protest-of-public-hametz-sales.html.
33 At www.independent.co.uk/news/uk/home-news/mothers-detained-in-immigration-centre-hold-naked-protest-807802.html.
34 *The Guardian*, Tuesday 16 December 2008, at www.guardian.co.uk/world/2008/dec/16/france-art-life-models-protest.
35 Rebecca MacKinnon, Assistant Professor at the University of Hong Kong's Journalism and Media Studies Centre, who is working on a book tentatively titled *Internet Freedom and Control: Lessons from China for the World*, wrote on her blog: 'The most common method used by academics to map or track what bloggers are talking about in various countries is by counting the use of various key-words and putting them into categories, then figuring out how the various con-versations – tagged by subject matter – seem to cluster. The Chinese Internet presents a special problem for this kind of research, because in order to avoid censorship, people frequently talk about one thing when all their peers know they're talking about something completely different.' At http://rconversation.blogs.com/rconversation/2008/07/wengan-riots-pu.html.
36 At www.tibet.ca/en/newsroom/wtn/6183.
37 At www.straitstimes.com/Breaking%2BNews/SE%2BAsia/Story/STIStory_303757.html.
38 Ibid.
39 At http://news.bbc.co.uk/1/hi/world/asia-pacific/4599533.stm.
40 At www.treehugger.com/files/2007/07/lush_goes_naked.php.
41 At www.news.com.au/dailytelegraph/story/0,22049,23702849-5001021,00.html.
42 At www.thecancerblog.com/tag/beautiful/.
43 At www.greenpeace.org/international/news/naked-glacier-tunick-08182007.
44 http://skeptoid.com/episodes/4059.
45 At www.ynet.co.il/english/articles/0,7340,L-3642845,00.html.

4 The Prime Minister of Britain has Nothing to Conceal

1 Ed Cray, *General of the Army: George C. Marshall, Soldier and Statesman* (New York, 2000), p. 269.
2 Robert Dallek, *Flawed Giant: Lyndon Johnson and his Times, 1961–73* (Oxford, 1998): 'During a private conversation with some reporters who pressed him to explain why we were in Vietnam, Johnson lost his patience. According to Arthur

Goldberg, LBJ unzipped his fly, drew out his substantial organ and declared, "This is why!'"

3 H&E Naturist, December 2006, p. 46.
4 Charlotte Gill, 'Revealed: Cherie's nude portrait that Tony Tried to Ban', Daily Mail, 11 December 2006, at www.dailymail.co.uk/news/article-421698/Revealed-Cheries-nude-portrait-Tony-tried-ban.html.
5 Karol Wojtyla, Love and Responsibility, trans. H. T. Willetts (New York, 1981), pp. 176–92.
6 Thomas Carlyle, The French Revolution, A History (London, 1837).
7 Thomas Carlyle, Sartor Resartus: The Life and Opinions of Herr Teufelsdrockh (London, 1833–4), chap. 9.
8 Harold Bloom, ed., Thomas Carlyle (New York, 1986).
9 At www.independent.co.uk/news/uk/this-britain/focus-and-here-is-the-naked-news-from-brighton-theres-too-much-nudity-on-tv-555794.html.
10 At www.pinknews.co.uk/news/articles/2005-987.html.
11 http://news.bbc.co.uk/1/hi/entertainment/789086.stm
12 At www.booknotes.org/Transcript/?ProgramID=1501.
13 Nancy Gibbs and Michael Duffy, The Preacher and the Presidents: Billy Graham in the White House (Nashville, TN, 2008).
14 The incident now has its own entry on Wikipedia, which provided this quotation from the Times. See http://en.wikipedia.org/wiki/Conor_Casby.
15 Henry David Thoreau, Walking (Minneapolis, MN, 2008).
16 Walt Whitman, Specimen Days (Mineola, NY, 1995).
17 The Rational Dress Society Gazette, 1881.
18 Cec Cinder, The Nudist Idea (Riverside, CA, 1998), p. 376.
19 Sonia Orwell and Ian Angus, eds., The Collected Essays, Journalism and Letters of George Orwell, 4 vols (New York, 1968), vol. 1, p. 216
20 George Orwell, The Road to Wigan Pier [1937] (London, 1970).
21 Edward Carpenter, Civilization: Its Cause and Cure (London, 1889).
22 The book was self-published in Stuttgart at the beginning of 1906 under the full title Nakedness in an Historical, Hygienic, Moral and Artistic Light. An English translation was only published, with an extensive introduction by Dr Cec Cinder, by The Ultraviolet Press in 2005. Heinrich Scham, writing under the name of Heinrich Pudor, later accused Ungewitter of plagiarizing his insubstantial 1893 pamphlet 'Nackende Menschen: Jauchzen der Zukunst'. Clearly influenced by Nietzsche, 28-year-old Scham self-published his slim collection of aphorisms from a London address, 13 Kensington Park Road, and a comparison of his work with Ungewitter's makes it clear why he was never considered the 'father of nudism'. An English translation, Naked People: A Triumph-Shout of the Future, again with an introduction by Cinder, was published by Reason Books in 1998.
23 An inspiration to the FKK was Georg Lichtenberg, the scientist, philosopher and inventor of the standard paper sizes we use today (such as A4). Lichtenberg, was a proponent of naked 'air baths', and in 1795, a hundred years before the founding of the FKK, had published his Das Luftbad (The Air-Bath), which advocated frequent exposure of all of the skin to the invigorating benefits of fresh air. As early as 1777 James Boswell in his Life of Johnson had acquainted his readers with the idea of these baths, which the Scotsman Lord Monboddo had enjoyed as much as his contemporary Benjamin Franklin: 'Lord Monboddo told me that he awaked every morning at four, and then for his health got up and walked in his room naked, with the window open, which he called taking an air bath.' Some believe that the very first inspiration for nudism in Germany can be traced via Lichtenberg to Monboddo: 'That protagonists for the "cult of the nude" in Germany at the turn of the century were well aware of what they

owed to Monboddo is instanced by the fact that the first really active nudist
league in Berlin was called the 'Monboddo league'. Peter Quirin in *Sun and
Health* magazine, February 1964.

24 For an exploration of the influence of Lebensreform ideas, including nudism,
on the Hippie movement, see Gordon Kennedy, ed., *Children of the Sun: A Pictorial
Anthology From Germany to California, 1883–1949* (Ojai, CA, 1998).

25 Cinder, *The Nudist Idea*, p. 253.

26 The *Kampfring für völkische Körperkultur* (later *Bund für Liebeszucht*).

27 The story of the relationship between nudism and Nazism is complex and
treated in detail in Karl Toepfer, *Empire of Ecstasy: Nudity and Movement in German
Body Culture, 1910–1935* (Weimar and Now: German Cultural Criticism, no. 13)
(Berkeley, CA, 1997); Chad Ross, *Naked Germany: Health, Race and the Nation*
(Oxford, 2004); John Alexander Williams, *Turning to Nature in Germany: Hiking,
Nudism, and Conservation, 1900–1940* (Stanford, CA, 2007); and Cinder, *The Nudist
Idea*, chaps 1–4.

28 *Sun Bathing Review – Journal of the Sun Societies*, 1/2 (Summer 1933), p. 6.

29 Cinder, *The Nudist Idea*, p. 418.

30 Ibid., p. 419.

31 'Beyond Safe Havens: Oregon's Terri Sue Webb', Spring 2002 edition of *Nude
and Natural* magazine. Quoted at www.bodyfreedom.org.

32 Introduction to Maurice Parmelee, *Nudism in Modern Life* (Mays Landing, NJ,
1941), p. 2.

33 For a history of the nudist movements in Europe and the United States see
Cinder, *The Nudist Idea*; for Australia see Magnus Clarke, *Nudism in Australia: A
First Study* (Melbourne, 1982); for Canada see James Woycke, *Au Naturel: The
History of Nudism in Canada* (Etobicoke, ON, 2003).

34 Britain's longest running nudist magazine began life in 1900 as *Health Culture*,
devoted to simple, natural living, with articles on subjects such as exercise and
vegetarianism. Later it became *Health and Vim* and then in 1921 *Health and
Efficiency*. Nudism only became a feature of the magazine from 1922 onwards,
and in recent times it changed its name again to *H&E Naturist*.

35 Robert Verkaik, 'Vincent's Naked Ambition: Vincent Bethell's Determination
to Take His Clothes Off in Public, and His Refusal to Wear Anything for a
Court Appearance, Has Dismayed Magistrates. Is he a Crank or a Civil Rights
Campaigner?' *The Independent*, Tuesday, 29 August 2000.

36 Julia Hartley-Brewer, 'Nothing to Lose but our Clothes: Vincent Bethell is
Ready to Go to Jail for the Right to Bare All', *Guardian*, 15 October 1999.

37 Bob Janes, 'Case Against Naked Cyclist Dropped', *H&E Naturist*, November
2006, p. 5.

38 In 1983 the Naturist Society in the USA commissioned the respected Gallup
Organization to survey Americans on three questions pertaining to nude recreation. Gallup polled a representative sample of 1,037 men and women over the
age of 18. Interviews were conducted by telephone between 13 and 30 May 1983.
The three questions asked were: (1) Do you believe that people who enjoy
nude sunbathing should be able to do so without interference from officials as
long as they do so at a beach that is accepted for that purpose? (71.6% said yes);
(2) Local and state governments now set aside public land for special types of
recreation such as snowmobiling, surfing, and hunting. Do you think special
and secluded areas should be set aside by the government for people to enjoy
nude sunbathing? (39.1% said yes); and (3) Have you personally ever gone skinny-
dipping or nude sunbathing in a mixed group of men or women either at a beach,
at a pool, or somewhere else? (14.7% said yes). (From the Gallup Organization,
Inc., 'Attitudes Toward Nude Sunbathing: A Custom Survey Conducted For

The Naturists', June 1983.) By 2000 another Gallup poll showed that 25% of all American adults had been skinny dipping at least once. In Britain, British Naturism commissioned research by NOP Omnibus in 2001. 1823 interviews were conducted, face to face, with adults aged 16+. 82% felt it right to make nudity legal on some beaches. 24% admitted to having skinny-dipped.

39 *The Free Beach News*, issue 145, May–June 2002.
40 Stuart Ward, *Strange Days Indeed: Memories of the Old World* (Montague, CA, 2007).
41 Susan Stanton, *Being Naked: Attitudes Toward Nudity Through the Ages* (St Clair Shores, MI, 2001).

5 The Death of Shame

1 'Parson's Pleasure' only acquired this name in the twentieth century. It was known as Patten's Pleasure in the seventeenth century and Loggerhead in the nineteenth century.
2 Numerous variations of this story exist. See Leslie Mitchell, *Maurice Bowra: A Life* (Oxford, 2009).
3 Cec Cinder, *The Nudist Idea* (Riverside, CA, 1998), p. 443.
4 Seton befriended Native Americans and learnt many of their ways, and in his books he warned his fellow Americans of the dangers of their treament of the native population. He founded a group called The Woodcraft Indians, which in 1917 changed its name to the Woodcraft League of America. Similar to the Boy Scouts movement, it encouraged outdoor activities for children, and over the years exerted a formative influence on the entire American summer-camp movement. Unlike the Boy Scouts, though, it based its activities around Native American lore rather than the more militaristic and Christian ideals of the Scouts. The founder of the British Woodcraft movement, Ernest Westlake, was inspired by the writings of Edward Carpenter and by paganism. In 1919 he bought Sandy Balls, 120 acres bordering the River Avon in the New Forest. Sandy Balls is now run as a holiday centre. See www.sandy-balls.co.uk.
5 John Mollenkopf, 'Crash Syndrome' in *Carletonian*, Carleton College, 26 January 1967.
6 Transcript from Australian TV show *Where Are They Now?* on Channel 7, 12 March 2006, at www.streakerama.com/michael_obrien.html.
7 At www.streakerama.com/intro.htm.
8 Andy McSmith, 'Bare Necessities: The Naked Truth about Streaking', *The Independent*, 9 August 2007.
9 Sarah R. Phillips, *Modeling Life: Art Models Speak About Nudity, Sexuality, and the Creative Process* (New York, 2006), p. 31.
10 Kathleen Rooney, *Live Nude Girl: My Life as an Object* (Little Rock, AR, 2008), p. 3.
11 Uwe Ommer, *Do it Yourself* (Cologne, 2008).
12 A goal of mystics is to realize the essential unity that lies behind our everyday experience which divides all phemonena into Self or Other, and the use of a mirror can help to dissolve that division, so that Self and Other, Observer and Observed are united. The technique of Preksha meditation, taught by one branch of the Indian Jain tradition, is said to have originated when the Emperor Bharat, son of the first enlightened Jain teacher Lord Rshaba, passively observed himelf in a mirror. In doing this, he 'mastered the Self, attained Self-perfection and became omniscient.' ('The Agamic Source of Preksa Meditation', in M. A. Previous, 'Jainology and Comparative Religion and Philosophy, Paper III, Yoga of Meditation and Critique of Karma Theory', Jain Vishva Bharati University, Ladnun, p. 50.)
13 Ruth Barcan, *Nudity: A Cultural Anatomy* (Oxford, 2004), p. 255.

14 Cinder, *The Nudist Idea*, p. 155.
15 Ibid.
16 See Nicholas de Jongh, *Politics, Prudery and Perversions: The Censoring of the English Stage, 1901–1968* (London, 2001).
17 Scott Miller, *Rebels with Applause: Broadway's Ground-Breaking Musicals* (New York, 2001).
18 Michael Billington, 'Taboo or Not Taboo?', *The Guardian*, 15 February 2007.
19 Ibid.
20 '40 Years of *Hair*', *Newark Star-Ledger*, 19 July 2008.
21 For a history of the arrival of the naked body in British cinema see Tom Dewe Mathews, *Censored: The Story of Film Censorship in Britain* (London, 1994).
22 Karl Eric Toepfer, 'Nudity and Textuality in Postmodern Performance', *PAJ: A Journal of Performance and Art - PAJ 54*, XVIII/3 (September 1996), pp. 76–91.
23 After three days in court, the prosecution withdrew its evidence and the case was closed. Both sides claimed victory – Mary Whitehouse because the judge asserted that the Sexual Offences Act could be applied to events that occurred on stage and that a simulated sexual act could still amount to gross indecency, the play's producer because no conviction occurred.
24 Billington, 'Taboo or not Taboo?'.
25 John Lichfield, 'Quelle horreur! Paris Divided by Theatrical Obsession with Nudity', *The Independent*, 5 April 2005.
26 Quoted in Clive Barnes, 'Attitudes: Nudity in Dance', *Dance Magazine*, November 2003.
27 Ibid.
28 Gia Kourlas, 'The Bare Essentials of Dance', *New York Times*, 12 February 2006.
29 Ibid.
30 Ibid.
31 Sharon Verghis, 'Out of Step over Shock of the Nude', *The Sydney Morning Herald*, 14 September 2005.
32 Quoted in Philip Carr-Gomm, 'Nakedness and Our Ability to Share Intimacy' at http://philipcarrgomm.wordpress.com/2008/01/19/nakedness-and-our-ability-to-share-intimacy.
33 Anthony Tommasini ,'Take it off, Brünnhilde: On Opera and Nudity', *New York Times*, 17 September 2008.
34 From *Operachic*, 18 December 2008, at http://operachic.typepad.com/opera_chic/salome/.
35 Tony Paterson, 'The Naked (and the Wrinkled) Truth about Verdi's Masked Ball', *The Independent*, 12 April 2008.
36 Alan Travis, 'How Two Dames Saved *Oh! Calcutta!*', *The Guardian*, Saturday 23 December 2000.
37 Ibid.
38 Jonathan Ward, 'Come in My Mouth: The Story of the Adult Musicals of the '70s', in *Perfect Sound Online Music Magazine*, at www.furious.com/perfect/adultmusicals.htm.

6 The Hero's Return

1 In 1965 a new kind of magazine appeared in the USA under the generic title of 'Jaybird magazines', inspired by both the nudist and the hippie worlds. They featured photos, usually sexually oriented and often humorous, of both male and female nudes. In 1972 the US courts banished such titles to adult book-stores. By then magazines available on newsstands, such as *Playboy* and *Penthouse*,

had begun to reveal the pubic hair of their female models – gradually revealing
more as the two magazines went head to head, an era Hugh Hefner christened
'the Pubic Wars'. See Dian Hanson, *Naked as a Jaybird* (Cologne, 2003).

2 'In the Studio: Spencer Tunick', by Spencer Tunick, *The Daily Telegraph*, 16 May
2006. In a personal communication with the author (23 July 2009), Tunick
described himself as 'a contemporary artist making installations that I document
with photography and video'.
3 At www.nakedworlddoc.com.
4 Ibid.
5 Kelly Farrell, 'Naked Nation – *The Full Monty*, Working-Class Masculinity, and
the British Image', *Men and Masculinities*, VI/2 (2003), pp. 119–35.
6 Ibid.
7 Thomas Conner, 'Elfman: Mirren's Naked Talent', *Chicago Suntimes* blog, 25
February 2007, at http://blogs.suntimes.com/awards/2007/02/elfman_
mirrens_naked_talent.html.
8 'Crazy Jane Talks with the Bishop', by W. B. Yeats.
9 From notes kindly provided by the Council's archivist Michael Farrar.
10 CBS challenged the fine on the grounds that the broadcast was unintentional
and thus exempt from indecency regulation. In 2008 the United States Court
of Appeals for the Third Circuit voided the fine, but in May 2009 the Supreme
Court vacated that judgement and sent the case back to the Third Circuit for
reconsideration.
11 Zoe Williams, 'Topless or Not?', *The Guardian*, 23 July 2009.
12 Alain de Botton, *Status Anxiety*, Channel 4 TV documentary, available on DVD from
Revolver Entertainment, 2005.
13 Interview with by Shauna Miller, 3 April 2009 in the *Decider DC*, at
http://dc.decider.com/articles/annie-sprinkle,25907/.
14 C. Carr, 'A Public Cervix Announcement', in *On Edge: Performance at the End of the
Twentieth Century* (Middletown, CT, 2008).
15 Abraham Maslow, *Eupsychian Management* (Homewood, IL, 1965); republished as
Maslow on Management (New York, 1998).
16 See Ian Nicholson, 'Baring the Soul: Paul Bindrim, Abraham Maslow and "Nude
Psychotherapy"', *Journal of the History of the Behavioral Sciences*, XLIII/4 (Fall 2007),
pp. 337–59.
17 See www.paullowe.miamedia.org.
18 Aileen Goodson, *Therapy, Nudity and Joy: The Therapeutic Use of Nudity Through the Ages*
(Los Angeles, CA, 1991), p. 120.
19 At http://news.bbc.co.uk/1/hi/magazine/7915369.stm.

ACKNOWLEDGEMENTS

In addition to the fieldwork described in the Postscript, research on the internet and in books has proved invaluable. In particular Ruth Barcan's *Nudity: A Cultural Anatomy* and Kathleen Rooney's *Live Nude Girl* stand out in my memory as valuable sources of inspiration, as were the many friends who contributed their ideas and personal anecdotes. In particular I would like to thank my father, Francis, and my agent, Tony Morris, for regularly feeding me with relevant articles and press cuttings; my wife, Stephanie, and daughters Sophia and Charlie for their insights and suggestions on reading sections of the manuscript; Pamela Tudor-Craig for sharing her knowledge of St Francis; Maria Ede-Weaving for contributing her text; Hala Faisal, Bert Schlauch, Jack Gescheidt, Iseult Weston, Donna Sheehan and Paul Reffell for their photographs and support; Russell Ash, Anna Carlisle, Cec Cinder, David Craver, Jim C. Cunningham, Michael Farrar, Tarquin Gotch, Graham Harvey, Ronald Hutton, Paul LeValley and Annie O'Temro for their generous contributions of specialist knowledge; and Robin Bierstedt, L. R. Fredericks, Susan Jones, Jonathan Miller and Thea Worthington for their detailed comments on reading drafts of some or all of the chapters.

PHOTO ACKNOWLEDGEMENTS

The author and publishers wish to express their thanks to the below sources of illustrative material and/or permission to reproduce it.

Advertising Archives: p. 252; The British Library, London: p. 77; www.doubletake-microwear.com: p. 239 (photo: Tom Murdock); www.durbano.com: p. 237 (photo: Gerhilde Skoberne); Richard Cocks: p. 242 bottom; courtesy of the England Gallery, London, www.englandgallery: p. 245; courtesy of Janet Farrar: p. 24; photo © 2009 Jack Gescheidt, TreeSpiritProject.com: p. 110; Getty Images: pp. 6, 15, 22 bottom, 23 bottom, 58, 61, 80, 83, 91, 94 top, 96, 99, 117, 124, 128, 129 top, 141, 142, 165, 166, 167, 168, 170, 175, 180, 183, 188, 192, 198, 201, 202, 206, 208, 210, 211, 213, 214, 215, 217, 218, 222, 225, 228, 230, 235, 249, 253, 261; Neil Gillespie: p. 229; Gypsy Boots: p. 157; Barry Hipwell: p. 247; photo © International Nath Order: p. 63; Lush Cosmetics: p. 124; NASA: p. 231 top; NudeHotYoga.com: p. 23 top; Mirrorpix: p. 176; Simon Monk: p. 241; Museum Meermanno-Westreenianum, The Hague: p. 53 (10 A 11, fol. 93v); National Archives, Washington, DC: p. 90; The NEE Party, Antwerp: p. 140; Aleister Crowley photo copyright © Ordo Templi Orientis, JAF Box 7666, New York, NY 10116: p. 64; Carlos Felipe Pardo: p. 111; PETA: p. 106, 108; PA Photos: pp. 120, 231 bottom; Stevee Postman: pp. 36, 37; Rex Features: pp. 16 (Ben Swinnerton/Newspix), 17 top (Austral Int.), 17 bottom (SIPA Press),18 (Neal Haynes), 19 (Double PR), 20 (Mivy James), 21 top, 21 bottom (Miquel Benitez), 22 top, 65 (SIPA Press), 94 bottom, 107 (SIPA Press), 126–7 (Action Press), 129 bottom (SIPA Press), 137 (Nils Jorgensen), 143 (Charles Sykes), 147 (Olycom SPA), 150 (Mike Thomas), 181 (Tom E. Osthuss/Allover Press, Norway), 182 (Nigel R. Barklie), 185 (David Butler), 186 (Action Press), 187 (Giuseppe Aresu), 189 top (Stockroll), 189 bottom (Koster/Ward), 190 (Erik G. Pendzich), 194, 216 , 227 (Terry Logan), 233 (Extrapress), 240 (Picture Perfect), 242 top (Jonathan Player), 244 (Matt Faber), 246 (Erik G. Pendzich), 250 top (Nils Jorgensen), 250 bottom (Richard Young), 254 (Abel B'Hahn), 262 (SIPA Press), 263 (Denis Cameron); Estate of John David Roberts, by courtesy of The William Roberts Society: p. 172; Topfoto: p. 178; Photo Scala, Florence: p. 75; Bert Schlauch: p. 100; Science and Society Picture Library: p. 162 (NMeM Daily Herald Archive); courtesy of Donna Sheehan and Paul Reffell: pp. 102–3; Skuds: p. 238; The Vancouver Sun, Vancouver: p. 113 (George Diack); courtesy of Iseult Weston: pp. 44, 45.

INDEX

Page numbers in *italics* refer to illustrations